South Asia Economic and Policy Studies

Series editors

The Series aims to address evolving and new challenges and policy actions that may be needed in the South Asian Region in the 21st century. It ventures niche and makes critical assessment to evolve a coherent understanding of the nature of challenges and allow/facilitate dialogue among scholars and policymakers from the region working with the common purpose of exploring and strengthening new ways to implement regional cooperation. The series is multidisciplinary in its orientation and invites contributions from academicians, policy makers, practitioners, consultants working in the broad fields of regional cooperation; trade and investment; finance; economic growth and development; industry and technology; agriculture; services; environment, resources and climate change; demography and migration; disaster management, globalization and institutions among others.

More information about this series at http://www.springer.com/series/15400

Selim Raihan
Editor

Structural Change and Dynamics of Labor Markets in Bangladesh

Springer

Editor
Selim Raihan
University of Dhaka
Dhaka, Bangladesh

and

SANEM
Bangladesh

ISSN 2522-5502 ISSN 2522-5510 (electronic)
South Asia Economic and Policy Studies
ISBN 978-981-13-2070-5 ISBN 978-981-13-2071-2 (eBook)
https://doi.org/10.1007/978-981-13-2071-2

Library of Congress Control Number: 2018950950

This Springer imprint is published by the registered company Springer Nature Singapore Pte Ltd.
The registered company address is: 152 Beach Road, #21-01/04 Gateway East, Singapore 189721, Singapore

Preface

Bangladesh's achievement in economic growth over the last decade has been quite robust. The country has recently been upgraded from a low-income country (LIC) to a lower-middle-income country (LMIC) as per the World Bank's classification. There is an aspiration to graduate from the LDC status by 2024 as per the United Nations' classification. The Seventh Five-Year Plan sets an ambitious target of 8 percent growth in GDP by 2020. There are also steep development targets to be achieved under the Sustainable Development Goals (SDGs) by 2030. All these will require an enormous leap forward from the current level of economic growth rate and sustaining it in the future. The situation also demands a considerable structural change in the economy, leading to large-scale economic diversification, promotion of labor-intensive and high-productivity sectors, in both farm and nonfarm sectors, and interventions to enhance productivity, job, and income in traditional and informal activities where there are large pools of surplus labor.

Against this backdrop, this volume titled *Structural Change and Dynamics of Labor Markets in Bangladesh* covers a wide range of issues related to labor markets in Bangladesh. These include structural change and employment creation, factors affecting the choice between farm and nonfarm employment, employment status and well-being of rural households, factors influencing female labor force participation, unpacking unpaid family labor, dynamics of employment in the urban informal sector, social protection programs impacting on labor force participation behavior, impact of both international and internal remittances on the domestic labor market, some estimates of the first demographic dividend in Bangladesh, role of education and skill development in the transition from 'good-enough' job to 'decent' job, issue of agricultural seasonality in skill training, and policy simulations using social accounting matrix and computable general equilibrium frameworks.

We wish to extend our sincere gratitude to IDRC, Canada, for their financial support to successfully publish this volume. It is our pleasure to thank Edgard Rodriguez, IDRC, Canada, for his support and advice. We are pleased to recognize the contributions from authors and co-authors of the chapters in this volume. The list includes Selim Raihan, Bazlul Haque Khondker, Simeen Mahmud, Sayema Haque Bidisha, Abu Parves Shonchoy, Nafiz Ifteakhar, Mir Tanzim Nur Angkur,

Muhammad Moshiur Rahman, Fatima Tuz Zohora, Syer Tazim Haque, Israt Jahan, Mahtab Uddin, and Andilip Afroze.

Finally, we would like to thank Sk. Ashibur Rahman Anjon, Raisa Tamanna Khan, Sunera Saba Khan, Nabila Hasan, Wahid Ferdous Ibon, and Md. Jillur Rahman for their excellent support services.

Dhaka, Bangladesh

Selim Raihan

Contents

Editor and Contributors

About the Editor

Dr. Selim Raihan is Professor in the Department of Economics, University of Dhaka, and Executive Director of the South Asian Network on Economic Modeling (SANEM). He holds a Ph.D. from the University of Manchester, UK. He possesses vast expertise in research on international trade, labor market dynamics, poverty, economic growth, and political economy analysis of growth and development. He has a long experience in teaching international trade, economic modeling, quantitative economics, econometrics, development economics, and poverty dynamics at the University of Dhaka. He is Editor of a monthly digest *Thinking Aloud*, published from SANEM. He has a number of publications in reputed journals and has also written several books and chapters published by reputed publishers in London, New York, New Delhi, and Dhaka. He has worked for several national and international organizations including the Asian Development Bank, the World Bank, UNDP, UNESCAP, UNCTAD, IFPRI, the Commonwealth Secretariat, FAO, the European Commission, ILO, IDRC, DFID.

Contributors

Ms. Andilip Afroze is Research Associate at the South Asian Network on Economic Modeling (SANEM). She obtained her bachelor's and master's degrees from the Department of Economics, University of Dhaka. Her major areas of interest include labor economics, international trade, and development economics.

Mir Tanzim Nur Angkur is Lecturer in the Department of Economics, East West University, and Research Associate at the South Asian Network on Economic Modeling (SANEM). He obtained his bachelor's and master's degrees from the Department of Economics, University of Dhaka. His research interests lie in the areas of international trade, global value chain, and informal sector.

Dr. Sayema Haque Bidisha is Associate Professor in the Department of Economics, University of Dhaka, and Research Director at the South Asian Network on Economic Modeling (SANEM). She has specialized in applied labor economics, agriculture economics, and development policy.

Mr. Syer Tazim Haque is Research Associate at the South Asian Network on Economic Modeling (SANEM). He obtained his bachelor's and master's degrees from the Department of Economics, University of Dhaka. His areas of interest are international trade, labor market issues, and development economics.

Mr. Nafiz Ifteakhar is Lecturer at the Institute of Health Economics, University of Dhaka, and Research Associate at the South Asian Network on Economic Modeling (SANEM). He obtained his bachelor's and master's degrees from the Department of Economics, University of Dhaka. His research interests include poverty, food security, international trade, international labor migration, and international finance.

Ms. Israt Jahan is Research Associate at the South Asian Network on Economic Modeling (SANEM). She obtained her bachelor's and master's degrees from the Department of Economics, University of Dhaka. She has been working in the fields of development economics, international trade, and macroeconomics.

Dr. Bazlul Haque Khondker is Professor in the Department of Economics, University of Dhaka, Bangladesh, and Chairman of the South Asian Network on Economic Modeling (SANEM). He has specialized in the areas of distributional consequences of macroeconomic policies, national transfer accounts, and macroeconomic modeling.

Ms. Simeen Mahmud was Fellow at the BRAC Institute of Governance and Development, BRAC University. Her research interests included population dynamics, in particular fertility change, women's work and empowerment, citizenship, social policy with a focus on health and education, and development policy and gender.

Mr. Muhammad Moshiur Rahman is Research Associate at the South Asian Network on Economic Modeling (SANEM). He obtained his bachelor's and master's degrees from the Department of Economics, University of Dhaka. Labor market, international trade, international labor migration, and economic modeling are his main areas of interest.

Dr. Abu Parves Shonchoy is Research Fellow at the Institute of Developing Economies (IDE-JETRO), Japan, and Adjunct Assistant Professor at the Graduate School of Public Policy (GraSPP), University of Tokyo. He is a development economist with interests in impact evaluation and microeconometrics.

Mr. Mahtab Uddin is Lecturer in the Department of Economics, University of Dhaka, and Research Associate at the South Asian Network on Economic Modeling (SANEM). He obtained his bachelor's and master's degrees from the Department of Economics, University of Dhaka. His areas of interest include micro-econometrics, labor economics, international trade, and development economics.

Ms. Fatima Tuz Zohora is Research Associate at the South Asian Network on Economic Modeling (SANEM). She obtained her bachelor's and master's degrees from the Department of Economics, University of Dhaka. Her areas of research interest include labor market issues and international trade.

Abbreviations

APS	Average Propensities to Spend
BA	Bachelor of Arts
BBS	Bangladesh Bureau of Statistics
BIHS	Bangladesh Integrated Household Survey
CES	Constant Elasticity of Substitution
CET	Constant Elasticity of Transformation
CFW	Cash for Work
CGE	Computable General Equilibrium
ECI	Economic Complexity Index
ESR	Economic Support Ratio
EU	European Union
FDI	Foreign Direct Investment
FE	Fixed Effect
FFW	Food for Work
GDP	Gross Domestic Product
GFCF	Fixed Capital Formation
GR	Gratuitous Relief
GSP	Generalized Systems of Preference
HIES	Household Income and Expenditure Survey
HSC	Higher Secondary School Certificate
IFPRI	International Food Policy Research Institute
ILO	International Labor Organization
I-O	Input-Output
IV	Instrumental Variable
LCD	Life-Cycle Deficit
LFP	Labor Force Participation
LFPR	Labor Force Participation Rate
LFS	Labor Force Survey
LIC	Low-Income Country
LMIC	Lower-Middle-Income Country

LPM	Linear Probability Model
MFA	Multi Fibre Arrangement
MICE	Multiple Imputations by Chained Equations
NGO	Non-Government Organization
NSSS	National Social Security Strategy
NTA	National Transfer Account
OECD	Organization for Economic Co-operation and Development
OLS	Ordinary Least Squares
OPS	Open Market Sales
PEP	Partnership for Economic Policy
PSU	Primary Sampling Unit
RE	Random Effect
RMG	Ready-Made Garments
RR	Relative Risk
RRR	Relative Risk Ratio
SAM	Social Accounting Matrix
SNA	System of National Accounts
SSC	Secondary School Certificate
TFR	Total Fertility Rate
UN	United Nations
UNDP	United Nations Development Program
UNFPA	United Nations Population Fund
VGD	Vulnerable Group Development
VGF	Vulnerable Group Feeding
WSD	Widowed/Separated/Divorced

List of Figures

What Determines the Choice Between Farm and Nonfarm Employments in the Rural Bangladesh?

How Does Employment Status Matter for the Well-Being of Rural Households in Bangladesh?

Dynamics of Employment in the Urban Informal Sector in Bangladesh

Some Estimates of First Demographic Dividend in Bangladesh: An Application of the Bangladesh National Transfer Account

Does Participation in Vocational Training Differ on Agricultural Seasonality?

How Does Remittance Affect Labor Force Participation Behavior and Employment Choice in Bangladesh?

Economy-Wide and Employment Effects of Different Scenarios in Bangladesh: Application of a CGE Model

List of Tables

Female Labor Market Participation in Bangladesh: Structural Changes and Determinants of Labor Supply

Unpaid Family Labor: A Hidden Form of Labor Market Discrimination of Women in Bangladesh

Dynamics of Employment in the Urban Informal Sector in Bangladesh

Some Estimates of First Demographic Dividend in Bangladesh: An Application of the Bangladesh National Transfer Account

How Does Social Protection Affect Labor Force Participation in Bangladesh?

How Do Education and Skill Development Affect the Transition from "Good-Enough" Job to "Decent" Job?

Economy-Wide and Employment Effects of Different Scenarios in Bangladesh: Application of a CGE Model

Key Messages

1. Bangladesh economy has undergone significant structural changes over the last four decades. The share of agriculture in GDP has declined, while the relative significance of industry and service sectors has increased. These structural changes have been associated with both positive trends and persistent employment challenges such as lack of diversification, poor working conditions, low productivity, and a high degree of informality.
2. Economic diversification can play an important role in the structural transformation of the economy from producing low value-added products to high value-added products. Promotion of labor-intensive and high-productivity sectors, in both farm and nonfarm, is therefore fundamental. This should be coupled with interventions to enhance productivity, jobs, and incomes in traditional and informal activities where there are large pools of surplus labor.
3. However, strategies specified in the different policies in Bangladesh for economic and export diversification lack clear guidelines as regards implementation and, therefore, result in ineffective strategies. In case of export diversification, it has been a matter of serious concern that though there are significant incentives provided to the export sector in Bangladesh, there is a formidable difficulty in actually accessing such incentives and they helped little in diversifying the export basket. Furthermore, though the latest industrial policy identifies a number of high-priority and priority sectors for economic diversification, there are several policy-induced and supply-side constraints that have constricted the development of these sectors. Unless and until these policy-induced and supply-side constraints are addressed, the agenda for further productive economic diversification will remain unfulfilled.
4. Major supply-side constraints include poor physical infrastructure, inefficiencies at ports and related internal road transportation, lack of investment fund and working capital, high interest rate, shortage of skilled workers, technological bottlenecks, lack of entrepreneurial and management skills, and very high invisible costs of doing business.

5. In the discourse on infrastructure and economic growth, the dominant area of discussion is on the quantity and quality of infrastructure and how countries differ in these respects. While most of the countries emphasize a lot on investing in raising the quantity (and quality) of infrastructure, there is a fundamental concern whether rising supply of infrastructure ensures the access to infrastructure. This problem is manifested through the fact that due to a variety of reasons the enhanced supply of infrastructure may not solve the problem of 'entitlement failure' in terms of effective access to infrastructure, as the people/sectors in dire need of improved infrastructure may not have the access even with an increased supply.
6. Some of the supply-side constraints related to weak infrastructure in Bangladesh are broadly 'general' in nature, and some are critically 'sector specific'. Yet, policy-makers are so inclined to improvement in the broad general infrastructure, i.e., the enhanced supply of electricity, improvement in roads, improvement in port facilities, that the developments of critical sector-specific infrastructure are largely overlooked. Embarking on developing broad general infrastructure is relatively easy, whereas solving sector-specific infrastructure problems involves identifying priorities in the policy-making process and addressing a number of political and economic issues. Failure to deal with sector-specific infrastructure problems leads to a scenario where a large number of potential inclusive growth-enhancing sectors fail to enjoy the benefit from the improvement in broad general infrastructure and thus end up with 'entitlement failure'.
7. Manufacturing is now an overwhelmingly salient component of Bangladesh's export composition, thanks largely to the rapid expansion of the garments industry. Garments has been an important contributor to growth and employment generation in Bangladesh. However, the garments industry of Bangladesh is now at a crossroads. There have been concerns with regard to compliance issues and workplace safety in the garments industry in Bangladesh, and in the last few years, these issues have become very critical for the future of this industry. These concerns should be addressed in a positive way as an opportunity to build industry's reputation in the global market. In this context, issues like wage, workplace security, fringe benefits, and workplace environment need to be resolved on a priority basis. In addition, there is a critical need for enhancing labor productivity, moving up to the higher value-added products through introducing new technology along the production line spurring innovation and enhancing Bangladesh's competitiveness by reducing the cost of doing business.
8. As far as economic diversification is concerned, the productive rural nonfarm sector can be very instrumental. The rural nonfarm sector also has a crucial role in reducing poverty and increasing the well-being of rural households. Education, improvement in rural infrastructure, and development of productive rural nonfarm sector provide a positive stimulus to raise employment in the rural nonfarm sector.

9. The rate of female labor force participation in Bangladesh is still very low. Evidence suggests that female labor force participation reduces the likelihood of household poverty; resources in female's hands have a range of positive outcomes for human capital and capabilities within the household. Thus, there is a strong rationale for ensuring female participation in the economy's growth process. Education, skill development, public and private sector initiatives in investment in the care economy, and different social protection programs can be very useful in increasing female labor force participation.
10. 'Decent' job should be regarded as a dynamic and progressive phenomenon. There could be three stages for moving toward 'decent' job. The first stage is the 'good-enough' job, which shows the transition from 'no job' to 'job' or from unpaid family job to paid job. The second stage is the 'good' job, which shows the transition from 'good-enough' job to job with better return, formal job security, and enhanced workers' rights. The third stage is the 'decent' job, which shows the transition from 'good' job to a state of productive employment in compliance with agreed international standards of working environment and workers' rights.
11. The economic growth process in Bangladesh, over the past two decades, has been in a position to generate employment in agriculture, rural nonfarm sector, urban informal sector, and the urban formal sector, mostly in garments. Apart from garments, employment in all other sectors has largely been for males, mostly informal in type. The nature of these jobs has been largely 'good enough'. The rise in employment in agriculture, in both crop and non-crop sectors, has been associated with virtually no progress toward 'good' job. Rises in employment in the rural nonfarm and urban informal sectors have also happened without much progress toward the creation of 'good' jobs in these sectors. For males, such expansion has helped moving out from unemployment or unpaid family labor to 'good-enough' jobs. For females, employment in the garments sector, in most cases, is a manifestation of the transition from no labor force participation or unpaid family jobs to paid jobs. Such paid jobs in most of the garment factories are largely 'good enough' in nature. All these suggest that jobs in Bangladesh are predominantly 'good enough' in nature.
12. In the near future, for the promotion of inclusive growth, the challenge of the Bangladesh economy, as far as the quality of employment is concerned, is how to make a transition from the current state of 'good-enough' jobs to large-scale 'good' jobs. In the medium to long term, the prospect of inclusive growth in Bangladesh would depend on how the growth momentum would be able to generate a successful transition toward a state of 'decent' job.
13. Imposition of terms and conditions for 'decent job' agenda may not be enough in promoting 'decent job' as the workers may themselves lack the quality to be absorbed in the transformation process due to their lower productivity. Hence, supply-side policies like spreading education and skill development programs to the mass population, removing socioeconomic barriers over educational attainments, and enhancing the diversity of training programs, taking into consideration domestic and global labor market demands, should be adapted.

Most importantly, to ensure the proper escalation of labor productivity, emphasis must be on the improvement of the quality of education and training as well.

14. The critical issue of local agricultural seasonality should be taken into consideration for any typical skill development training program. As socioeconomic attributes of participants systematically vary during the period of seasonality than normal time, understanding the seasonality and adequately addressing this into the design of the program are warranted to achieve a targeted population. Otherwise, programs will face issues like mistargeting, attrition, and dropouts.
15. Bangladesh is passing through a critical phase of the demographic dividend. However, the country is still far from making the best use of it. For making the best use of the demographic dividend, the critical policy areas should include investment on youth development, expanding access to family planning, investment in infrastructure, public health, education, especially female education and skill development. In addition, decisive policy emphasis should be on promoting both labor-intensive and skill-intensive jobs, savings, and openness to trade and foreign investment.
16. For further economic growth acceleration and employment generation in Bangladesh, there is a need for reforms in policies and institutions. This will require increased domestic private investment and foreign direct investment, targeting broader economic and export diversification. Emphasis should be not only on raising the level of investment but also on the efficiency of investment through the removal of a number of supply-side bottlenecks in the economy. There is a need for a new paradigm of macro-, trade, and investment policies with effective and time-bound support to emerging dynamic sectors.
17. There is a need for a well-designed and effective industrial policy, wherein monetary and fiscal incentives for the emerging dynamic sectors should be transparent and time-bound. In addition, industrial policy needs to address issues of education and skill development for facilitating higher capabilities for economic diversification, attracting FDI, and integrating with the global value chain.
18. Institutional reforms should be considered as a key to overall policy reforms. Improving the bureaucracy quality, ensuring property rights, managing corruption, and ensuring contract viability through reduction in the risk of contract modification or cancelation are examples of such institutional reforms. Furthermore, reducing political uncertainties or establishing political stability and generating political capital for economic diversification are critically important.

Structural Change in Bangladesh: Challenges for Growth and Employment Creation

Selim Raihan

1 Introduction

Bangladesh economy has undergone significant structural changes over the last four decades. The share of agriculture in GDP has declined from over 60% to less than 20%, while the relative significance of industry (including manufacturing), currently estimated to be 28% of GDP, and service sectors has increased substantially. The composition of the manufacturing sector during the 1990s and 2000s has become increasingly readymade garments (RMG) oriented. Driven by the expansion of the RMG industry, the share of employment in the manufacturing sector in Bangladesh rose from 9.5% in 1999–00 to 16.4% in 2013. As found in all low-income countries, the unemployment rate does not accurately capture deficiencies in the labor market (the rate was just 4.3% in 2013). Rather, the majority of workers are found in informal employment and suffer from under-employment. Gender disparities persist despite the rise in the share of female workers. In summary, robust economic growth in Bangladesh has been associated with both positive trends and persistent employment challenges such as lack of diversification, poor working conditions, low productivity, and a high degree of informality.

This chapter contains excerpts from the author's previous publications as op-eds in the newspapers and websites (see: https://www.thedailystar.net/op-ed/how-tackle-entitlement-failure-infrastructure-211636, and http://sanemnet.org/workers-the-heart-of-the-garment-industry-in-bangladesh/).

S. Raihan (✉)
Department of Economics, University of Dhaka, Dhaka, Bangladesh
e-mail: selim.raihan@gmail.com

S. Raihan
South Asian Network on Economic Modeling (SANEM), Dhaka, Bangladesh

S. Raihan (ed.), *Structural Change and Dynamics of Labor Markets in Bangladesh*, South Asia Economic and Policy Studies,
https://doi.org/10.1007/978-981-13-2071-2_1

Against this backdrop, this paper analyzes the nature of structural transformation in Bangladesh and elaborates on the major challenges for future growth acceleration and employment creation.

2 The Nature of Structural Transformation in Bangladesh

Over the past four decades, notwithstanding many external and internal shocks, Bangladesh has increased its per capita income by fourfold. As shown in Fig. 1, Bangladesh has been able to maintain healthy rates of growth in real GDP during the 2000s and the first half of 2010s. Bangladesh's economic growth rates in recent years (more than 6%) have been higher than most of the South Asian countries and many of the sub-Saharan African countries. Such economic growth has been associated with some important structural changes in the economy.

Structural change of the economy is the shift in resources from the less productive sectors of the economy to the more productive sectors, diversification and sophistication of production and exports, and discovery of new products (Felipe 2009). There have been some significant structural transformations in the Bangladesh economy in recent decades. Figure 2 shows that the share of agriculture, forestry, and fishing in GDP declined from 25.6% in 1999–2000 to 19.75% in 2011–12. The share of industry increased from 16.5 to 20.3% during the same period. While the share of construction increased from 7.9 to 9.3%, that of the service sector remained little over 50% during this period.

Table 1 presents the changes in the subsectoral shares of GDP during 1999–00 and 2011–12. Among the manufacturing subsectors, the sectors which have

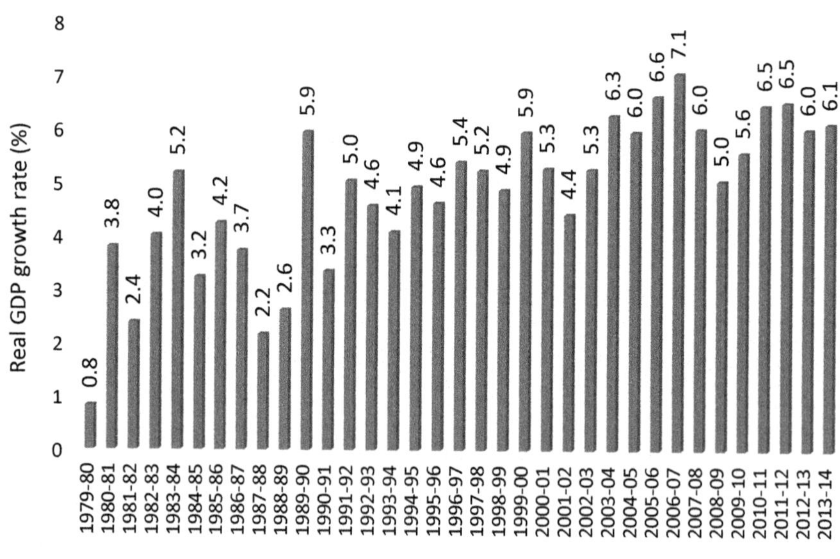

Fig. 1 Real GDP growth rate. *Source* World Bank, WDI

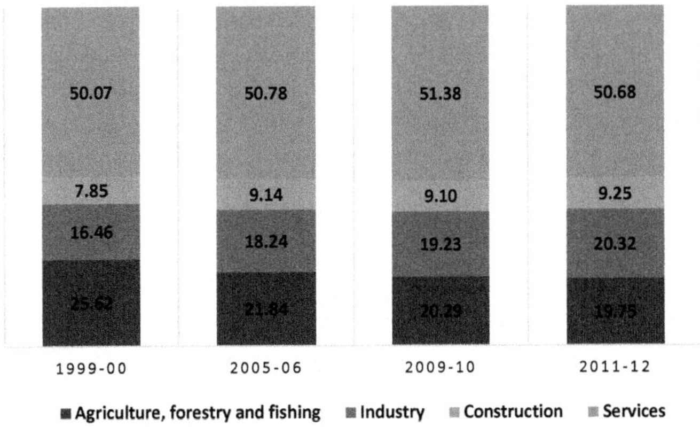

Fig. 2 Broad sectoral shares of GDP at constant (1995–96) prices (%). *Source* Author's calculation from the National Accounts data of BBS

Table 1 Subsectoral shares of GDP at constant (1995–96) prices (%)

Subsector	1999–00	2005–06	2009–10	2011–12
Agriculture, forestry and fishing	25.62	21.84	20.29	19.75
Mining and quarrying	1.03	1.16	1.29	1.26
Food and beverage	1.84	1.96	1.70	1.64
Tobacco	0.88	1.01	0.96	0.85
Textile and wearing apparel	4.38	5.09	5.78	7.20
Leather and footwear	0.50	0.41	0.38	0.34
Wood and wood products	0.29	0.22	0.25	0.33
Printing and publishing	0.46	0.44	0.41	0.35
Chemical, rubber and plastic	0.95	1.24	1.45	1.34
Petroleum and petroleum products	0.01	0.01	0.01	0.00
Metal and mineral products	1.33	1.36	1.34	1.32
Electrical machinery	0.10	0.13	0.12	0.12
Other manufacturing	4.69	5.21	5.53	5.57
Construction	7.85	9.14	9.10	9.25
Electricity, gas, water and waste management	1.44	1.65	1.60	1.72
Trade, hotel and restaurants	14.01	14.77	15.09	14.96
Transportation, storage and communication	9.22	10.07	10.79	10.70
Financial intermediation, real estate and other business activities	11.28	10.31	9.79	8.90
Public administration and defense	2.55	2.71	2.84	2.91
Education	2.21	2.49	2.71	2.83
Human health and social work activities	2.20	2.27	2.38	2.45
Other service activities	7.17	6.52	6.17	6.21
Total	100.00	100.00	100.00	100.00

Source Author's calculation from the National Accounts data of BBS

increased their shares over time are textile and wearing apparels, chemical, rubber and plastics, and other manufacturing involving mainly the small-scale industries. However, manufacturing subsectors such as food and beverage, tobacco, leather and footwear, and printing and publishing experienced fall in their shares. Shares of subsectors like petroleum and petroleum products and metal and mineral products remained stable. In case of services, most of services subsectors, except financial intermediation, real estate and other business activities, and other service activities, experienced rise in their shares during the same period.

Within the manufacturing sector, the shares of different subsectors in the manufacturing GDP are presented in Fig. 3. It is obvious that during 1999–00 and 2011–12, the major gainer has been the textile and wearing apparel subsector, which by 2011–12 increased its share of the manufacturing GDP to 37.8% from 28.4% in 1999–00. The rise in the share of textile and wearing apparel subsector during 2009–10 and 2011–12 has been quite remarkable, as its share increased by more than 5% points during that short span. While chemical, rubber and plastics, electrical machinery and other manufacturing could increase their shares by some margins during 1999–2000 and 2009–10, all other subsectors experienced fall in shares during that period. During 2009–10 and 2011–12, all manufacturing subsectors, except textile and wearing apparel, experienced fall in their shares in the manufacturing GDP. This suggests that over the years, in terms of subsectoral shares in value addition, the manufacturing sector has become more and more concentrated around the textile and wearing apparel sector.

In terms of the share in employment, quite a reverse picture emerges. Figure 4 shows that the combined share of agriculture, forestry, and fishing in 2013 was still quite high (45.1%) which however declined from more than 50% (50.8%) in

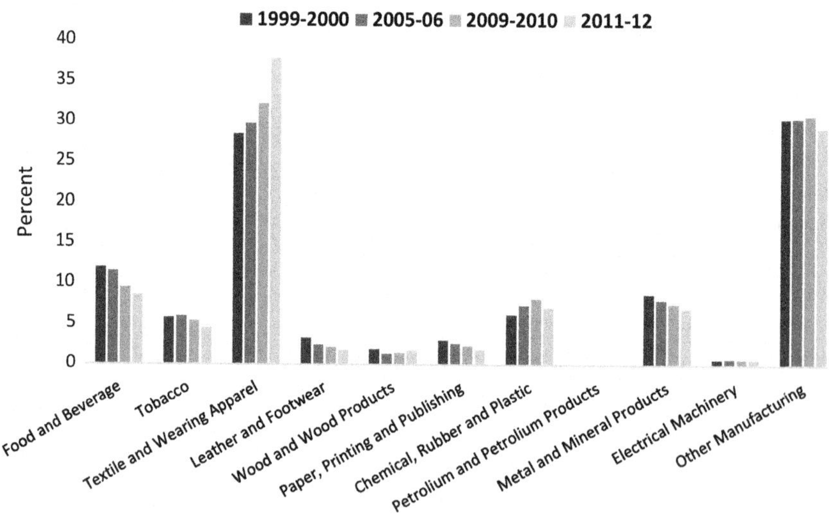

Fig. 3 Shares of different subsectors in the manufacturing GDP (%). *Source* Author's calculation from the National Accounts data of BBS

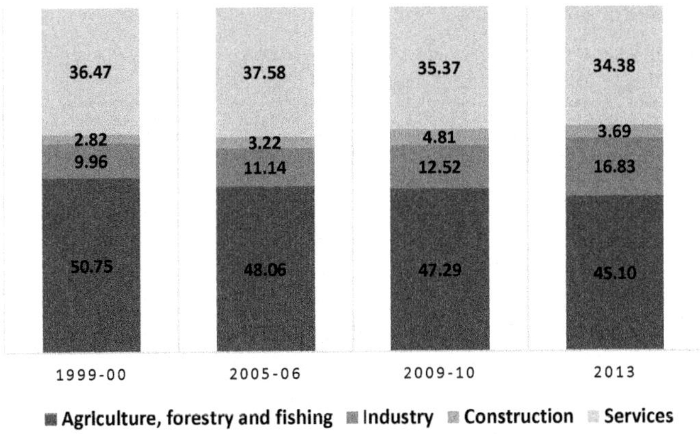

Fig. 4 Broad sectoral shares of employment (%). *Source* Author's calculation from the Labor Force Survey data

1999–00. Industry's share in total employment increased from around 10% in 1999–00 to 16.8% in 2013. The share of construction sector also increased quite significantly during 1999–00 and 2009–10 (from 2.8 to 4.8%) but declined to 3.7% in 2013. The share of services sector however declined from 36.5 to 34.4% during 1999–00 and 2013.

The subsectoral shares of employment are presented in Table 2. Among the manufacturing subsectors, all sectors, except leather and footwear and other manufacturing, experienced rise in their shares in total employment during 1999–00 and 2013. Among the services subsectors, except education and health subsectors, all subsectors experienced fall in their shares during the period under consideration.

Within the manufacturing sector, the shares of different subsectors in manufacturing employment are presented in Fig. 5. There is no clear pattern and trend.

Table 2 Subsectoral shares of employment (%)

Subsector	1999–00	2005–06	2009–10	2013
Agriculture, forestry and fishing	50.75	48.06	47.29	45.10
Mining and quarrying	0.45	0.11	0.20	0.40
Food and beverage	1.33	1.20	1.48	2.19
Tobacco	0.10	0.27	0.27	0.32
Textile and wearing apparel	3.73	4.57	7.46	8.35
Leather and footwear	0.49	0.22	0.16	0.16
Wood and wood products	0.81	0.95	1.09	2.27
Printing and publishing	0.17	0.24	0.12	0.28
Chemical, rubber and plastic	0.29	0.58	0.21	0.39
Petroleum and petroleum products	0.01	0.00	0.01	0.01

(continued)

Table 2 (continued)

Subsector	1999–00	2005–06	2009–10	2013
Metal and mineral products	0.63	1.10	0.75	1.20
Electrical machinery	0.14	0.06	0.04	0.17
Other manufacturing	1.81	1.84	0.74	1.08
Construction	2.82	3.22	4.81	3.69
Electricity, gas, water and waste management	0.38	0.19	0.23	0.34
Trade, hotel and restaurants	15.86	16.55	15.42	14.45
Transportation, storage and communication	6.34	8.39	7.42	6.45
Financial intermediation, real estate and other business activities	0.67	1.54	0.94	0.77
Public administration and defense	2.03	1.86	0.99	1.32
Education	2.67	2.76	2.37	3.23
Human health and social work activities	0.75	0.71	0.79	1.20
Other service activities	7.77	5.58	7.21	6.62
Total	100.00	100.00	100.00	100.00

Source Author's calculation from the Labor Force Survey data

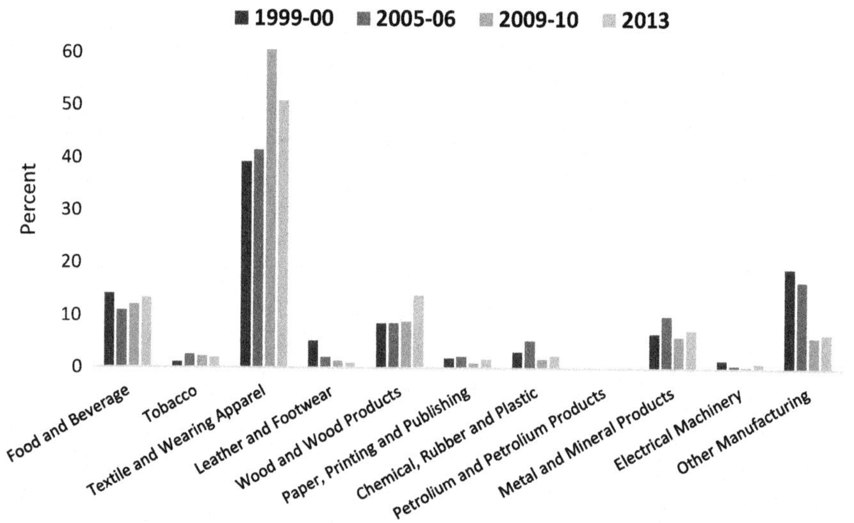

Fig. 5 Shares of different subsectors in manufacturing employment (%). *Source* Author's calculation from the Labor Force Survey data

Though the textile and wearing apparel is the major subsector of employment, as its share increased from 39% in 1999–00 to 60.5% in 2009–10, its share in total manufacturing employment declined to 50.8% in 2013. The subsector which experienced some significant rise in employment share during 2009–10 and 2013 is the wood and wood products, which had shares of around 8.5 to 8.9% during

1999–00 and 2009–10 but increased its share to 13.9% by 2013. Employment shares of other manufacturing subsectors fluctuated. However, there has been quite a remarkable drop in the share of other manufacturing, as its share declined from 19% in 1999–00 to 6.6% in 2013. The aforementioned analysis suggests that even with a decline in share in recent time, textile and wearing apparel is the major source of manufacturing employment in Bangladesh.

Despite some important structural transformation in the economy, the economic structure is still far from a well-diversified one. Figure 6 shows the trend in the calculated Herfindahl–Hirschman concentration index of value-added for three major sectors in the economy. It appears that in case of agriculture, forestry, and fishing, though the concentration index declined in general during 1989–90 and 2011–12, since 2004–05, the concentration ratio did not fall and in fact in recent years the concentration ratio increased. In case of manufacturing, there has been a gradual rise in the concentration index and since 2006–07, the pace in such rise increased quite considerably. This suggests that the manufacturing sector in recent years has become less and less diversified. Interestingly, the services sector in Bangladesh has remained well diversified and the situation did not change during 1989–90 and 2011–12.

Such lack of diversification in the overall economy is also reflected in the export basket of Bangladesh. Figure 7 shows the movement of the composition of export in different time periods. It is clearly evident that with the remarkable growth in total exports during 1995 and 2013, the export basket became more and more concentrated around readymade garments (RMG). The growth of Bangladesh's RMG exports had largely been attributable to international trade regime in textiles and clothing, which, until 2004, was governed by the multi-fiber arrangement

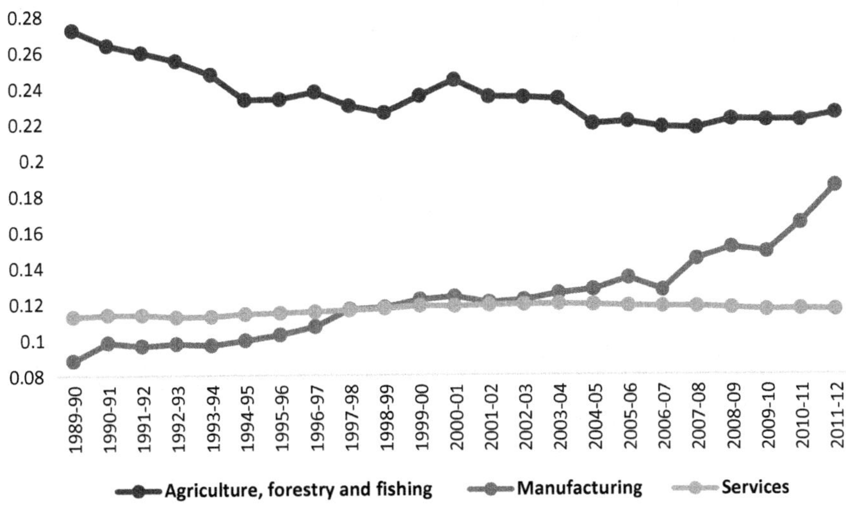

Fig. 6 Herfindahl–Hirschman concentration index of value-added. *Source* Author's calculation from the National Accounts data of BBS

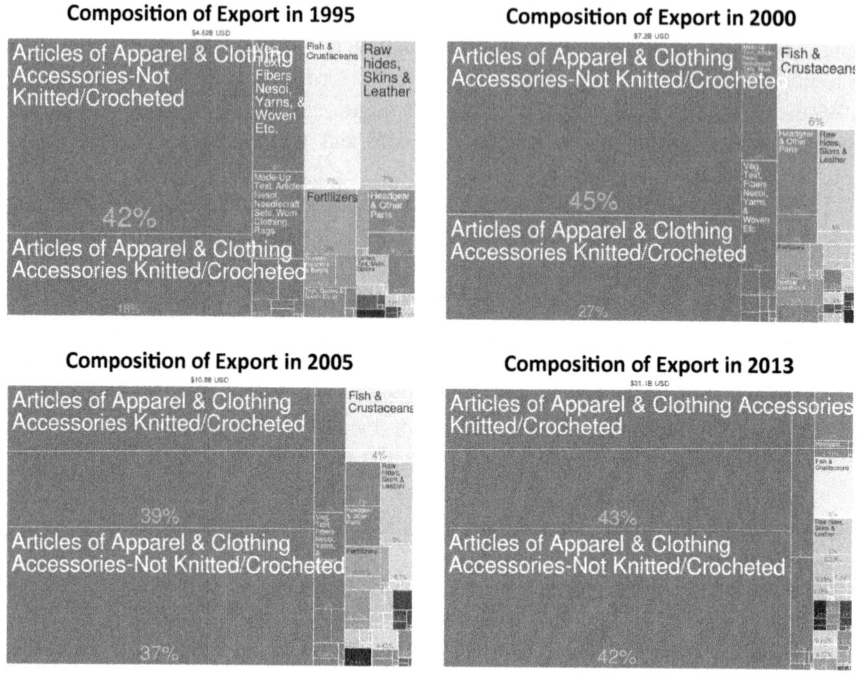

Fig. 7 Change in export composition. *Source* http://atlas.media.mit.edu/en/

(MFA) quotas. The quota system restricted competition in the global market by providing reserved markets for a number of developing countries including Bangladesh, where textiles and clothing items have not been traditional exports. The duty-free access for Bangladesh's RMG products in the EU has also greatly supported the growth of the sector.

One of the associated concepts of economic diversification is the economic complexity index. Hidalgo and Hausmann (2009) defined economic complexity index (ECI) as a measure of the production characteristics of large economic systems, usually whole countries. The goal of this index is to explain an economic system as a whole rather than the sum of its parts. The ECI looks to explain the knowledge accumulated in a country's population (the networks that people form) and that is expressed in the country's industrial composition. To achieve this goal, the ECI combines metrics of the diversity of countries and the ubiquity of products to create measures of the relative complexity of a country's exports. Figure 8 shows the trend in the ECI for Bangladesh between 1974 and 2012. It is observed that the ECI for Bangladesh has always been negative, except in 1978, suggesting very low level of economic complexity. The ECI had a fluctuating trend with improvements in some years. During 2000 and 2012, in general, ECI declined with some year-to-year fluctuations.

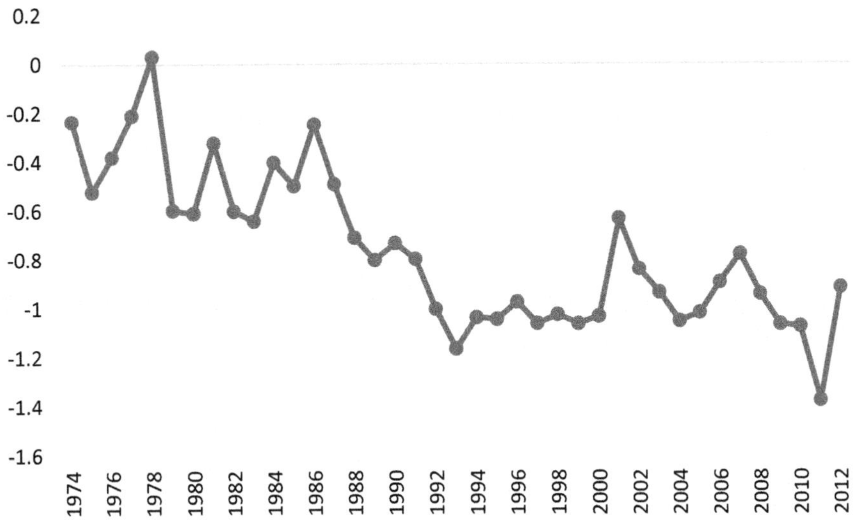

Fig. 8 Economic complexity index for Bangladesh. *Data Source* http://atlas.media.mit.edu/en/

3 Challenges for Economic Growth and Employment Creation in Bangladesh

3.1 Reform in the Policies and Institutions for Economic Diversification

Bangladesh's achievement in economic growth over the last one decade has been quite robust. The country has recently been upgraded from low-income country (LIC) to lower middle-income country (LMIC) as per World Bank's classification. There is an aspiration of graduating from the LDC status by 2024 as per UN classification. The 7th five-year plan sets the target of 8% GDP growth rate by 2020. There are also steep development targets under the Sustainable Development Goals (SDGs) to be achieved by 2030. This requires a huge leap forward from the current level of growth rate. This also requires a considerable structural change in the economy leading to large-scale economic diversification. Economic diversification is commonly viewed as a necessary condition for a sustained and long-term growth of the economy and job creation. Diversification is argued to be playing an important role in structural transformation of the economy from producing low value-added products to high value-added products. Promotion of labor-intensive and high-productivity sectors, both in the farm and nonfarm sectors, are therefore fundamental. This should be coupled with interventions to enhance productivity, jobs, and incomes in traditional and informal activities where there are large pools of surplus labor.

However, it is important to note that strategies specified in the different policies in Bangladesh for economic and export diversification lack clear guidelines as regards to implementation, and therefore, result in ineffective strategies. In the case of export diversification, it has been a matter of serious concern that though there are significant incentives provided to the export sector in Bangladesh, there is formidable difficulty in actually accessing such incentives and they helped little in diversifying the export basket. Furthermore, though the latest industrial policy identifies a number of high priority and priority sectors for economic diversification, there are several policy-induced and supply-side constraints that have constricted the development of these sectors. Unless and until these policy-induced and supply-side constraints are addressed, the agenda for further productive economic diversification will remain unfulfilled.

One strong view related to the policy for diversification of exports is its heavy emphasis on extensive tariff liberalization with the aim of reduction in anti-export bias. The policy conclusion that emerges from this stance is for low and uniform tariffs and a seamless export–import regime that facilitates least-cost transactions at the border. Tariff liberalization, under this view, is seen as a kind of 'auto' driver of export expansion and diversification of the export basket. While the importance of tariff liberalization for export promotion and diversification cannot be undermined, and in Bangladesh there is a need for further tariff rationalization and liberalization, tariff liberalization alone cannot by itself be sufficient to trigger 'auto' large supply responses in terms of expanding export volumes and diversifying the export basket. A number of supply-side constraints can prevent local producers from expanding exports, and the lack of an enabling environment can strangle entrepreneurship and innovation. Studies have indicated that Bangladesh faces several supply-side constraints. High lead time is an important challenge. Inefficiencies at ports and related internal road transportation further aggravate the problem. Among others, lack of investment fund and working capital, high interest rate, poor physical infrastructure, shortage of skilled workers, technological bottlenecks, lack of entrepreneurship and management skills, poor law and order situation, lack of information, invisible costs of doing business, etc. are major impediments to export prospects and export diversification. Therefore, the policy options and support measures for exports are much more difficult and involved than the mere reduction of tariffs.

It is important to note that in the discourse of policy reforms for economic diversification, the political economy perspective is generally ignored and reform of institutions is largely overlooked. A favorable overall incentive structure through the management and distribution of 'rent' is important for diversification. Experiences from many developing countries show that the dominant sector becomes the main beneficiary of different incentives (both formal and informal) while for other sectors, such schemes appear to be less effective primarily due to various structural bottlenecks as mentioned before. In this process, the dominant sector grabs the lion's share of the 'rent' being generated through such incentives.

This situation also raises a critical question as to whether 'rents' are needed for the promotion of other sectors. Experiences from successful countries highlight the importance of providing effective incentives to other sectors and removing structural bottlenecks in order to generate some 'rents' in those sectors. However, it should be kept in mind that while generating such 'rent', there is a need for a well-designed and effective industrial policy wherein monetary (interest rate subsidies) and fiscal incentives (reduced taxes or tax holidays) for the emerging dynamic export sectors should be transparent and time-bound. In addition, industrial policy needs to address the issues of education and skill development for facilitating higher capabilities for economic diversification, attracting FDI and integrating with the global value chain.

Experiences from different countries also suggest that institutional reforms should be considered as a key to overall policy reforms. Improving the bureaucracy quality, ensuring property rights, managing corruption, ensuring contract viability through reduction of the risk of contract modification or cancelation are examples of such institutional reforms. Furthermore, reducing political uncertainties or establishing political stability and generating political capital for economic diversification are critically important.

3.2 *Transition from 'Good-Enough' Job to 'Decent' Job*

Though there are many views on 'inclusive growth', the key consensus is that 'inclusive growth' is a growth process which reduces poverty and inequality, promotes 'decent' jobs, reduces social exclusion, and promotes economic and social cohesion. One of the major pillars of inclusive growth is 'decent' job, where 'decent' job is referred to a productive job for women and men in conditions of freedom, equality, security, and human dignity. It also involves opportunities for work that deliver a fair income; provides security in the workplace and social protection for workers and their families (ILO 2011).

Bangladesh economy had been growing at a rate over 5% over the last two decades. There are arguments that such growth in Bangladesh has been largely 'inclusive' in nature and Bangladesh has been successful in generating 'good' jobs by improving farm–nonfarm, rural–urban interindustry inter-sectoral labor mobility at a relatively low skill level that had poverty reducing and social cohesion enhancing effects (Hossain et al. 2012). Such claims demand careful examination as it is not clear how 'good' job is defined in the context of Bangladesh economy. It is equally important to understand what needs to be done in the transition towards a regime of 'decent' jobs, a critical factor for the promotion of 'inclusive growth' in the country.

'Decent' job should be regarded as a dynamic and progressive phenomenon. There could be three stages for moving towards 'decent' job. The first stage is the 'good-enough' job which shows the transition from no job to job or from unpaid family job to paid-job. The second stage is the 'good' job which shows the transition from 'good-enough' job to job with better return, formal job security, and enhanced workers' rights. The third stage is the 'decent' job, which is the transition from 'good' job to a state of productive employment in compliance with agreed international standards of working environment and workers' rights.

The economic growth process in Bangladesh, over the past two decades, has been in a position to generate employment in agriculture, rural nonfarm sector, urban informal sector, and the urban formal sector, mostly in RMG. Apart from RMG, employment in all other sectors has largely been for males, mostly informal in type. The nature of these jobs has been largely 'good-enough'. Rise in employment in agriculture, both in the crop and non-crop sectors, has been associated with agricultural growth and rise in agricultural real wage, with virtually no progress towards 'good' job. Rises in employment in the rural nonfarm and urban informal sectors have also happened without much progress towards the creation of 'good' jobs in these sectors. For males, such expansion has helped moving out from unemployment or unpaid family labor to 'good-enough' jobs. For females, employment in the RMG sector, in most cases, is a manifestation of the transition from no labor force participation or unpaid family jobs to paid-jobs. Such paid-jobs in most of the RMG factories are largely 'good-enough' in nature. Thus, the RMG sector has been able to generate very large 'good-enough' jobs, which however has also contributed to the reduction in poverty and generating growth in Bangladesh.

It should also be kept in mind that though the economic growth process over the past two decades has been able to increase the rate of female labor force participation in Bangladesh, the rate is still very low. Evidence suggests that female labor force participation reduces the likelihood of household poverty; and resources in females' hands have a range of positive outcomes for human capital and capabilities within the household. Thus, there is a strong rationale for ensuring females' participation in the economy's growth process. Education, skill development, public and private sector initiatives in investment in the care economy as well as different social protection programs can be very useful in increasing female labor force participation.

While discussing 'inclusive growth', it is equally important to understand the quality of structural transformation that has happened in the process of economic growth in Bangladesh. Though the share of industrial sector in GDP has increased from around 20% in the early 1990s to around 30% by late 2000s, with a simultaneous reduction in the share of agricultural sector, there is still a long way to go for the creation of large-scale 'good' jobs in the urban sectors. This will require both quantitative and qualitative changes in the current pattern of structural transformation of the economy. The economy is yet to have a strong and diversified manufacturing base, which requires supporting macroeconomic, trade and industrial policies and removal of policy-induced and supply-side constraints.

In the near future, for the promotion of inclusive growth, the challenge of the Bangladesh economy, as far as the quality of employment is concerned, is how to make a transition from the current state of 'good-enough' jobs to large-scale 'good' jobs. In the medium to long-term, the prospect of inclusive growth in Bangladesh would depend on how the growth momentum would be able to generate successful transition towards a state of 'decent' job.

3.3 The Future of the RMG Industry in Bangladesh

Manufacturing is now an overwhelmingly salient component of Bangladesh's export composition, thanks largely to the rapid expansion of the RMG industry. From a small base of only around US$32 million in 1984, garment exports have grown to around US$25 billion by 2014, accounting for more than three-quarters of export earnings. RMG has been an important contributor to growth and employment generation in Bangladesh. Female participation in the formal labor market underwent a major shift with the rise of the RMG industry in Bangladesh. It provides direct employment to over 4 million people, 70% of whom are female. More than 50% of the manufacturing labor force is now employed in this sector, and the sector accounts for 30% of the investment in manufacturing. Therefore, the story of the growth of the manufacturing sector in Bangladesh over the past two decades has been the story of the success of the RMG sector.

There is no denying the fact that the success story of the RMG industry in Bangladesh lies in its comparative advantage generating from the country's large pool of unskilled labor. Considering the fact that Bangladesh's Asian neighbors and competitors such as India, Pakistan, Sri Lanka, and China also have large pool of unskilled labor, it is certainly astounding how Bangladesh has been able to retain its comparative advantage till date and has enjoyed continued export growth. While cheap labor has been the single most important advantage of Bangladesh, the local industry has flourished in spite of numerous challenges, e.g., high cost of doing business, weak infrastructure, weak governance, and labor unrests.

There have been concerns with regard to the compliance issues and the workplace safety in the RMG industry in Bangladesh, and in the last couple of years, these issues have become very critical for the future of this industry. There is strong international pressure, in the form of the threat of canceling large preferences in the markets of Western countries, if labor conditions are not improved. Quality competitiveness is getting increased priorities over price competitiveness, and of course, quality of a product embodies the standard of living of labor being used in the production process. These concerns should be addressed in a positive way as an opportunity to build industry's reputation in the global market. This calls for, among many other things, to deal with labor issues in the garment industry carefully. In this context, issues like wage, workplace security, fringe benefits, workplace environment, etc. need to be resolved on a priority basis. Current labor practices prevalent in the garment industry need to be improved in order to make the sector sustainable. Improvement of the labor condition is closely linked to the enhancement of the productivity of labor. There is equally a need to invest in training workers to move up to the higher value-added garment products. The BGMEA and the government should collaborate with each other, with help from relevant international agencies, to be able to work effectively in this area.

The RMG industry of Bangladesh is now at a crossroad. It is now time to focus on how Bangladesh could retain its comparative advantage and continue its success story. Reliance on only the mass pool of unskilled labor doing things in the old way would be not sufficient. Careful examination of Bangladesh's comparative advantage in the RMG industry reveals the fact that the nature of this advantage is primarily static in nature. This suggests, retaining the static comparative advantage will be highly challenging in the future given the increased competition from other countries, growing stringent compliance issues, and the fact that to what extent the country will be able to enhance its competitiveness in doing business. Therefore the sector should aim for generating dynamic comparative advantage which would ensure the sustainability of this sector in the future. There is a critical need for enhancing labor productivity, moving up to the higher value-added products through introducing new technology along the production line spurring innovation, and enhancing Bangladesh's competitiveness by reducing the cost of doing business.

It is also essential to keep in mind that comparative advantage does not necessarily translate into competitive advantage. Given an environment of high cost of doing business, in order to maintain the competitive advantage, there is a tendency of putting downward pressure on workers' wages and benefits. In this context, for the workers' welfare, there is a critical need for reducing the cost of doing business in Bangladesh. Otherwise, this will eventually determine the competitive advantage of Bangladesh's garment industry and exports. Addressing these issues requires strategic planning and its adroit implementation.

The future of the RMG industry will be critical for Bangladesh's socioeconomic development. Although the evidence on trade–growth and trade–poverty relationships as found in academic studies is still far from being conclusive, the growth of RMG exports has been associated with the overall economic growth of the country accompanied by a remarkable progress on poverty alleviation. Even without going deep into such hotly debated subjects as whether the export sector has been the 'engine' of growth and to what extent the growth has been equitable to reach the poorest groups, it can be said that the RMG-led export growth process has established a direct link between trade and poverty in Bangladesh by creating massive employment opportunities. And the sustainability of this industry also depends on how carefully and properly the issues related to the welfare of the workers are addressed.

3.4 Tackling 'Entitlement Failure' in Infrastructure

In the discourse on infrastructure and economic growth, the dominant area of discussion is on the quantity and quality of infrastructure and how countries differ in these respects. While most of the countries emphasize a lot on investing in raising the quantity (and quality) of infrastructure, there is a fundamental concern whether rising supply of infrastructure ensures the access to infrastructure. This problem is manifested through the fact that due to a variety of reasons, enhanced supply of infrastructure may not solve the problem of 'entitlement failure' in terms of effective access to infrastructure, as the people/sectors in dire need of improved infrastructure may not have the access even with an increased supply.

There appears to be a consensus among researchers and policy makers that infrastructure is a key contributing factor to economic growth. The importance of infrastructure for economic development originates from the fact that it provides both final consumption services to households and key intermediate consumption items in the production process. The deficiency of some of the most basic infrastructure services is an important dimension of poverty; and therefore, increasing level of infrastructure stock has a direct bearing on poverty reduction. Furthermore, while it is generally accepted that economic diversification is a necessary condition for a sustained and long-term growth of the economy and job creation, infrastructure development is a prerequisite for economic diversification.

What is the significance of economic diversification as far as 'inclusive growth' is concerned? If inclusive growth is defined as the inclusiveness in economic opportunities, economic diversification can help attain inclusive growth. However, several supply-side constraints related to weak infrastructure can restrict economic diversification. Some of these constraints are broadly 'general' in nature and some are critically 'sector-specific'. Interconnection and complementarities between general and sector-specific infrastructures are key elements for increasing service efficiency, supporting the adoption of innovative technologies, promotion of economic diversification, and supporting inclusive growth.

Yet, policymakers in the developing countries are so inclined to improvement in the broad general infrastructure, i.e., enhanced supply of electricity, improvement in roads, improvement in port facilities, etc., that the developments of critical sector-specific infrastructure are largely overlooked. Embarking on developing broad general infrastructure are relatively easy, whereas solving sector-specific infrastructure problems involves identifying priorities in the policy making process and addressing a number of political economic issues. Failure to deal with sector-specific infrastructure problems leads to a scenario where a large number of potential inclusive growth-enhancing sectors fail to enjoy the benefit from the improvement in broad general infrastructure, and thus end up with 'entitlement failure'.

One such example is the leather industry in Bangladesh which accounts for around one billion US$ in exports and which has huge potentials in generating employment and growth by increasing export of higher value-added products. However, this sector has not yet reached its full potential primarily due to operating constraints stemming from its production base in Hazaribagh of Dhaka city where there are minimal waste management systems and inadequate industrial layout planning. The Hazaribagh-centric tannery industry is now legally bound to relocate all the factories to a new environmentally compliant tannery estate (under construction) on the outskirts of Dhaka city. However, such relocation has been stuck for many years with unresolved decisions on cost sharing of various components of the new industrial estate. Yet, there is no denying the fact that unless this relocation is effectively done, the leather sector will continue to suffer from 'entitlement failure' despite significant improvements in broad general infrastructure.

Factors responsible for such entitlement failure include the lack of resources to undertake sector-specific infrastructure development, lack of reliable data to determine finance and manpower requirements of projects, lack of infrastructure development framework that adequately delineate links between general and sector-specific infrastructure requirements, inadequate planning, inadequate supporting institutions, and unstable political environments. However, on top of all these, the major critical factor behind the failure to address sector-specific infrastructure problems is the inability of the political system to deliver a political consensus around strategic plans for such sector-specific infrastructure and stable policy frameworks to support their implementation.

How to deal with this entitlement failure? A major part of the sector-specific infrastructure problems needs to be solved through public investment. The priorities in the industrial and related policies need to be realigned to the country's long-term economic growth strategy in the changing world economy. There is a need for generating political capital for such realignment. However, the task of developing such infrastructure facilities cannot be left to the government alone. It is binding on policy makers to come forward with strategies and mechanisms to encourage private sector participation in such sector-specific infrastructure developments. Such mechanisms should not only provide paper strategies but also practical ways of turning into tangible projects through the provision of adequate finance.

3.5 Making Most of the Demographic Dividend

For long, debates among economists and social scientists on the impact of population change on economic development centered on positions that population growth either restricts, promotes, or is independent of economic development. Despite the merits of these views, a critical issue is largely ignored which is the age structure of the population that can change dramatically as the population grows. As people's economic behavior varies at different stages of life, changes in a country's age structure can have substantial effects on its economic performance. This latter view relates to a 'demographic dividend' which can exert a large positive effect on the economy stemming from a favorable age structure of the country.

The demographic dividend is not, however, automatic. With the right kind of policy environment, this demographic dividend can attain the targeted objectives. This brings to the fundamental question: how to make the most of the demographic dividend?

A simple association between the demographic dividend and per capita income, as is shown in the scatter-plot in Fig. 9, can shed some light on this issue. The scatter-plot is generated with the data of 124 countries for the period between 1950 and 2010 with five-year intervals. The demographic dividend is calculated from the data of the United Nations (Department of Economic and Social Affairs-Population Division) and is defined as the ratio of working age population to the dependent population. The per capita income data are from the World Bank WDI. Since demographic dividend might have a lag effect on per capita income change, we assume that the data of demographic dividend for any particular year corresponds to

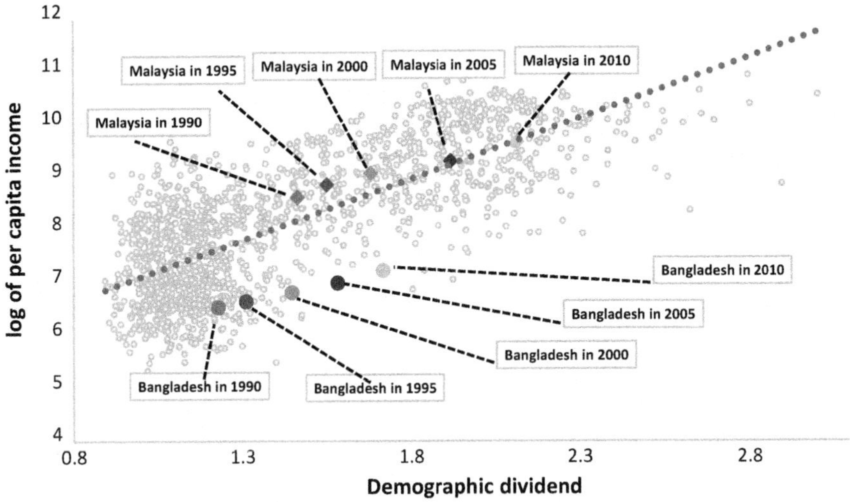

Fig. 9 Demographic dividend and economic growth. *Note* The scatter-plot is generated with the data of 124 countries for the period between 1950 and 2010 with five-year intervals (Color figure online). *Data source* United Nations Department of Economic and Social Affairs-Population Division and World Bank, WDI

the average per capita income data for the subsequent five years. For example, demographic dividend data for 1950 corresponds to the average of per capita income data for 1951–1955. The trend line (red-dotted) shows a very strong positive association between the demographic dividend and per capita income. Though simple, even this scatter-plot tells us a very interesting story. If we compare Malaysia with Bangladesh, we find that both Malaysia and Bangladesh, between 1990 and 2010, were experiencing rising demographic dividends which contributed to the rise in their per capita incomes. However, Bangladesh has always been much below the trend line; whereas Malaysia was always on or above the trend line. This suggests that compared to Bangladesh, Malaysia was much better able to utilize its demographic dividend to raise its per capita income during the period under consideration. For Bangladesh, the concern is that the country is yet to exploit the demographic dividend it has, and over time, the distance from the trend line has enlarged. Interestingly, in 2010, Bangladesh had the demographic dividend similar to that Malaysia had in 2000, but Bangladesh in 2010 had one-seventh of the per capita income of what Malaysia had in 2000.

The lesson for Bangladesh is that for making the best use of the demographic dividend to successfully capitalize on shifts in country's age structures to gain a boost in economic productivity, the critical policy areas should include investment in youth development, expanding access to family planning, investment in infrastructure, public health, education, especially female education, and skill development. Also, decisive policy emphasis should be on promoting both labor-intensive and skill-intensive jobs, savings and openness to trade and foreign investment.

4 Conclusion

The analysis in this paper suggests that, for further economic growth acceleration and employment generation in Bangladesh, there is a need for reforms in the policies and institutions, promoting the transition from ‘good-enough’ job to ‘decent’ job, investment in infrastructure and tackling ‘entitlement failure’ in infrastructure, and making most of the demographic dividend through investment in youth development, public health, education, and skill development.

All these will require increased domestic private investment and FDI targeting broader economic and export diversification. Emphasis should be not only on raising the level of investment but also on the efficiency of investment through the removal of a number of supply-side bottlenecks in the economy. There is a need for a new paradigm of macro, trade and investment policies with effective and time-bound support to emerging dynamic sectors.

Reform of economic and political institutions for efficiency gains is critically important. Improving the bureaucracy quality, managing corruption, reducing political uncertainties and establishing political stability, generating political capital for larger private sector investment and accelerated economic growth, are all part of the institutional reform.

References

Felipe, J. (2009). *Inclusive growth, full employment and structural change: Implications and policies for developing Asia.* Manila: Asian Development Bank.

Hidalgo, C. A., & Hausmann, R. (2009). The building blocks of economic complexity. *Proceedings of the National Academy of Sciences, 106*, 10570–10575.

Hossain, M., Sen, B., & Sawada, Y. (2012). *Jobs, growth and development: making of the "other" Bangladesh.* WDR 2013 Background Paper.

International Labor Organization. (2011). *Working with the ILO—Decent work and system wide coherence.* Geneva: International Labor Organization.

What Determines the Choice Between Farm and Nonfarm Employments in the Rural Bangladesh?

Selim Raihan and Syer Tazim Haque

1 Introduction

With a small geographic size and huge population, employment generation for all economically active population is a major challenge in Bangladesh. Though agriculture has been the major employment generating sector, the rural economy in Bangladesh has been experiencing a transition over the past two decades. While unpaid family work in the rural areas is still highly farm-based, paid employment is mainly experiencing the transition, shifting more towards the nonfarm activities. World Bank (2004) reported that the rural nonfarm sector in Bangladesh accounted for about 40% of rural employment during early 2000s. Recent labor force surveys reveal some strong evidence of growth in the rural nonfarm economy. The growth of the rural nonfarm sector is very evident, because, with the limited arable land and intensification of the ones that are available reaching its peak, agricultural sector is least likely to absorb the growing rural labor force. With these contexts in frame, the current paper provides an overview of the potential determinants of the nonfarm participation in rural Bangladesh, and makes a systematic analysis of the determinants of employment-switch between farm and nonfarm sectors in rural Bangladesh. In this paper, we use data from the Household Income and Expenditure Surveys (HIES) of Bangladesh Bureau of Statistics (BBS) as the HIES data provides detailed household-level socioeconomic information, which is helpful for such analysis.

This chapter contains excerpts from the authors' previous publication as an op-ed in a newsletter (see: http://sanemnet.org/sanemafeefcontainer/uploads/2014/10/Thinking-Aloud_VI_N6.pdf).

S. Raihan (✉)
Department of Economics, University of Dhaka, Dhaka, Bangladesh
e-mail: selim.raihan@gmail.com

S. Raihan · S. T. Haque
South Asian Network on Economic Modeling (SANEM), Dhaka, Bangladesh

S. Raihan (ed.), *Structural Change and Dynamics of Labor Markets in Bangladesh*, South Asia Economic and Policy Studies,
https://doi.org/10.1007/978-981-13-2071-2_2

2 Literature Review

Studies conducted in the contexts of many developing countries found evidence of rural nonfarm sector contributing to the growth of rural economy and reducing poverty (Hymer and Resnic 1969; Binswanger 1983; Islam 1984; Saith 1992; Ranis and Stewart 1993; Hayami and Kikuchi 2000; Berdegué and Escobar 2002). In general, these studies found that rural nonfarm sector, through employment generation, helped in diversifying the earning source of the rural households. Not only did many households find their employment in the vibrant rural nonfarm sectors, but also many households undertook the nonfarm activities as secondary jobs for smoothing consumption in the lean agricultural seasons. Indeed, smoothing consumption is found to be a major problem in many agrarian societies and there is a large body of literature to support this claim (Khandker 2009).

There are some debates on the definition of rural nonfarm sector. Hossain (2004) considered a narrow definition of the rural nonfarm activities which included only nonagricultural activities and excluded non-crop farming activities such as livestock, fisheries, and forestry. Davis and Bezemer (2003) however emphasized that the definition of rural nonfarm sector depends on what definition of agriculture is being used. Agriculture may include crop production and non-crop activities such as forestry, fisheries, livestock rearing, horticulture (flowers and vegetables) or it may include crop activities only and exclude the non-crop part. Lanjouw and Lanjouw (1997) defined rural nonfarm economy as being all those income generating activities (including income in kind) that are not agricultural but located in rural areas. Keeping in mind the aforementioned debate, in this paper, we have defined rural nonfarm economy comprising all those nonagricultural activities which generate income to rural households, either through wage employment or self-employment.

3 Pattern and Trend of the Nonfarm Employments in Rural Bangladesh

The transition from farm to nonfarm occupation started taking place in the early 1980s. But, during the 1990s nonfarm sector became more prominent and started contributing more to income generation. By the year 2000, about 40% of the income for the rural households was derived from the nonfarm sources (BBS 2000). Along with the household-level contribution, nonfarm sector contributed substantially to GDP as well accounting for about one-third of it where the agricultural sector contributed to about a quarter (World Bank 2004).

The diversification of employment over time took place in two major ways. There had been a structural change in the agricultural employment during this

Table 1 Share of farm and nonfarm employments in total rural employment (%)

Sectors	1995	2000	2005	2010
Farm employment	**60.36**	**63.12**	**56.76**	**55.16**
Of which				
Crop agriculture	54.63	55.19	52.9	49.24
Non-crop agriculture	5.73	7.93	3.86	5.92
Nonfarm employment	**39.64**	**36.88**	**43.24**	**44.84**
Total	**100.00**	**100.00**	**100.00**	**100.00**

Source HIES data different years

period and the other change was brought upon by shifting out of labor from the agricultural sector. It appears from Table 1 that in rural Bangladesh, there has been a decline in the share of farm employment from 60.36% in 1995 to 55.16% in 2010 and simultaneous rise in the nonfarm employment from 39.64 to 44.84% during the same period. Even with the farm employment, there has been a shift from crop agriculture to non-crop agriculture as the share of crop agriculture declined from 54.63 to 49.24% and that of non-crop agriculture (with some fluctuations) increased from 5.73 to 5.92% during the period under consideration.

A further disaggregation can be done to analyze the occupational structure in the nonfarm activities. Table 2 shows the participation of head of the households (who were in occupation) in various activities. The share of 'agricultural, animal husbandry, forestry and fisheries' declined from 64.04% in 1995 to 56.52% in 2010. Among the nonfarm activities, there have been notable rises in the shares of 'production and related workers and transport workers' and 'service workers' during that period. While the shares of 'professional, technical and related workers', and 'sales workers' remained more or less stable, the share of 'clerical and related workers and govt. executive' declined drastically during 2005 and 2010.

Table 2 Household heads' major occupation in the rural area (% of total)

	1995	2000	2005	2010
Professional, technical and related workers	4.49	5.50	7.19	5.85
Administrative and managerial works	0.11	0.21	0.10	2.31
Clerical and related workers and govt. executive	2.14	8.09	8.86	1.58
Sales workers	13.00	10.68	12.30	10.84
Service workers	3.94	5.08	7.09	6.58
Production and related workers and transport workers	11.37	9.13	7.78	16.32
Agricultural, animal husbandry, forestry and fisheries	64.94	61.31	56.69	56.52
Total	**100.00**	**100.00**	**100.00**	**100.00**

Source HIES data different years

4 Overview of the Potential Drivers of Employment Switch in Rural Bangladesh

Available literature suggests that there could be a number of push and pull factors which can determine the employment switch between farm and nonfarm activities in rural Bangladesh. These are land ownership, age, education, relative wages, and rural infrastructure. Before, going into any systematic analysis with regard to the impact of these factors on the choice of employment, this section provides an overview of these potential drivers of employment switch.

4.1 Land Ownership

Figure 1 shows a rise in the share of households with less than 0.5 acres of land during 1995 and 2010 from 56.49 to 59.97% (though the share rose quite dramatically to 65.6% in 2000). It also appears that the share of households with higher average land size had been declining. This clearly indicates the growing trend of landlessness in rural Bangladesh and the concentration of land in the hands of fewer households over time.

4.2 Age Distribution

Hossain (2004) found that the nonfarm participation was higher among younger households. Rahman (2013) also found that younger generation had a preference to

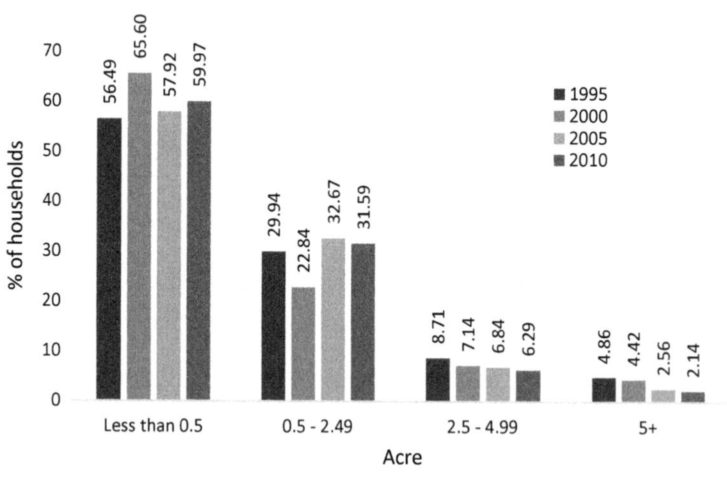

Fig. 1 Distribution of rural households by size of owned land. *Source* HIES data different years

participate in the nonfarm activities in the rural areas. It is also evident from Table 3 that during 1995 and 2010, in general, though the participation in the nonfarm activities increased among all age groups, such rise had been much higher for the younger age groups compared to the older age groups.

4.3 Education

Higher level of educational attainment can stimulate the choice in favor of nonfarm employment (Islam 1997; Hossain 2004). Figure 2 shows that during 2000 and 2010, 'no education' among rural adults declined from around 62–55%, while the share of adults with education above the primary level increased over time. This suggests that though majority of the rural adults are yet deprived of education, the scenario is gradually changing.

It is also observed that there are differences in education attainment between farm and nonfarm households (as classified by the occupation of the household head). Figure 3 shows the differences in mean years of schooling of the adults between farm and nonfarm households. Mean years of schooling is found to be higher for the nonfarm households for all three years compared to farm households. Also, the rise in mean years of schooling during 2000 and 2010 had been higher for nonfarm households (47%) compared to the farm households (41%).

4.4 Real and Relative Wages

One important finding of Hossain (2004) was that nonfarm activities are more productive in nature and provides a higher return. Hence that mobility across sectors can be interpreted as is fueled from a pull factor. Figure 4 highlights the differences in nominal and real wage across broad sectors during 1991–92 and 2011–12. Though all broad sectors observed increase in nominal wages, fisheries sector is found to be at the bottom. Manufacturing and construction had been on the top in all those years. The gap between manufacturing and agriculture widened during the mid-2000s; however, such gap got reduced in recent years. Similar pattern emerges in the case of real wages as well.

Table 4 provides disaggregated sectoral level relative wages with respect to the daily wage in crop cultivation. It is clear that between 2000 and 2005, the gaps between the wage of crop cultivation and wages of most of the nonfarm activities widened; though between 2005 and 2010, such gaps were reduced. However, in 2010, wages in all nonfarm activities were considerably higher than that of the crop cultivation.

Table 3 Farm and nonfarm participation by age distribution

Age group	1995			2000			2005			2010		
	Farm	Nonfarm	Total	Farm	Nonfarm	Total	Farm	Nonfarm	Total	Farm	Nonfarm	Total
15–24	61.56	38.44	**100**	60.48	39.52	**100**	50.32	49.68	**100**	48.34	51.66	**100**
25–34	55.07	44.93	**100**	58.85	41.15	**100**	50.28	49.72	**100**	48.51	51.49	**100**
35–44	55.32	44.68	**100**	60.15	39.85	**100**	56.05	43.95	**100**	53.65	46.35	**100**
45–54	61.74	38.26	**100**	65.89	34.11	**100**	60.78	39.22	**100**	60.63	39.37	**100**
55–64	71.77	28.23	**100**	74.83	25.17	**100**	70.31	29.69	**100**	68.99	31.01	**100**
65+	75.47	24.53	**100**	78.64	21.36	**100**	73.78	26.22	**100**	71.69	28.31	**100**

Source HIES data different years

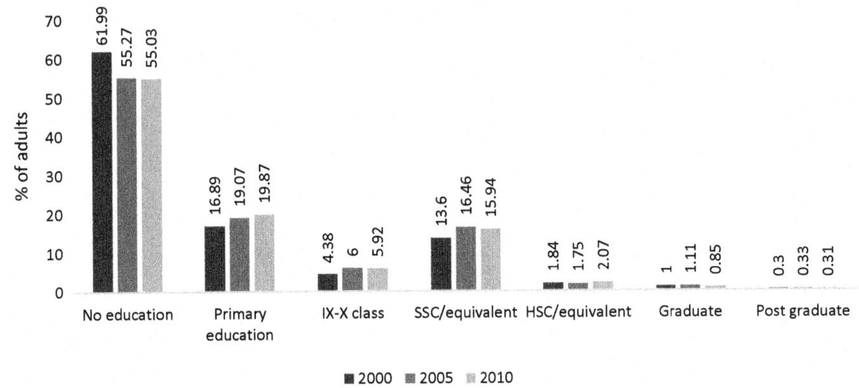

Fig. 2 Progress in the educational attainment in rural areas during 2000 and 2010. *Source* HIES data different years

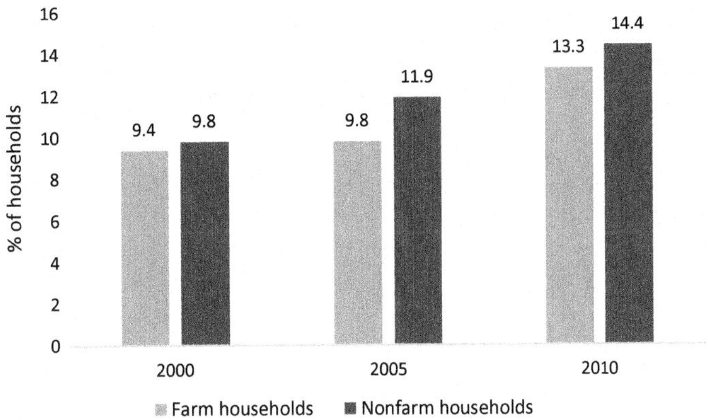

Fig. 3 Difference in mean years of schooling of adults. *Source* HIES data different years

Fig. 4 Over time changes in wage rates (1991–92 = 100). *Source* BBS. The original data has 1969–70 as the base. We have adjusted it for 1991–92 as the base. The real wage rates have been calculated by dividing the nominal wage with national CPI

Table 4 Daily relative sectoral wages in rural areas with respect to wage in the crop cultivation

Sector	2000	2005	2010
Crop cultivation	1.0	1.0	1.0
Livestock rearing	0.4	2.2	0.9
Poultry rearing	1.1	3.1	1.2
Fisheries	1.2	1.8	1.2
Forestry	1.4	1.5	0.8
Mining and quarrying	1.1	1.6	1.0
Food processing	0.8	1.9	1.3
Textile	1.2	2.6	1.0
Wearing apparel	0.6	5.1	1.4
Leather	1.0	4.4	1.5
Wood and furniture	1.5	1.8	1.1
Paper, printing and publishing	1.1	6.6	1.8
Chemical, rubber and plastic	1.7	7.3	1.4
Transport equipment	0.8	2.5	1.0
Electricity gas and water	2.4	10.0	1.5
Construction of building	1.8	1.5	1.1
Electrical installation (under specialized construction)	1.6	2.6	1.8
Repairing of vehicles	0.7	2.6	1.1
Wholesale and retail and other trade	1.0	3.0	1.3
Land transport	1.6	2.8	1.1
Water transport	1.1	3.9	1.2
Postal courier	0.6	6.2	1.9
Hotel and restaurants	0.9	2.5	1.3
Administrative and support activities	0.8	9.5	1.8
Education	2.1	7.4	1.8
Health	2.8	7.4	1.8
Other service	1.0	2.9	1.2
Activities of household as employers	0.6	1.8	1.5

Source Authors' calculation from LFS data

4.5 Infrastructure

Infrastructure can be an important catalyst in generating nonfarm employment (Islam 1997; Hossain 2004; Deichmann et al. 2008). Figure 5 shows that there has been a significant improvement in rural paved roads during 2002–03 and 2011–12. Though all three categories of rural roads, namely Upazilla road, Union road and Village road experienced positive growth, the expansion of the Village road in recent years has been quite remarkable.

Figure 6 clearly shows that there has been a remarkable rise in the share of rural households with access to electricity. In 1995, only 10.32% of rural households had

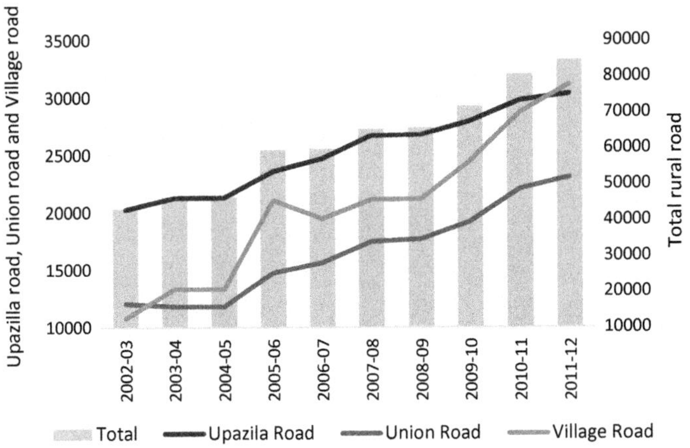

Fig. 5 Growth in rural paved roads (in kilometers). *Source* Statistical Pocketbook of BBS, various years

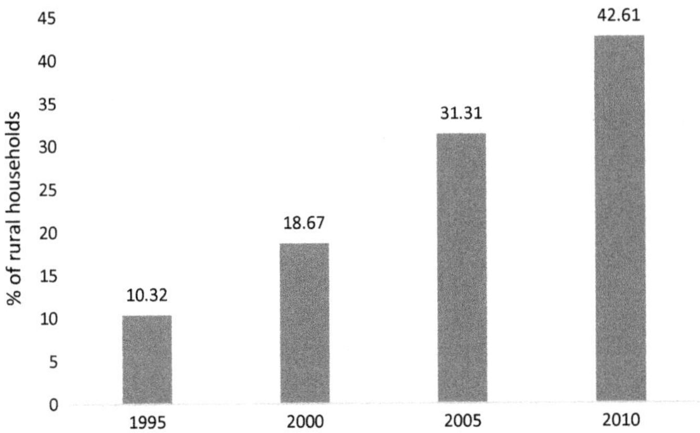

Fig. 6 Percent of rural households with access to electricity. *Source* HIES data different years

access to electricity, and by 2010, the share increased to 42.61%. Figure 7 indicates that the nonfarm households had much greater access to electricity than the farm households during the period under consideration.

The development of rural infrastructure in recent years is also manifested by the remarkable rise in the mobile phone subscribers in the rural areas. Figure 8 shows that between 2005 and 2010, both for farm and nonfarm households the access to mobile phone increased quite dramatically. The nonfarm households seem to have larger access to mobile phone than their counterparts.

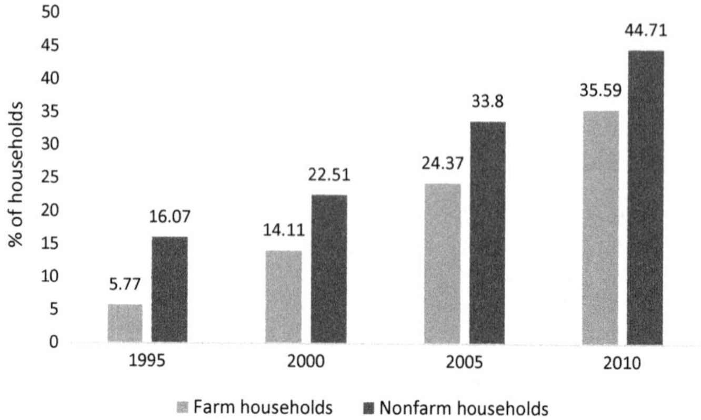

Fig. 7 Percent of rural farm and nonfarm households with access to electricity. *Source* HIES data different years

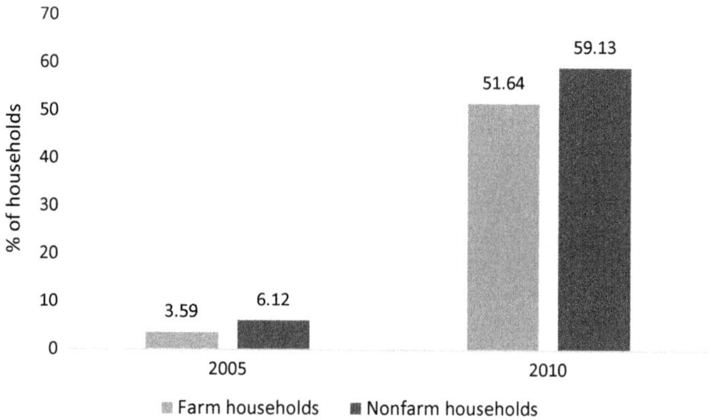

Fig. 8 Percent of rural farm and nonfarm households with access to mobile phone. *Source* HIES data different years

5 Determinants of Employment Switch in Rural Bangladesh: A Pseudo Panel Econometric Analysis

One of the major limitations of most of the empirical studies on the rural nonfarm sector employment in Bangladesh is that they used cross-section data and could not take into account a longer time horizon, and control for endogeneity and heterogeneity bias. This is where the current study differs from others as the study develops a pseudo panel database considering four rounds of HIES data over a time span of 15 years, and this allows to control for the aforementioned biases.

Since the HIES does not survey the same households in different years, constructing a normal panel is not possible. However, to capture the dynamics of employment-switch over time, the necessity of a panel data cannot be stressed any further. Therefore, this study constructs a pseudo panel data set using four rounds of the HIES from 1995 to 2010. Since this paper only focuses on the rural households, a pseudo panel data for the rural households is constructed separately. Data of rural households for each survey year is divided into 100 cohorts where the cohorts are defined based on percentile ranking of monthly consumption expenditure of households. As there are 100 cohorts in each survey year, four rounds of data generate 400 observations in total.

In the panel regression, the dependent variable is the relative nonfarm participation (the ratio of the number of adults participating in the rural nonfarm activities to the number of adults participating in the rural farm activities within any percentile cohort). This variable shows the switch between rural nonfarm and farm employments. The explanatory variables are relative nonfarm income, average age of adults within any percentile cohort, average years of schooling of adults within any percentile cohort, the labor force participation (LFP) rate of adults within any percentile cohort, rural infrastructure, as represented by the share of households with access to electricity in total households within any percentile cohort, and the size of land holding within any percentile cohort. All variables are expressed in natural logarithms.

This study uses a two-stage instrumental variable regression method to tackle the endogeneity problem arising from the variable relative nonfarm income (ratio of nonfarm to farm income). At the first stage, a regression is run considering the factors affecting the relative nonfarm income to get the endogeneity corrected predicted values of relative nonfarm income. The results of the first stage regression are presented in Table 5. Selection of appropriate instrumental variable (IV) for this model is complicated because any variable that affects the farm–nonfarm participation is likely to affect relative nonfarm income. However, the relative nonfarm

Table 5 Results from the first stage fixed effect regression

Explanatory variables	Dependent variable: relative nonfarm income (ratio of nonfarm to farm income)
	Fixed effect coefficients
Age of household head	−0.54 (0.70)
Age of adults in the household	2.74[a] (0.20)
Average years of schooling of household head	0.90[a] (0.03)
Average years of schooling of adults	0.27[a] (0.08)
LFP rate of adults	−1.81[a] (0.37)
% of households with access to electricity	0.68[c] (0.41)
Constant	−8.66[b] (2.75)
Number of observation	400
F	354.95
Prob > F	0.000

Note a, b and c indicate statistical significance at the 1, 5 and 10% levels respectively. The figures in parentheses are the standard errors

income comprises of both nonfarm income and capital or asset income. This, in particular, is the key to IV selection. From empirical testing, it is found that household head's education did not have any statistically significant impact on farm–nonfarm employment switch but household head's education showed a positive correlation with nonfarm income. Therefore, household head's education has been used as the IV in the two-stage regression.

In the second stage, the predicted value of the relative nonfarm income is used as the explanatory variable, along with other explanatory variables, in the fixed effect regression model of farm–nonfarm employment switch. The results are shown in Table 6. Average age of the adults has a negative significant effect and average education of the adults has a positive significant effect on the relative nonfarm participation, suggesting younger and educated adults tend to participate more in the nonfarm activities than in farm activities. A 10% decline in the average age of adults and a 10% increase in the average years of schooling of the adults lead to the rise in the relative nonfarm participation by 5.7% and 1.7%, respectively. Relative nonfarm income has a positive impact: a 10% rise in the relative nonfarm income leads to the rise in relative nonfarm participation by 1.6%. The rural LFP rate has a positive effect, as a 10% rise in rural adults' LFP rate leads to the rise in relative nonfarm participation by 3.8%. Rural infrastructure, as represented by the share of households with access to electricity in total households in the rural area, has a positive impact, as 10% rise in such ratio leads to 8.8% rise in the relative nonfarm participation. Finally, landholding has a negative impact: a 10% rise in the average size of landholding leads to reduction in relative nonfarm participation by 0.1%.

Table 7 reports the regression on computed z-scores of the variables in the second stage regression from Table 6. It is found that as far as the employment in the rural nonfarm sector relative to the farm sector is concerned, the largest positive

Table 6 Results from second stage fixed effect regression

Explanatory variables	Dependent variable: relative nonfarm participation
	Fixed effects coefficients
Age of adults	−0.57[a] (0.13)
Average years of schooling of adults	0.17[b] (0.08)
Relative nonfarm income (predicted)	0.16[a] (0.02)
LFP rate of adults	0.38[c] (0.22)
% of households with access to electricity	0.88[a] (0.31)
Average land size	−0.01[c] (0.007)
Constant	1.59[b] (0.52)
Number of observation	400
F	25.17
Prob > F	0.000

Note a, b and c indicate statistical significance at the 1, 5 and 10% levels respectively. The figures in parentheses are the standard errors

Table 7 Regression on computed Z-scores from the second stage fixed effect regression

Explanatory variables	Dependent variable: Z score of relative nonfarm participation
	Fixed effects coefficients
Z score of age of adults	−0.54[a] (0.12)
Z score of average years of schooling of adults	0.30b (0.14)
Z score of relative nonfarm income (predicted)	0.50[a] (0.08)
Z score of LFP rate of adults	0.10[c] (0.06)
Z score of % of households with access to electricity	0.31[a] (0.12)
Z score of average land size	−0.01[c] (0.005)
Constant	−4.25e−08 (0.03)
Number of observation	400
F	25.28
Prob > F	0.000

Note a, b and c indicate statistical significance at the 1, 5 and 10% levels respectively. The figures in parentheses are the standard errors

effect comes from the rise in the relative nonfarm income followed by the improvement in rural infrastructure and education of the adults, and the largest negative effect stems from age of the adults.

6 Conclusion

Notwithstanding its falling share in economic output, agriculture still accounts for the major share of employment in Bangladesh. As employment generation in the formal urban manufacturing sector is mostly concentrated in the textile and garment sectors, where an overwhelming majority of wage laborers are women as against of a male-dominated rural farm labor market, the traditional theoretical argument of formal manufacturing sectors pulling rural laborers may not be forthcoming although the 'push factors' continue to generate migration to urban areas. On the other hand, the capacity of agriculture in absorbing additional labor force is extremely limited because of declining arable land (due to population pressure), the cropping intensity already reaching the peak, and further technological progress likely to be capital-intensive yielding low-employment elasticity of output. Therefore, the rural–urban labor market linkages would not be enough for productively absorbing the surplus workforce. Rather, it is the rural nonfarm economy, which should act as the engine of employment generation.

The analysis in this paper suggests that younger and more educated people participate more in the rural nonfarm sector. Also, improvement in rural infrastructure plays a positive stimulus. Another very important finding is that nonfarm employment offers a higher income potential compared to farm employment which works as a major pull factor for the employment in the nonfarm sector. It also appears that the decline in the landholding works as a major push factor for nonfarm participation.

References

Bangladesh Bureau of Statistics. (2000). *Household income and expenditure survey*. Dhaka: Bangladesh Bureau of Statistics (BBS).

Berdegué, J. A., & Escobar, G. (2002). Rural diversity, agricultural innovation policies and poverty reduction. *Agricultural Research & Extension Network*, Paper No. 122.

Binswanger, H. P. (1983). Agricultural growth and rural non-farm activities. *Finance and Development*, 38–40.

Davis, J., & Bezemer, D. (2003). *Key emerging and conceptual issues in the development of the rural non- farm economy in developing countries and transition economies*. DFID unpublished mimeo Report. 2.

Deichmann, U., Shilpi, F., & Vakis, R. (2008). *Spatial specialization and farm-nonfarm linkages*. Policy Research Working Paper 4611, World Bank.

Hayami, Y., & Kikuchi, M. (2000). *A rice village saga: Three decades of green revolution in the Philippines*. New York: Barnes and Nobles.

Hossain, M. (2004). *Rural non-farm economy in Bangladesh: A view from household surveys*. Dhaka: Centre for Policy Dialogue (CPD).

Hymer, S., & Resnick, S. (1969). A model of an agrarian economy with nonagricultural activities. *The American Economic Review, 59*(4), 493–506.

Islam, R. (1984). Non-farm employment in rural Asia: Dynamic growth or ploretarization? *Journal of Contemporary Asia, 14*, 306–324.

Islam, N. (1997). *The non-farm sector and rural development: Review of issue and evidence*. Food, Agriculture and the Environment Discussion Paper. 22.

Khandker, S. R. (2009). *Poverty and income seasonality in Bangladesh*. Policy Research Working Paper WPS4923, World Bank.

Lanjouw, J., & Lanjouw, P. (1997). *The construction of poverty lines: Methods and assumptions*. Mimeo: Yale University.

Rahman, M. (2013). Socio-economic determinants of off-farm activity participation in Bangladesh. *Russian Journal of Agricultural and Socio-Economic Sciences, 1*(13).

Ranis, G., & Stewart, F. (1993). Rural non-agricultural activities in development: Theory and applications. *Journal of Development Economics, 40*, 75–201.

Saith, A. (1992). *The rural non-farm economy: Processes and policies*. Geneva: International Labor Organization.

World Bank. (2004). *Summary report. Vol. 1 of Bangladesh—Promoting the rural non-farm sector in Bangladesh*. Washington, DC: World Bank.

How Does Employment Status Matter for the Well-Being of Rural Households in Bangladesh?

Selim Raihan and Fatima Tuz Zohora

1 Introduction

In rural Bangladesh, a great challenge is to tackle the low pay, poor-quality jobs that are unrecognized and unprotected by law, widespread underemployment, the absence of rights at work, inadequate social protection, and the lack of representative voice. There is no denying the fact that efficient labor markets can contribute to raising the quantity and quality of employment. However, there remains a big question whether poverty in rural Bangladesh is concentrated in certain employment categories. Against this background, this paper examines the link between different forms of employment and well-being of rural households in Bangladesh.

This paper uses the data from the Bangladesh Integrated Household Survey (BIHS) of IFPRI. This data are nationally representative data of rural Bangladesh for the year 2011–2012 where the sample size is 6,500 households in 325 primary sampling units (PSUs). The reason for using the BIHS database for this study is that this is the latest available survey data on rural Bangladesh. This study has attempted systematic analysis in understanding the association between employment status and well-being of rural households in Bangladesh.

From the BIHS data, the study has used consumption expenditures as the principal indicator of household economic status or well-being and has used per capita consumption expenditure as the proxy for income. The total consumption expenditure is measured as the sum of total food consumption and total nonfood

S. Raihan (✉)
Department of Economics, University of Dhaka, Dhaka, Bangladesh
e-mail: selim.raihan@gmail.com

S. Raihan · F. T. Zohora
South Asian Network on Economic Modeling (SANEM), Dhaka, Bangladesh

S. Raihan (ed.), *Structural Change and Dynamics of Labor Markets in Bangladesh*, South Asia Economic and Policy Studies,
https://doi.org/10.1007/978-981-13-2071-2_3

expenses excluding lumpy expenditures. Income (expenditure) deciles have been created by dividing the households into ten groups from the lowest to the highest in terms of households' total income. Employment statuses have been constructed for those household heads who are able and eligible to participate in the labor market. By definition, the labor force consists of everyone above the age of 15 who are employed (including individuals working without pay) or unemployed but actively seeking employment. Household head, not counted in the labor force, includes students, retired people, disabled people, and discouraged workers who are not seeking work.

2 Literature Review

The 2013 World Development Report calls jobs a cornerstone for development that connects living standards, productivity, and social cohesion—all critical for achieving inclusive growth (World Bank 2013). There is also a consensus in economic literature that access to good, steady jobs, and living wages are key to alleviate rural poverty in countries like Bangladesh. However, when it comes to using rural employment promotion as a tool for promoting rural development, both the quantitative and qualitative aspects of employment need to be taken into account for promoting both productive employment and decent work in a mutually reinforcing manner. In this regard, it is very important to address numerous types of labor relations and various forms of labor force participation at disaggregated level, which may include wage earners in both farm and nonfarm sectors, self-employed both in farm and nonfarm sectors, unpaid family workers, and unemployed.

Several studies emphasized the link between the nature of employment and poverty. Gutierrez et al. (2007), using a sample of 104 short-run growth spells in developing countries between 1980 and 2001, found that, in the short run, though the overall employment intensity of growth did not matter for poverty reduction, the sectoral pattern of employment growth and productivity growth were important for poverty reduction. Krongkaew et al. (2006), in the case of Thailand, showed that poverty reduction in Thailand was attained through a combination of high growth and productive employment, and the probability of being poor was related to farm income, place of residence, household size, and male household head. In the case of rural employment and poverty, Chadha (2008) and Kumar et al. (2011) found that increased employment in the rural nonfarm sector had a significant positive effect on reducing rural poverty in India.

Mahmud (1996) observed that, in the case of Bangladesh, the process of labor shift from agriculture to rural nonfarm sector showed an uncertain balance of the "push versus pull" factors that might have kept rural poverty situation from deteriorating, without making much improvements in the situation either. Rahman and

Islam (2003) found that the poor in Bangladesh were more likely to be casual workers and were in informal sectors, and the probability of a household being poor decreased with the increase in employment in nonfarm sectors. The study also found that wageworkers were more prone to poverty than the self-employed. In addition, Rahman (2004) observed that those in wage employment in the agricultural sector faced higher chances of poverty due to the lower average income of wage employed compared to that of self-employed. The study suggested that rural nonfarm self-employment should be an important mechanism for improvement of income of those closer to the poverty threshold. Furthermore, the study by Islam (2004) showed that the shift from agriculture to manufacturing sector had positive implication on reducing poverty, but agriculture also had a prominent role in pro-poor growth in developing countries. The study argued that relative prices of agricultural products with respect to nonagricultural products would be an important factor for pro-poor growth. Osmani and Latif (2013) investigated the major determinants of poverty for the year 2000–2010 in Bangladesh and found that poverty reduction was more for the self-employed and nonfarm workers than that for agricultural wage labors.

3 Overview of Pattern of Employment and Well-Being in Rural Bangladesh

3.1 Distribution of Employment Categories

The distribution of the different employment categories in the labor force is shown in Fig. 1. In the x-axis, 10 deciles are organized in ascending order on the basis of monthly consumption expenditure of the rural households. Therefore, first decile is the poorest one and the 10th decile is the richest one. The figure summarizes that, while wage employment is mostly concentrated in the poorer deciles, self-employment is concentrated mostly in the richer deciles. Salaried employed maintains smaller shares among poorer deciles.

Figure 2 presents the distribution of deciles by employment categories in the rural area. Individuals who work as wage labor are mostly from poorer deciles. More than 50% of total wage employment in the farm sector is from the poorest three deciles. In the case of wage employment in the nonfarm sector, around 40% are from the poorest three deciles. In the case of self-employment, for both the farm and nonfarm sectors, the distributions of 10 deciles are largely even and similar. For both these categories of employment, the bottom three deciles have around 27–28% shares. Salaried employment is mostly from the decile 4 and above. Unpaid family job is mostly from the decile 3 and above. In the unemployed category, the decile 1 has the highest share (21.3%) followed by the decile 6 (20%).

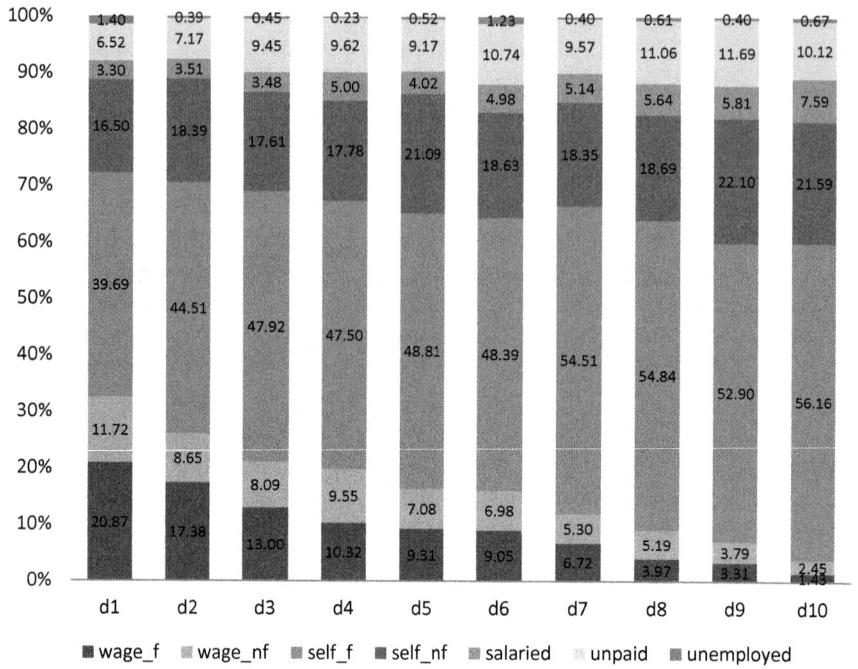

Fig. 1 Distribution of employment categories by income deciles. *Note* di = deciles, where i = 1, 2, …, 10; wage_f = wage employment farm; wage_nf = wage employment nonfarm; self_f = self-employment farm; self_nf = self-employment nonfarm; salaried = salaried employment; unpaid = unpaid family job; unemployed = unemployed. *Source* Calculated from the Bangladesh Integrated Household Survey (BIHS) data of IFPRI 2011–12

3.2 *Land Ownership and Employment Categories*

Figure 3 shows the average landholding per capita by employment categories in the rural areas of Bangladesh. People who are unpaid have the highest per capita land (0.33 acres) followed by people working as self-employed in the farm sector (0.32 acres). People employed as wageworkers, both in the farm and nonfarm sectors, have the least per capita land, 0.12 and 0.10 acres, respectively. Self-employed people in the nonfarm sector, salaried and unemployed people have per capita landholdings of 0.16, 0.18 and 0.17 acres, respectively.

Figure 4 shows the figures of land income as percentages of households' total income for different income deciles. The poorest decile has the lowest share of 16%. This share has an increasing trend up to the fourth decile with a figure of around 22% for that income decile. With some fall in the share for decile 5 and decile 6, the share rises to around 22% for both decile 7 and decile 8. For the top income decile, the share is little over 16%.

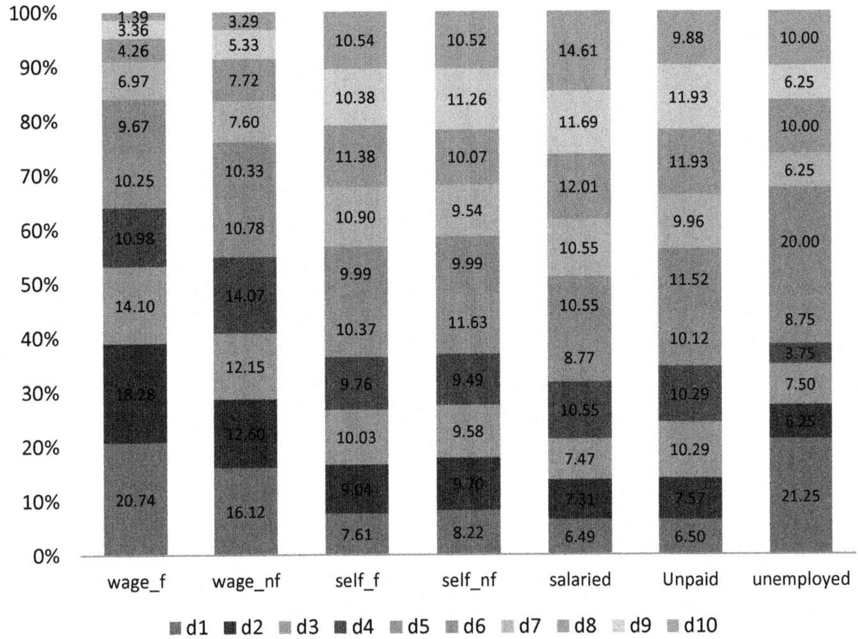

Fig. 2 Distribution of income deciles by employment categories. *Note* di = deciles, where I = 1, 2, ..., 10; wage_f = wage employment farm; wage_nf = wage employment nonfarm; self_f = self-employment farm; self_nf = self-employment nonfarm; salaried = salaried employment; unpaid = unpaid family job; unemployed = unemployed. *Source* Calculated from the Bangladesh Integrated Household Survey (BIHS) data of IFPRI 2011–12

Fig. 3 Average landholding per capita (acres). *Note* wage_f = wage employment farm; wage_nf = wage employment nonfarm; self_f = self-employment farm; self_nf = self-employment nonfarm; salaried = salaried employment; unpaid = unpaid family job; unempd = unemployed. *Source* Calculated from the Bangladesh Integrated Household Survey (BIHS) data of IFPRI 2011–12

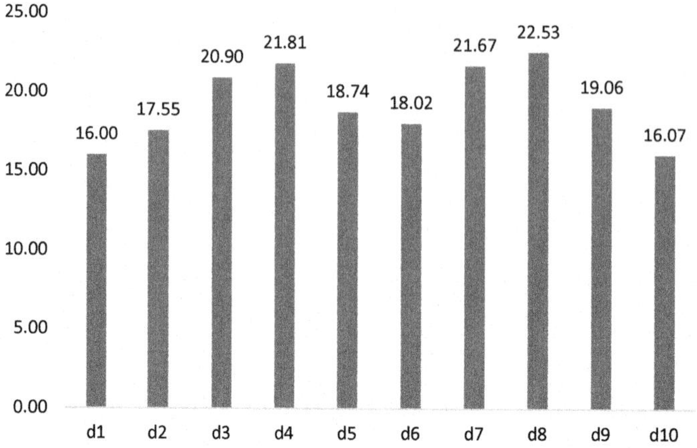

Fig. 4 Percentage of land income in total income. *Note* di = deciles, where I = 1, 2, ..., 10. *Source* Calculated from the Bangladesh Integrated Household Survey (BIHS) data of IFPRI 2011–12

3.3 Education and Employment Categories

Figures 5 and 6 show the educational status of the male and female workers by employment categories in the rural areas. Males with no education seem to be highly concentrated in the wage employment in both farm and nonfarm sector. They are also densely present in the self-employment activities. In the salaried employment category, the dominant share is of the males with less than secondary level but higher than primary education. However, males with HSC and beyond HSC account for around 25% of the salaried employment.

On the other hand, females with no education seem to be highly concentrated in wage employment (Fig. 6). Females with less than primary education have a dominant share in the case of unemployed (55.56%). In the case of the unpaid family job for the female adults, around 28% of them are with less than secondary but higher than primary education.

3.4 International Remittances

Figure 7 shows the shares of international remittance income in total income of rural households by heads' employment categories. Households with heads in the wage employment, both in the farm and nonfarm sectors, have the least shares of remittance income in total income, which is around 1%. Households with heads in the farm self-employment have on average the second highest share (12.66%). The highest share is actually observed in the case of unemployed category.

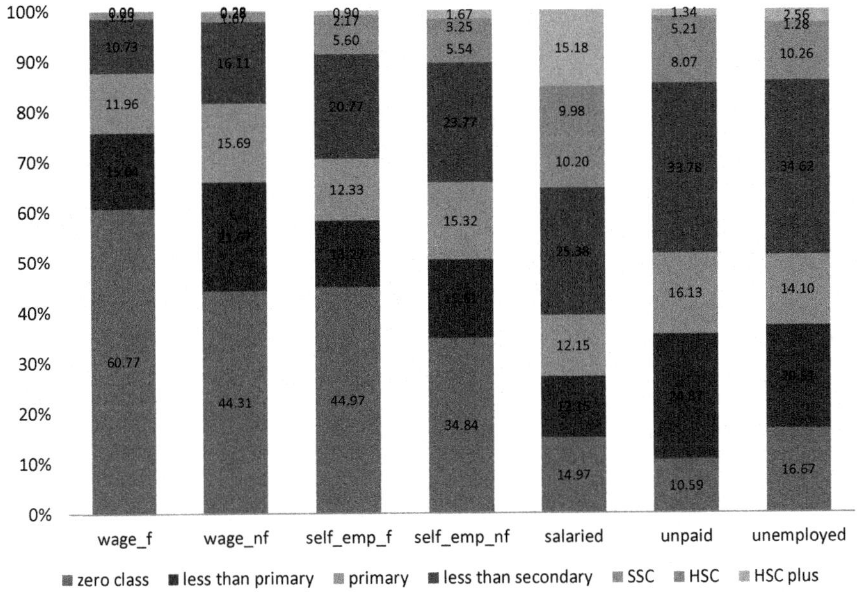

Fig. 5 Education by employment categories (male). *Note* wage_f = wage employment farm; wage_nf = wage employment nonfarm; self_f = self-employment farm; self_nf = self-employment nonfarm; salaried = salaried employment; unpaid = unpaid family job; unemployed = unemployed. *Source* Calculated from the Bangladesh Integrated Household Survey (BIHS) data of IFPRI 2011–12

Figure 8 presents the figures of remittance income share in total income of rural households by income deciles. Remittance share varies between 2% and more than 18%, where the richest decile having a share of more than 18% and the poorest decile having a share of less than 2%.

4 Does Employment Status Matter in Rural Well-Being? Insights from Econometric Exercises

In order to investigate the factors affecting well-being of rural household in Bangladesh, the paper has used the cross section multinomial logistic regression models. The income status of the household is considered as the dependent variable, where per capita consumption expenditure is used as a proxy for households' income status. For the explanatory variables, the paper has used different categories of employment of household head, e.g., wage labor in the farm and nonfarm sector, self-employed in the farm and nonfarm sector, salaried worker, and unpaid worker; all of these are dummy variables, where "unemployed" has been considered as the base employment status. Other explanatory variables are age of household head,

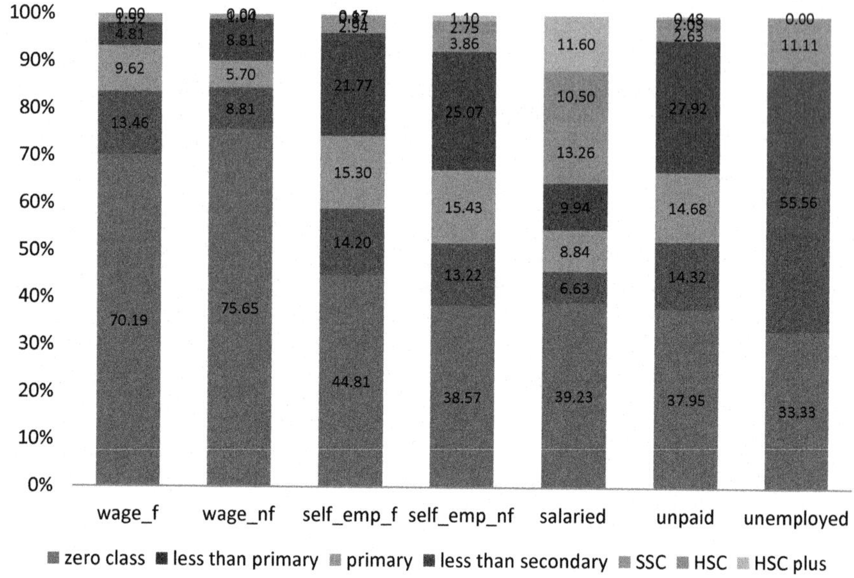

Fig. 6 Education by employment categories (female). *Note* wage_f = wage employment farm; wage_nf = wage employment nonfarm; self_f = self-employment farm; self_nf = self-employment nonfarm; salaried = salaried employment; unpaid = unpaid family job; unemployed = unemployed. *Source* Calculated from the Bangladesh Integrated Household Survey (BIHS) data of IFPRI 2011–12

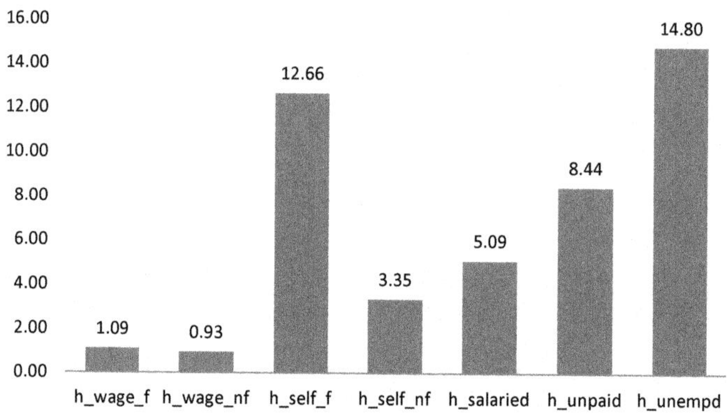

Fig. 7 Percent share of remittance income in total income by household heads' employment category. *Note* h_wage_f = head's wage employment in farm; h_wage_nf = head's wage employment in nonfarm; h_self_f = head's self-employment in farm; h_self_nf = head's self-employment in nonfarm; h_salaried = head's salaried employment; h_unpaid = head's unpaid family job; h_unemployed = head is unemployed. *Source* Calculated from the Bangladesh Integrated Household Survey (BIHS) data of IFPRI 2011–12

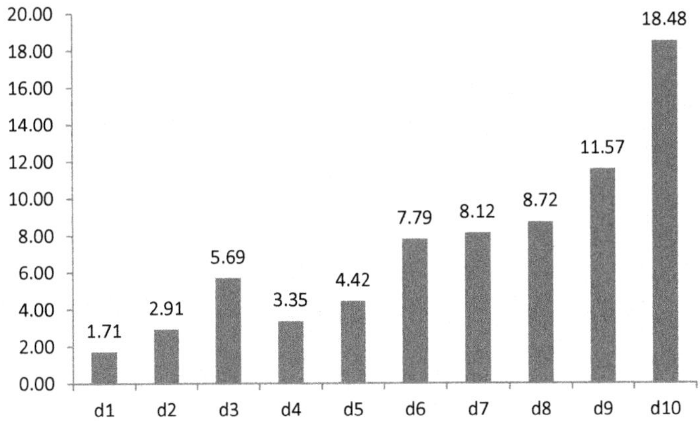

Fig. 8 Percentage of remittance income in total income by deciles wise. *Note* di = deciles, where I = 1, 2, …, 10. *Source* Calculated from the Bangladesh Integrated Household Survey (BIHS) data of IFPRI 2011–12

years of education of the head, number of dependent members per household, per capita landholding, and a dummy variable on whether the household receives international remittance or not.

To compare the regression result with the base income category the paper has used the method of relative probability calculation; parameters with statistically significant coefficients greater than 1 have higher probabilities than the base category, and parameters with statistically significant coefficients less than 1 have low probabilities than the base category. To see the regression results in the probability scale, marginal effects of the coefficients are also presented in this paper rather than the actual coefficient values.

4.1 Comparison with Respect to the Base Category

The results, using decile 1 as the base category, are presented in Table 1. It appears that wage employment in the farm sector has statistically significant association with all income deciles between 6 and 10. However, such employment status does not have any statistically significant association with income deciles between 2 and 5. For a wage-worker in the farm sector, relative probabilities to be in deciles 6, 7, 8, 9, and 10 are, respectively, 39%, 44%, 75%, 85%, and 90% lower than to be in decile 1. The result depicts the fact that wage employment in the farm sector is more concentrated among the poorer households and does not play any pivotal role in shifting up the status of a household. The result is quite analogous for the wage employed in the nonfarm sector too: if the household head is employed in nonfarm activities, the relative probability to be in the deciles 9 and 10 are 62% and 78% lower (respectively) than to be in decile 1.

Table 1 Ratio of relative probabilities from multinomial logistic regression (base: decile 1)

Explanatory variables	Dependent variable: income status								
	Income deciles								
	2	3	4	5	6	7	8	9	10
Farm wage employment	1.120 (0.249)	0.988 (0.262)	0.714 (0.264)	0.688 (0.268)	0.612[a] (0.262)	0.455[c] (0.272)	0.254[c] (0.290)	0.153[c] (0.301)	0.096[c] (0.352)
Nonfarm wage employment	0.925 (0.278)	1.119 (0.289)	1.278 (0.281)	1.004 (0.291)	0.820 (0.289)	0.826 (0.293)	0.711 (0.295)	0.377[c] (0.310)	0.223[c] (0.367)
Farm self-employment	1.126 (0.253)	1.478 (0.259)	1.318 (0.256)	1.447 (0.257)	1.143 (0.250)	1.253 (0.247)	1.166 (0.244)	0.698 (0.236)	0.660[a] (0.240)
Nonfarm self-employment	1.423 (0.253)	1.903[b] (0.261)	1.860[b] (0.258)	2.240[c] (0.258)	1.840[b] (0.252)	1.687[b] (0.253)	1.717[b] (0.250)	1.326 (0.241)	1.328 (0.246)
Salaried employment	0.692 (0.393)	1.013 (0.389)	1.295 (0.367)	0.908 (0.388)	1.309 (0.358)	1.246 (0.361)	1.229 (0.356)	0.618 (0.358)	0.787 (0.354)
Unpaid family labor	0.000 (960.37)	0.335 (0.888)	0.000 (1031.3)	0.000 (1027.4)	0.000 (1057.1)	0.000 (1075.9)	0.187[a] (0.969)	0.193[a] (0.898)	0.056[b] (1.125)
Household head's age	1.006 (0.004)	1.008[a] (0.004)	1.005 (0.004)	1.006 (0.004)	1.005 (0.004)	1.010[b] (0.004)	1.012[c] (0.004)	1.013[c] (0.004)	1.013[c] (0.004)
Number of dependent members per household	0.756[c] (0.044)	0.700[c] (0.045)	0.624[c] (0.047)	0.573[c] (0.048)	0.533[c] (0.049)	0.509[c] (0.050)	0.470[c] (0.052)	0.414[c] (0.054)	0.306[c] (0.060)
Years of education of the head	1.104[c] (0.020)	1.118[c] (0.020)	1.146[c] (0.020)	1.164[c] (0.020)	1.182[c] (0.020)	1.209[c] (0.020)	1.219[c] (0.020)	1.308[c] (0.020)	1.353[c] (0.020)
Per capita landholding	7.711[c] (0.544)	37.22[c] (0.507)	51.81[c] (0.502)	55.22[c] (0.500)	97.09[c] (0.492)	171.4[c] (0.483)	173.5[c] (0.483)	246.9[c] (0.480)	369.4[c] (0.479)
Dummy for international remittance (1 = recipient)	2.545[b] (0.444)	4.577[c] (0.418)	4.494[c] (0.423)	5.655[c] (0.416)	8.770[c] (0.405)	12.120[c] (0.399)	14.407[c] (0.397)	18.036[c] (0.397)	26.039[c] (0.397)

(continued)

Table 1 (continued)

Explanatory variables	Dependent variable: income status								
	Income deciles								
	2	3	4	5	6	7	8	9	10
Constant	–0.138 (0.328)	–0.499 (0.337)	–0.167 (0.335)	–0.174 (0.338)	–0.044 (0.332)	–0.416 (0.335)	–0.340 (0.333)	–0.287 (0.330)	–0.306 (0.339)
Number of observation	6503								
LR chi2 (99)	2592.64								
Prob > chi2	0								
Pseudo R2	0.0866								
Log-likelihood	–13677.38								

Note Coefficients are expressed as the exponentials of the coefficient (e^{coeff}) from mlogit; c, b, and a indicate statistical significance at the 1, 5, and 10% levels, respectively. The figures in parentheses are the standard errors

Table 1 suggests that in case of self-employment, if the household head is engaged in the farm sector, the relative probability of that household to be in decile 10 is 44% lower than to be in the base decile 1. This association is insignificant for all other deciles meaning that self-employment in the farm sector does not necessarily improve the income status. On the contrary, if the household head is self-employed in the nonfarm sector, the relative probabilities to be in deciles 3, 4, 5, 6, 7, and 8 compared to the base category are higher by 90%, 86%, 124%, 84%, and 72%, respectively. It shows that self-employment in nonfarm sector has a strong transitory power to improve household well-being. In addition to these, when considering salaried employment, the study finds no significant influence of salaried employment over shifting the well-being status from income decile 1 to higher income deciles. On the other hand, if the household head is employed as an unpaid worker the relative probability to be in deciles 8, 9 or 10 is more than 80% lower than to be in the decile 1.

In Table 1, among other variables, household characteristics like age of the head, dependent member per household, per capita landholding, and remittance status hold significant impact on the nature of economic status of the household. If the age of the household head increases by one additional year, the relative probability to be in the top four deciles compared to the decile 1 increases by around 1.2 percentage points. It is also seen that, with the rise in number of dependents in a family, the relative probability of the household to be in a higher decile compared to decile 1 becomes lower. For example, if the number of dependents in a family increases by 1 additional person, the relative probability to be in decile 2 compared to decile 1 is 25% lower. Whereas, if the number of dependent increases by 1 additional person the relative probability to be in decile 10 compared to decile 1 is 70% lower.

The results in Table 1 also suggest that education and international remittances play a role of pull factor in case of shifting household status from the lowest decile to upper deciles. An increase in the years of education of the household head by one additional year increases the relative probability to be in decile 2 compared to decile 1 by 10 percentage points; whereas, for the same increment, the relative probability to be in decile 10 compared to decile 1 increases by 35%. In case of remittances, households that receive remittance have more than threefold relative probability to be in decile 4 or above. For the remittance-receiving households, the relative probability to be in decile 10 compared to the decile 1 is more than 25 times higher than a household that does not receive remittances. Along with these, per capita landholding is appeared as an important household characteristic that can help a household to be on the higher deciles.

Hence, the results using relative probability method indicate that household head who works as wage labor in the farm and nonfarm sector has high relative probability of being in the lower deciles compared to the highest two income deciles. Similarly, the household head who is working as a self-employed in the farm sector has a high probability to be in the lower deciles compared to the highest two deciles. Head who works as self-employed in nonfarm sector has high relative probability to be in the income deciles 2–8 rather than being in the base income decile 1. However, the household head who works as a salaried worker is more likely to be in the middle-income group. Being an unpaid head has a significant influence to be in the lowest decile rather than being unemployed head. Besides, increase in dependent member per household linked with a high probability of being in the lower deciles. Increase in years of education, per capita landholding, and remittance has a significant impact to be in the higher income deciles rather than being in decile 1. To switch from the current income status to the immediate deciles group employment status has no significant role but household characteristic plays an important role.

4.2 *Average Marginal Effects Result of Multinomial Logit*

From the calculated average marginal effects, reported in Table 2, we see that households with head working as wage labor in the farm sector have a significant probability to be in decile 1. On an average, the probability of being in decile 1 increases by 3.7 percentage points if household head is a wage labor in the farm sector, while, the probability of being in decile 1 is 4.2 percentage points lower if the head works as a self-employed in the nonfarm sector. However, head engaged as wage employed in the nonfarm sector, self-employed in the farm sector, salaried worker or unpaid has no significant impact to be in decile 1. In addition, age of head, dependent member per household, education, per capita landholding, and remittance status have significant impacts on decile 1. If the age of head increases by 1 year, the probability of being in decile 1 decreases by 0.06%. On the other hand, if the dependent member per household increases by one additional member, the probability of being decile 1 increases by 4%. In addition, increase in the years of education or per capita landholding reduces the probability of being in the lowest decile. Analogously, households that receive remittances have lower probability to be in the decile 1.

Table 2 also shows that employment status, except wage labor in the farm sector, has no significant relationship with the probability of being in decile 2. The probability of being in decile 2 will increase by on an average 6.1 percentage points if the head is a wage labor in the farm. However, number of dependent person per household, education of the household head, per capita landholding, and remittance status of the household have significant impacts on decile 2. On an average, if dependent member per household increases by one, the probability of being in decile 2 will increase by 1.9%. On the other hand, 1-year increase in the education of the household head reduces the probability of being in decile 2 by 0.3%. Rise in per capita landholding by one acre reduces the chance of being in decile 2. The remittance-receiving households have less chance to be in decile 2 as well. Like decile 2, households with head employed as wage labor in the farm is a significant factor to be in decile 3. Household characteristics like dependent member per household and education of head have a significant impact on decile 3. In terms of

Table 2 Average marginal effect estimation of the multinomial logit

Explanatory variables	Dependent variable: income status									
	Coefficients									
(Base: decile 1)	1	2	3	4	5	6	7	8	9	10
Farm wage employment	0.037[b] (0.015)	0.061[c] (0.016)	0.056[c] (0.017)	0.030[a] (0.017)	0.030[a] (0.018)	0.024 (0.017)	0.004 (0.018)	–0.048[b] (0.019)	–0.085[c] (0.020)	–0.111[c] (0.022)
Nonfarm wage employment	0.010 (0.016)	0.007 (0.018)	0.030 (0.019)	0.046[b] (0.018)	0.024 (0.019)	0.008 (0.019)	0.013 (0.019)	0.002 (0.019)	–0.052[c] (0.020)	–0.091[c] (0.023)
Farm self-employment	–0.014 (0.015)	–0.001 (0.015)	0.026 (0.016)	0.015 (0.016)	0.025 (0.016)	0.003 (0.014)	0.014 (0.014)	0.008 (0.013)	–0.038[c] (0.011)	–0.038[c] (0.010)
Nonfarm self-employment	–0.042[c] (0.015)	–0.010 (0.016)	0.017 (0.017)	0.014 (0.016)	0.032[b] (0.016)	0.013 (0.015)	0.004 (0.015)	0.006 (0.014)	–0.018 (0.012)	–0.016 (0.011)
Salaried employment	0.001 (0.022)	–0.035 (0.026)	0.002 (0.025)	0.026 (0.023)	–0.008 (0.025)	0.028 (0.021)	0.023 (0.021)	0.022 (0.020)	–0.043[b] (0.018)	–0.017 (0.016)
Unpaid family labor	0.860 (24.40)	–0.654 (85.23)	0.794 (24.59)	–0.669 (94.32)	–0.669 (94.03)	–0.708 (96.89)	–0.747 (97.54)	0.691 (22.82)	0.647 (21.26)	0.455 (19.05)
Household head's age	–0.0006[b] (0.0002)	0.000 (0.0002)	0.0001 (0.0002)	–0.0002 (0.0002)	–0.0001 (0.0002)	–0.0002 (0.0002)	0.0001 (0.0002)	0.0003 (0.0002)	0.0004 (0.0002)	0.0003 (0.0002)
Number of dependent members per household	0.040[c] (0.002)	0.019[c] (0.002)	0.015[c] (0.002)	0.006[b] (0.003)	0.00008 (0.003)	–0.004 (0.0031)	–0.005[a] (0.003)	–0.011[c] (0.003)	–0.018[c] (0.003)	–0.042[c] (0.003)
Years of education of the head	–0.011[c] (0.001)	–0.003[c] (0.001)	–0.003[c] (0.001)	–0.001 (0.001)	–0.0005 (0.001)	0.0004 (0.0009)	0.001[a] (0.0009)	0.001[b] (0.0009)	0.007[c] (0.0008)	0.009[c] (0.0008)
Per capita landholding	–0.305[c] (0.035)	–0.141[c] (0.028)	–0.007 (0.021)	0.012 (0.019)	0.008 (0.018)	0.052 (0.015)	0.091[c] (0.012)	0.083[c] (0.011)	0.096[c] (0.009)	0.109[c] (0.007)
Dummy for international remittance (1 = recipient)	–0.140[c] (0.029)	–0.067[b] (0.022)	–0.021 (0.018)	–0.030 (0.018)	–0.013 (0.017)	0.023 (0.014)	0.044[c] (0.012)	0.056[c] (0.011)	0.064[c] (0.010)	0.083[c] (0.009)

Note c, b, and a indicate statistical significance at the 1, 5, and 10% levels, respectively. The figures in parentheses are the standard errors

significance, the result is same for deciles 4 also. Households with head working as wage labor in the farm sector and self-employed in nonfarm sector have significant probabilities to be in decile 5; no other variables have significant effect. None of the employment and household characteristics are significant determinant of being in decile 6.

Table 2 also suggests that in decile 7, there is no significant impact of employment status but the number of dependent persons, education level of household head, per capita landholding and remittance-receiving status plays a significant role to be in that decile. It is noticeable that the impact of these variables is reverse compared to the poorer deciles. On an average, if dependent member per household increases by one, the probability of being in decile 7 will be reduced by 0.5%. Instead, 1-year increase in education of the head will increase the probability of being in decile 7 by 0.1%. One acre increase in per capita landholding increases the probability to be in decile 7 by 9.1%. The remittance-receiving status increases the probability of being in decile 7 by 4.4 percentage points than non-remittance-receiving household. For a household head employed in the farm sector, the probability of being in decile 8 is lower by 4.8 percentage points. Other employment status has no significant impact on decile 8. Dependent member per household, education, landholding, and remittance hold similar impact on decile 8 like decile 7.

According to Table 2, the employment status has higher influences over the highest two deciles. If a household head works as a wage labor or a self-employed in the farm sector then that household has less chance to be in the deciles 9 or 10. On an average, if the household head works as a wage employed in the farm sector, the probability of being in deciles 9 or 10 will be lower by 8.5 and 11.1 percentage points, respectively. In case of wage labor in nonfarm sector, the probability of being in decile 9 and 10 is lower by 5.2 and 11.1 percentage points, respectively. Similarly, if the household head is self-employed in the farm sector, the probability of being in deciles 9 and 10 will be reduced by 3.8 percentage points. For decile 9, if the head works as a salaried employee, it will reduce the probability of being in decile 9 by 4.3 percentage points. The effectiveness of other variables like dependency, education, landholding, and remittances over the well-being status of the household is also found to be significant for deciles 9 and 10.

5 Conclusion

The paper aimed to inspect the relationship between the nature of employment and well-being of rural household in Bangladesh. The paper complements existing literature on the subject of a systematic analysis of rural poverty concentration on certain employment type with the latest available data. The major findings of the paper can be summarized as follows.

First, the wageworkers in the rural area are mostly from the poorest deciles. When the head of a household works as wage labor, the relative probability of being in the lower income group is higher than being in the higher income group. This is evident partly from the fact that employment nature of wageworker requires low skill and minimum education, and is a less effective employment status to bring a major change in the economic well-being of the rural people, whereas the self-employed status is a very common employment type in all income groups. Despite capturing the highest employment share in total employment in all deciles, the self-employment in the farm is not important employment criteria to switch from one income deciles to another.

Second, in the case of self-employment in the nonfarm sector, there is a lower chance to be in the poorer income deciles. Household head working as a salaried worker is mostly concentrated in the middle-income group. This category is not a significant employment status in switching from one income group to another. The unpaid household head has a positive link to be in the lower income group. The results appear to support the hypothesis that the nonfarm sector has a crucial role in reducing poverty and increasing the well-being of the rural household. Also, to switch from base decile 1 to subsequent deciles, household characteristics (i.e., age, education of the household head, dependent member per household, per capita landholding, and remittance status) act as important determinants.

The findings of the paper provide a significant indication of the sectors coexisting with increasing well-being and reducing rural poverty. This further specifies the importance of incorporation of rural concern in national policy along with well-designed employment policies to eradicate poverty highly linked with certain employment categories.

References

Chadha, G. K. (2008). *Employment and poverty in rural India: Which way to go now*. ISBN: 978–92-2-121676-6. Geneva: International Labour Organization.

Gutierrez, C., Orecchia, C., Paci, P., & Serneels, P. (2007). *Does employment generation really matter for poverty reduction?*. Washington, DC: World bank.

Islam, R. (2004). *The nexus of economic growth, employment and poverty reduction: An empirical analysis*. Discussion paper no. 14. Geneva: International Labour Organization.

Krongkaew, M., Chamnivickorn, S., & Nitithanprapas, I. (2006). *Economic growth, employment, and poverty reduction linkages: The case of Thailand*. Geneva: International Labour Organization.

Kumar, A., Kumar, S., Singh, K. D., & Shivjee. (2011). Rural employment diversification in India: Trends, determinants and implications on poverty. *Agricultural Economic Research Review*, 361–372.

Mahmud, W. (1996). *Employment patterns and income formation in rural Bangladesh: The role of rural non-farm sector*. Dhaka: Bangladesh Institute of Development Studies (BIDS).

Osmani, S. R., & Latif, M. A. (2013). *The Pattern and determinants of poverty in rural Bangladesh: 2000–2010*. Working paper no. 18. Dhaka: Institute of Microfinance (InM).

Rahman, R. I. (2004). *Employment route to poverty reduction in Bangladesh: Role of self-employment and wage employmnet*. Geneva: International Labour Organization.
Rahman, R. I., & Islam, K. M. (2003). *Employment poverty linkages: Bangladesh*. Discussion paper 193.134.194.19. Geneva: International Labour Organization.
World Bank. (2013). *World development report 2013: Jobs*. Washington, DC: World Bank.

Female Labor Market Participation in Bangladesh: Structural Changes and Determinants of Labor Supply

Simeen Mahmud and Sayema Haque Bidisha

1 Introduction

Bangladesh has experienced moderately sustained economic growth (annual GDP growth of 6–7%) over the past two decades, as well as a fairly rapid demographic transition that began earlier, leading to sustained and steep declines in fertility levels and mortality rates. An accompanying feature of these socioeconomic trends has been the rising participation of women in the labor market, with the female labor force participation expanding from around 8% in the mid-1980s to 30% in 2010. While rising female labor force participation in Bangladesh denotes progress for women in a relatively conservative society, and has significant implications for economic growth and poverty alleviation of the country, there remain critical aspects that need examination. First, women's workforce participation is still very low compared to men's, despite the fact that women attach value to having their own independent incomes. Moreover, compared to men, women remain locked into fewer sectors and types of activities that offer fewer hours of employment and lower remuneration. Often, women have little choice but to contribute as unpaid labor to the family enterprise. Second, and related to the first, is that increase in formal school enrolment, better health, lower burden of childbearing (more time) are not translating into secure full-time employment, indicating that expansion in participation is supply driven rather than demand driven.

S. Mahmud
BRAC Institute of Governance and Development, BRAC University, Dhaka, Bangladesh

S. H. Bidisha (✉)
Department of Economics, University of Dhaka, Dhaka, Bangladesh
e-mail: sayemabidisha@gmail.com

S. H. Bidisha
South Asian Network on Economic Modeling (SANEM), Dhaka, Bangladesh

S. Raihan (ed.), *Structural Change and Dynamics of Labor Markets in Bangladesh*, South Asia Economic and Policy Studies,
https://doi.org/10.1007/978-981-13-2071-2_4

Hence, female labor market participation and its dimensions deserve an in-depth analysis from both an academic point of view and also from a policy perspective. In this paper, we attempt to examine the change over time in the nature of the female workforce and to identify factors affecting the labor supply decision of women in Bangladesh using Labor Force Survey data of several rounds (2005 and 2010 in particular) conducted by the Bangladesh Bureau of Statistics.

2 Literature Review

In the context of Bangladesh, factors affecting female labor force participation are quite diverse in nature and are often unique to the socioeconomic structure of the country. Besides, it is not only within the country, but also across different economic classes that these factors differ. In addition, the research on female labor supply differs from that of male by the inclusion of a number of household-specific variables. For example, the impact of family income was considered in the analysis conducted by Blau and Kahn (2006). They measured the impact of the wage of both participants and their spouses while controlling for the income from other sources. On the other hand, in order to control for the security of household income, Klasen and Pieters (2013) used the share of household income earned in regular salaried employment and also by the number of underemployed men in the household. In addition to wage and income variables, controls like age, age squared, and number of children, were also included in most of the studies. In order to capture their care responsibilities as well as their decision-making power, Klasen and Pieters (2013) added a dummy variable which is whether the female is living with the in-laws or not. Heim (2007), included cubic in wage, dummies of race and several geographical variables.

A number of studies attempted to understand the linkages between female labor force participation and growth and to analyze the growth implication of women's involvement in the labor market. In the context of South Asia, despite the gradual rise in female labor force participation over the decades, there still exists a gender gap in labor market participation, where the experience is not homogenous females are lagging far behind males in case of labor force participation with male labor force participation rate (LFPR) being 84% in the region as opposed to the corresponding figure of 33% for female (World Bank, Gender Statistics). In terms of individual countries, the relationship between income/GDP and LFPR is mixed-on, on one hand, countries like Bangladesh, Nepal, or Pakistan have been experiencing moderate increase in female labor force participation with the course of development whereas, on the other hand, female labor market participation in India has shown a declining trend with the Sri Lankan experience being mixed. Klasen and Pieters (2012) with the help of Indian data during 1984–2004 found that, despite the recent economic boom, India's growth has not been translated to greater participation of women in the labor force. Lahoti and Swaminathan (2013) used state-level employment data for India from 1983–84 to 2009–10 and found no significant relationship between women's labor market participation and economic development. Rahman and Islam (2013), with the Labor Force Survey data of

Bangladesh while analyzing the relationship between women's labor force participation and poverty argued that poorer women might be confined to low-skilled, low paid jobs and poverty can also result in lower productivity and lower bargaining power of women-all of these factors can eventually lead into lower level of wage (Rahman and Islam 2013).

In the context of Bangladesh, although a few studies attempted to postulate the relationship between labor force participation of women and economic development and growth, the area is not a well-researched one. According to the estimates of the World Bank (2015), if labor force participation of females can be increased from the present level (36%) to that equal to men (82%) that would result in an increase in GDP growth to as high as 7.5% (from the present 5.7%). Therefore, female LFPR of 82% would result in a 1.8% point increase in GDP growth.

While estimating the determinants of female labor force participation, the most crucial methodological issue that needs to be dealt with is the determination of wage rate. A large number of studies have applied different methods for confronting this challenge. The study of Blau and Kahn (2006) in this regard has analyzed the impact of wage on female labor force participation by estimating two regression equations, where the first one includes the wage of only the women for capturing the *income effect,* whereas the second includes the wage of their spouses (if married) for incorporating the impact of spouses' wage on labor force participation. The idea behind treating spouses' income separately comes from the concept of *bargaining model* which predicts that labor and consumption behavior of husbands and wives are separately influenced by their own sources of income (Lundberg and Pollak 1994; Manser and Brown 1980). As they had unpaid participants in the sample, while studying the stagnation of female labor force participation in India, Klasen and Pieters (2013) used predicted wage in the analysis. In studying shrinking wage elasticity of married female labour force, Heim (2007) used predicted wage to capture the impact of wage on participation. We have followed the method described in the seminal work of Mroz (1987). Our study, however, differs from Mroz by adding an extra step to capture the extensive margins of elasticity. We have used Heckman 2-step procedure to get the selection corrected wage and the wage predicted from that model was used in the next step.

3 Overview of the Trend and Pattern of Labor Force Participation

3.1 Composition of the Female and Male Workforces and Trends Over Time

In Bangladesh, although women constitute nearly half of the total population and the economically active population, their representation in the workforce is much smaller, reflecting the far lower rates at which women participate in economic or market activities compared to men. Table 1 shows that female LFP rate increased

Table 1 Distribution of sample populations for the Labor Force Surveys, 1999, 2005, and 2010 (in million)

	1999			2005			2010		
	Male	Female	Total	Male	Female	Total	Male	Female	Total
Total population	66.6 (52.24)	60.9 (47.76)	127.5 (100)	70.04 (51)	67.3 (49)	137.3 (100)	74.2 (49.9)	73.5 (49.4)	148.7 (100)
Population 15+	38.3 (51.62)	35.9 (48.38)	74.2 (100)	43 (50.8)	41.6 (49.2)	84.6 (100)	47.8 (50.1)	47.7 (49.9)	95.5 (100)
Population in LF	32.2 (79.12)	8.6 (21.13)	40.7 (100)	37.3 (75.35)	12.1 (24.44)	49.5 (100)	39.5 (69.66)	17.2 (30.34)	56.7 (100)
Population employed	31.1 (79.74)	7.9 (20.26)	39.0 (100)	36.1 (76.16)	11.3 (23.84)	47.4 (100)	37.9 (70.06)	16.2 (29.94)	54.1 (100)
LFPR (pop in LF/pop 15+)	0.84	0.24	0.55	0.87	0.29	0.59	0.83	0.36	0.59

Note Figures in brackets are percentages
Source LFS various years

from 24% in 1999 to 36% in 2010. Compared to the earlier period of 1999–2005, the LFP rate rose faster during 2005 and 2010, averaging an annual increase of 1% in this period. In contrast, the male LFP rate declined slightly from 87% in 2005 to 83% in 2010, which could be reflecting rising rates of attendance of educational institutions by young men. Hence, there was relatively faster growth of the female labor force compared to the male labor force in this decade.

Women's participation in the labor market is considered to depend upon three sets of factors: to some extent upon individual market endowments (age and education level in response to existing labor demand); upon their household situation (marital status, presence of small children, head's occupation) which determines the labor time allocated to domestic/care work; and upon characteristics of the household head (sex, education, and occupation) which determines the extent to which the norms of the "female home maker" and "female seclusion" are adhered to within the family.

In this context, Table 2 presents labor force participation (LFP) rates in 1999, 2010, and 2005 according to selected individual socioeconomic and demographic characteristics. Women aged 25–44 years had the highest LFP rates, followed by younger women aged 15–24 years, while older women (45+ years) had the lowest rates. Since 1999, the LFP rate had increased for women of all age groups, except older women aged 45+ years, who experienced a rise in 2005 and then a decline. The greatest increase was recorded for women aged 25–44 years. Thus, the relationship between LFP rate and age was an inverted J in 2010, with LFP rates of the youngest women (aged 15–24 years) being higher than that of older women (aged 45+ years). In 2010, currently, married women had higher LFP rates (38%) compared to either single women or widowed/separated/divorced (WSD) women. Over the years, the LFPR increased most visibly among married women.

With respect to education level, the highest LFP rate in 2010 was among women with a BA degree or above, followed by women having 6–9 years of schooling. The lowest LFP rate was for women having a HSC or equivalent degree, much lower compared to the LFP rate among women with no education. Since 1999 LFP had increased for women with all education levels, with the least for women having a HSC degree. In fact, LFP increased most visibly among women with 6–8 years of schooling (from 21 to 42) and for women with a graduate degree and above. Thus, the earlier U-shaped relationship, with lowest participation rates among women having secondary education or with SSC/HSC degrees, had given way to a more complex relationship in 2010. In summary, younger women (15–25 years) were entering the labor market at a faster pace than older women (44+ years), but greatest increase in LFP was for married women in the prime working age group (25–44 years).

Besides individual endowments, household circumstances are also important determinants of female supply, either constraining or supporting women's labor supply for market work, by their impact on women's time allocation for "care work" and household tasks and the household need for income. According to Table 3 in 2010, the presence of small children (under 6 years) did not appear to affect women's LFP in either time period. The LFP had increased generally for

Table 2 Male and female labor force participation rates according to selected individual characteristics

	1999		2005		2010	
	Male	Female	Male	Female	Male	Female
Labor force participation rate	0.84	0.24	0.87	0.29	0.83	0.36
Age						
15–24	0.62	0.26	0.67	0.22	0.62	0.36
25–34	0.94	0.28	0.96	0.35	0.93	0.44
35–44	0.98	0.26	0.98	0.36	0.97	0.46
45 and above	0.84	0.18	0.86	0.27	0.83	0.18
Marital status						
Unmarried	0.63	0.29	0.67	0.19	0.61	0.28
Married	0.93	0.24	0.94	0.31	0.91	0.38
Separated/wid/div	0.43	0.27	0.55	0.32	0.47	0.21
Highest class passed						
No education	0.90	0.26	0.93	0.33	0.90	0.32
Class i–v	0.91	0.24	0.93	0.30	0.90	0.38
Class vi–viii	0.79	0.21	0.88	0.26	0.86	0.42
Class ix–x	0.79	0.21	0.76	0.21	0.69	0.37
SSC/equivalent	0.68	0.23	0.68	0.22	0.67	0.34
HSC/equivalent	0.68	0.23	0.67	0.26	0.50	0.25
Bachelor/equivalent	0.77	0.33	0.82	0.43	1.00	1.00
Master/equivalent			0.88	0.51	0.81	0.48
Medical/engineering degree			0.84	0.61	0.76	0.47
Technical/vocational education			0.77	0.37	1.00	1.00
Others			0.63	0.42	0.69	0.45
Literacy						
Literate	0.80	0.23	0.81	0.26	0.79	0.37
Not-literate	0.91	0.26	0.92	0.33	0.90	0.33

Source LFS various years

women in all head's education group. In 2010, the head's education up to the SSC level did not appear to have any association with female LFP rate, which hovered around 35–38. However, when the head had a HSC or higher degree there was a dip in the female LFP rate. The pattern was different in 1999, when LFP rate was relatively higher for women when the head had the highest education level (over BA degree).

With respect to household socioeconomic status, measured by the main source of household income and household landownership, the patterns were a bit complicated in 2010. In households, where self-employment (both in agriculture or non-agriculture) was the primary source of income, women had far higher participation rates compared to households with primary income either from service or labor selling. In landless and marginal households, women had lower participation rates than in small/medium landed households and also relatively lower compared

Table 3 Male and female labor force participation rates according to household characteristics

	1999		2005		2010	
	Male	Female	Male	Female	Male	Female
Labor force participation rate	0.84	0.24	0.87	0.29	0.83	0.36
Sex of the household head						
Male-headed household	0.84	0.23	0.86	0.29	0.84	0.36
Female-headed household	0.72	0.46	0.76	0.41	0.66	0.29
Presence of small children						
Without children under 5	0.79	0.25	0.82	0.31	0.79	0.35
With children under 5	0.89	0.24	0.90	0.29	0.88	0.36
Highest class passed by head						
No education	0.88	0.28	0.90	0.34	0.87	0.35
Class i–v	0.86	0.24	0.87	0.28	0.84	0.37
Class vi–viii	0.83	0.23	0.84	0.27	0.81	0.35
Class ix–x	0.80	0.20	0.83	0.26	0.77	0.38
SSC/equivalent	0.75	0.21	0.77	0.23	0.75	0.35
HSC/equivalent	0.74	0.19	0.74	0.23	0.68	0.30
Bachelor/equivalent	0.72	0.23	0.73	0.26	0.80	0.30
Master/equivalent	0.67	0.31	0.77	0.29	0.71	0.27
Medical/engineering degree	0.58	0.32	0.81	0.28	0.73	0.25
Technical/vocational education			0.77	0.29	0.81	0.24
Main source of income of HH						
Self-employed (agriculture)	0.84	0.25	0.86	0.30	0.83	0.57
Self-employed (non-agriculture)	0.85	0.22	0.88	0.28	0.86	0.61
Service	0.82	0.26	0.80	0.29	0.78	0.19
Day labor	0.94	0.27	0.93	0.34	0.91	0.16
Others	0.78	0.27	0.66	0.28	0.53	0.19
Landownership						
Landless	0.89	0.31	0.90	0.32	0.88	0.32
Marginal	0.86	0.24	0.87	0.30	0.84	0.29
Small	0.81	0.22	0.84	0.28	0.80	0.43
Medium	0.71	0.19	0.80	0.28	0.76	0.44
Large	0.77	0.22	0.78	0.31	0.72	0.38

Source LFS various years

to women in large landed households. These two factors could be correlated though.

In Table 4, further information about women's engagement in the labor market has been described. In both 2005 and 2010, the agriculture sector (including forestry and fishing) employed more than two-thirds of the female workforce. The second important industry category for women was manufacturing, accounting for 11% of female employment in 2010, up from 9% in 2005, followed by wholesale and retail trade, and the activities of private household sector. Between 2005 and 2010 slowly expanding industries included manufacturing, retail trade activities,

Table 4 Distribution (%) of employed women

	2005	2010
Total number of female employed in million (% in parenthesis)	11.3 (100)	16.2 (100)
Share in key Industry (%)		
Agriculture, forestry, and fishing	68.06	66.49
Manufacturing	8.98	10.74
Construction	1.03	1.47
Wholesale retail trade, repair	4.1	6.22
Transportation and storage	0.49	1.23
Financial and insurance activities	0.82	0.28
Professional, scientific and technical activities	0.01	0.14
Administrative and support service	0.11	0.26
Public admin, defense, social security	1.24	0.23
Education	3.46	1.97
Activities of households as employers	9.83	9.24
Status in employment categories (%)		
Paid employee (regular or irregular worker)	11.40	9.54
Employer, self-employed	21.26	25.75
Unpaid family worker	58.79	57.14
Day labor (agriculture or non-agriculture)	6.20	5.24
Domestic worker	2.36	2.32
Share of types of occupation (%)		
Employer/self-employed	21.26	25.75
Unpaid	58.79	57.14
Waged/salaried	19.96	17.10
Share of sectors of employment (%)		
Formal	9.47	10.48
Semi-formal	5.04	2.14
Informal	85.51	87.38

Source LFS various years

transport and storage, and construction, while shrinking industries were public administration, education, and health services, possibly reflecting a squeezing of public sector service employment. There were negligible proportions of women employed in other sectors, e.g., financial and insurance services, real estate activities, professional and scientific activities, public administration, defense, etc. Hence, there was visible segregation in the female labor market by industry category, which had not diminished between 2005 and 2010.

Contributing unpaid family worker was the overwhelming employment status for women, accounting for around 57% of female employment in both 2005 and 2010. Not only that, employed women were less likely in 2010 compared to 2005 to be either in salaried jobs (paid employee either regular or irregular) or in waged work as day laborers. On the other hand, they were more likely to be self-employed (employers or own account workers) in 2010 compared to 2005, while the proportion of domestic workers remained unchanged. Thus, the route to expansion in the female workforce and an increase in female labor force participation rate was through self-employment rather than waged/salaried employment. Additionally, even with a workforce that was expanding with the entrance of relatively more educated and younger women the dominant type of employment for women remained unpaid family work.

4 What Determines Female Labor Supply in Bangladesh?

4.1 Estimation of the Determinants of Labor Force Participation

Here, we want to understand how labor force participation of a woman is influenced by different socioeconomic and demographic factors. Given the dependent variable is a dichotomous one (1 if the respondent participates in the labor force and 0 otherwise), the most appropriate estimation technique is that of probit/logit. As shown in column 2 of Table 5, education has strong positive impact on labor market participation and all three education dummies have come out to be statistically significant with positive coefficient estimates. Another crucial determinant of labor market participation of females that distinguishes their decision from that of males is childbearing and subsequent involvement in care activities. As discussed, age of the child can also affect participation decisions as relatively younger children require more attention, and therefore can act as a discouraging factor for a woman to participate. According to our results, the presence of younger children less than 6 years of age acts as an obstacle toward female labor market participation—children under 6 years of age reduces female LFP by around 3.6%. On the other hand, our estimate shows that the coefficient of total number of children in the household increases participation. This result might have resulted from the fact that, greater number of children increases the financial requirements of a household and as a consequence induces a woman to join the labor market. As shown in column 2 of Table 5, higher family income has a significantly negative impact on participation and it reduces participation probability by around 7%. Possession of land by a household, on the other hand, increases the probability of participation—the magnitude of the coefficient is, however, quite small.

Column 2 of Table 5 also suggests that if the head of a household has higher education (university degree in this case) then that reduces the probability of participation of a woman belonging to that household. In case of head's occupation, although head's sector of occupation (agriculture vs. nonagriculture) has come out as immaterial (insignificant from a statistical point of view) in our analysis, a self-employed household head as opposed to a wage employed one increases participation probability of a woman residing in that household significantly and the large magnitude of head's self-employment coefficient might be a reflection of the

Table 5 Results of participation equation (without and with wage)

Column 1	Column 2	Column 3
Variable	Participation (without wage)	Participation (with wage)
Imputed wage		0.084[a] (0.004)
Age	0.016[a] (0.001)	0.036[a] (0.001)
Age^2	−0.0003[a] (0.000)	−0.0006[a] (0.000)
Primary and secondary passed	0.057[a] (0.006)	0.122[a] (0.007)
SSC and HSC passed	0.124[a] (0.013)	0.163[a] (0.013)
University passed	0.577[a] (0.018)	0.542[a] (0.021)
Marital status	−0.130[a] (0.010)	−0.130[a] (0.010)
Child	0.004[c] (0.002)	0.005[c] (0.002)
Child under 6 years	−0.036[a] (0.003)	−0.036[a] (0.003)
Net family income (natural log)	−0.069[a] (0.001)	−0.069[a] (0.001)
Household land	7.26E−05[a] (0.000)	7.26E−05[a] (0.000)
Urban	0.119[a] (0.006)	
Living with in-laws	−0.036[a] (0.007)	−0.036[a] (0.007)
Head primary and secondary passed	0.001 (0.001)	0.001 (0.006)
Head SSC and HSC passed	0.005 (0.010)	0.005 (0.010)
Head university passed	−0.037[b] (0.015)	−0.037[b] (0.015)
Head employed in agriculture	0.009 (0.005)	0.009 (0.005)
Head self employed	0.476[a] (0.004)	0.476[a] (0.005)
Chittagong division	0.051[a] (0.009)	0.051[a] (0.009)
Dhaka division	0.087[a] (0.009)	0.087[a] (0.009)
Khulna division	0.038[a] (0.010)	0.038[a] (0.010)
Rajshahi division	0.042[a] (0.009)	0.042[a] (0.009)
Sylhet division	0.010 (0.011)	0.010[a] (0.011)
Constant	1.525	−0.729
Pseudo R^2	0.293	0.293
Chi^2	0.000	0.000
N	42,646	42,646

fact that, women with self-employed household head are likely to be involved in the labor market with the head, and therefore are more likely to be engaged in self-employment activities or in unpaid family work.

Given that the wage received in the market is a crucial determining factor of labor market participation, in column 3 of Table 5 we have shown estimation result with wages included in the set of explanatory variables. In order to omit the upward bias of reported wage and to correct for the self-selection bias, we run a selection correction model known as Heckman two-step model wherein the first step we have estimated a probit model of participation and from this model whereas in the next step, while utilizing information from the first step, *imputed wage* is calculated and used in estimation. As shown in column 3 of Table 5, wage has a strong positive impact on participation decision whereas in terms of other coefficient estimates, the results of the participation model with wage show very similar estimates to the one without wage.

4.2 *Estimation of the Determinants of Employment Status*

While analyzing labor market experience of women, in addition to labor force participation, it is also important to understand the types of jobs with which they are engaged. This is particularly of interest because it is not only mere participation but also associated wage, job security, pension, other benefits, etc., that frames labor market status of a woman. In Table 4.6 the estimation results of a Multinomial Logit Model with four categories of employment status has been shown where the categories are: (i) unpaid family worker (category 0); (ii) regular wage employment (category 1); (iii) irregular wage employment (category 2) and (iii) self-employment (category 3). Here, unpaid family workers are chosen as the base category.

Estimation results presented in Table 4.6 show that, age, number of children, and number of children below 6 years of age, among others act as significant determinants in the decision of choice between regular as well as irregular wage employment and self-employment as opposed to unpaid family work. The impact of wage is, however, not symmetric for the wage employed (regular as well as

Table 6 Determinants of the choice of employment (multinomial logit model)

Column 1	Column 2	Column 3	Column 4
Variable	Regular employment	Irregular employment	Self-employment
Imputed wage	0.546[a] (0.046)	0.567[a] (0.081)	−0.154[a] (0.039)
Age	0.178[a] (0.017)	0.163[a] (0.030)	0.230[a] (0.016)
Age^2	−0.002[a] (0.000)	−0.002[a] (0.000)	−0.001[a] (0.000)
Secondary level passed	0.229[a] (0.081)	−0.072 (0.158)	−0.058 (0.069)
Marital status	−1.392[a] (0.098)	−1.106[a] (0.157)	−1.014[a] (0.098)
Child	0.057[c] (0.030)	0.078 (0.056)	0.085[a] (0.021)
Child under 6 years	−0.234[a] (0.051)	−0.315[a] (0.100)	−0.247[a] (0.038)
Net family income (natural log)	−0.347[a] (0.016)	−0.325[a] (0.018)	−0.274[a] (0.016)
Household land	0.00,006 (0.000)	−0.0005 (0.0005)	0.0001 (0.0001)
Living with in-laws	0.069 (0.096)	0.149 (0.178)	−0.067 (0.076)
Head self-employed	−4.091[a] (0.077)	−3.815[a] (0.138)	−1.180[a] (0.085)
Constant	1.659[a] (0.521)	−0.589 (0.881)	0.324 (0.477)
Pseudo R^2	0.372		
Chi^2	0.000		
N	13,886		

Note a, b, and c indicate statistical significance at the 1, 5 and 10% levels, respectively. The figures in parentheses are the standard errors

irregular) and the self-employed and as shown in Table 4.6, when the choice between unpaid family work and self-employment is considered, the impact is found to be negative and insignificant but it is positive and significant in case of both types of wage employment choices. The result of the coefficient estimate of wage in case of wage employment is prior to our expectation. The negative coefficient estimate of wage in self-employment might be related to the fact that we have "imputed" the wage for unpaid family workers, which might have resulted in *errors in measurement* of wage variable for the unpaid family workers and consequently have affected the sign and significance of related estimated coefficient.

Another interesting result is that of the coefficient of education variable. On one hand, holding a degree of above secondary education acts an important positive factor in choosing the job of regular wage employment as opposed to work as an unpaid family worker. On the other hand, the impact of education is not statistically significant when the decision is in between unpaid family work and self-employment as well as irregular wage employment. Given the informal nature of irregular wage employment as well as self-employment activities, the insignificant estimates of the relevant coefficients cannot be considered surprising or against our prior expectation.

5 Conclusion

The trend comparisons in the composition of the female workforce indicate that there has been an increase in women's labor force participation in a more mainstream manner to contribute to family incomes and reduce labor cost, compared to earlier when women's market work/economic activity was often undertaken by women without male support or very inadequate male incomes and seen to be more poverty driven.

These findings of this research have important policy implications. First, in terms of research, there is not sufficient understanding regarding the demand factors that influence women's employment choice, particularly with regard to the stagnant participation rates in regular salaried work and very slow rise in participation in casual waged work. This suggests a stagnating demand for female labor in the formal sector and very slow increase in demand in the informal sector. Moreover, the continued U shaped relation between female LFP and schooling level with a dip for women having HSC degree could either indicate that labor market returns from participation outside the home or family farm are not sufficiently high or that social barriers keep the opportunity cost of participation high. Both of which can explain why expansion in female LFP is driven by rising participation rates in unpaid work, which increases family welfare but implications for women's empowerment and well being are not immediately apparent.

This brings us to the policy issue. Rising female LFP, whatever the route, can be growth enhancing, since more women are spending time in productive activities, and because it means that the "demographic dividend" of a growing workforce is being reaped to some extent. But the implication of the expansion of female LFP as unpaid family labor on women themselves is not clear. No doubt rising social acceptance of women's economic activity and their contribution to family income and welfare, particularly in some regions of the country, is empowering for women. This improves women's social position and their value to family members. It also increases acceptance of women's visibility in the public and enhances women's capabilities such as physical mobility and public exposure. But the extent to which this type of employment has the potential to transform their position within the family and family gender norms remains to be seen. This is because regardless of the type of employment, the one factor that makes the most difference to women's lives in terms of giving them a sense of control over their lives and giving them self-esteem is having their own income.

References

Blau, F. D., & Kahn, L. M. (2006). *Changes in the labor supply behavior of married women: 1980–2000*. IZA Discussion Paper, 2180.

Heim, B. T. (2007). The incredible shrinking elasticities married female labor supply, 1978–2002. *The Journal of Human Resources, XLII*(4).

Klasen, S., & Pieters, J. (2012). *Push or pull? Drivers of female labor force participation during india's economic boom*. IZA Discussion Paper, 6395.

Klasen, S., & Pieters, J. (2013). *What explains the stagnation offemale laborforce participation in urban India?* IZA Discussion Paper, 7579.

Lahoti, R., & Swaminathan, H. (2013). Economic Growth and Female Labour Participation in India. Indian Institute of Management Bangalore, 414.

Lundberg, S., & Pollak, R. A. (1994). Non-cooperative bargaining models of marriage. *American Economic Review Papers and Proceedings, 84*(2), 132–137.

Manser, M., & Brown, M. (1980). Marriage and household decision-making: a bargaining analysis. *International Economic Review, 21*(1), 31–44.

Mroz, T. A. (1987). The sensitivity of an emperical model of married women's work to economic and statistical assumptions. *Econometrica, 55*(4), 765–799.

Rahman, R., & Islam, R. (2013). *Female labour force participation in Bangladesh: trends, drivers and barriers*. ILO, New Delhi: International Labour Organization.

World Bank. (2015). *Bangladesh Development Update*. Dhaka: World Bank.

Unpaid Family Labor: A Hidden Form of Labor Market Discrimination of Women in Bangladesh

Sayema Haque Bidisha and Selim Raihan

1 Introduction

In recent decades, Bangladesh has argued to have experienced significant rise in labor market participation of women–from less than 10% during mid-80s female labor force participation has increased to as high as 35.5% in 2015. This figure though quite impressive in comparison to many developing countries, including those of South Asia, there exist concern in terms of *quality* of work in which they are involved. In this context, unpaid family labor in particular is a common phenomenon of the labor market of Bangladesh where family members are engaged in productive activities of the household where such works do not get any monetary compensation. According to the Labor Force Survey (LFS) 2013 as high as 40.09% of the women who were in the labor force were employed as unpaid family workers, where the corresponding figure for men is only around 4.73%. Due to non-remunerative nature, this type of labor market activities cannot be considered to contribute toward financial empowerment of women and therefore should be treated differently from mainstream paid labor market activities.

Unpaid family labor although is a common phenomenon in South Asian countries, it is generally not observed in developed countries with properly functioning labor market. As a result, despite involvement of a significant percentage of workforce—mostly women in unpaid work—this component of the labor force has not been properly studied by the policy-makers or academicians. Besides, despite the non-remunerative feature of such work, the contribution of such labor is expected to be quite high given the magnitude of labor force engaged in such

S. H. Bidisha · S. Raihan (✉)
Department of Economics, University of Dhaka, Dhaka, Bangladesh
e-mail: selim.raihan@gmail.com

S. H. Bidisha · S. Raihan
South Asian Network on Economic Modeling (SANEM), Dhaka, Bangladesh

S. Raihan (ed.), *Structural Change and Dynamics of Labor Markets in Bangladesh*, South Asia Economic and Policy Studies,
https://doi.org/10.1007/978-981-13-2071-2_5

activities. The huge contribution of this unpaid family work especially in the context of Bangladesh therefore needs careful and thorough analysis of strategic policy formulation.

In this chapter, with the help of national-level Labor Force Survey data of Bangladesh, an attempt has been made to understand the key features of unpaid family labor and given the dominance of females in such activities, this analysis is restricted only to female unpaid family labor. Besides, through suitable econometric methodology, it has also analyzed and compared the factors determining the choice of unpaid family work by the females as opposed to paid work and/or being not in the labor force.

2 Conceptualizing Unpaid Family Labor in Bangladesh

Despite remarkable progress in a number of socioeconomic indicators, due to patriarchal and conservative social structure, women in Bangladesh are typically lagging behind men both from an economic and from sociocultural point of view. In terms of labor market, despite significant rise in labor force participation of women for the last couple of decades, as high as 67% of women are still out of the labor force with only 37% of female workforce engaged in wage employment (Bangladesh Bureau of Statistics 2013). In addition, most of the wage employed is concentrated in low-skilled, low-productive jobs with a very small percentage working in highly paid professional occupations.

Unpaid family labor, against this backdrop, can be argued as a specific mode of involvement in the labor market which, although considered as part of the labor force, should be treated separately from the mainstream activity due to its non-monetized nature. According to the definition of labor force survey of Bangladesh, an unpaid family worker is defined as "one who works at least one hour in the reference period (other than household work) without pay or profit in a family operated farm or in a business owned/operated by the head or other members of the household to whom he/she is related by kinship, marriage, adoption or dependency." In the context of Bangladesh, such work commonly includes those of, husking paddy, rearing poultry and livestock, vegetable gardening, etc., among others. According to 2013 Labor Force Survey (Bangladesh Bureau of Statistics 2013), 8.7% of the population above 15 years of age falls under this category where the corresponding figure for women is more than 13%.

From a labor market perspective, an individual's involvement in the labor market can be of two major types: paid (wage and self) employment and unpaid family work. In addition, there is a hidden and unrecognized (and unpaid) component of work, which is not considered as part of the labor market activities—these are domestic chores—performed mainly by women. Among these three categories, both unpaid family work and domestic works are outside of any monetary contribution but the difference is the former is counted in the national account and the contributors are included in the labor force, whereas the latter completely remains outside of any calculation of the gross domestic product and are not considered as part of labor force. In this paper, our focus is, however, on unpaid family worker.

Unpaid family work has certain interesting features that have made its analysis more interesting. For example, these works are done in an informal setup, often at home or in a family owned/controlled business entity under the ownership of a relative. In most of the cases, unpaid work is associated with households headed by self-employed persons who are involved in either farm or nonfarm activities and instead of hiring wage labor, she/he often engages his daughter/son/in-law/wife in such activity without any remuneration. Due to its highly informal setup, there is no specific payment scheme associated with such job and the laborer performs the task as part of family/household responsibility/obligation. Though the output of work performed by unpaid worker contributes to national income and the monetary benefit mainly goes to the household head owning the respective farm/business, the family worker does not get any monetary benefit or ownership. This type of participation in the labor force is not expected to contribute toward financial empowerment of the worker and therefore should be analyzed differently from the mainstream labor market activities.

3 Literature Review

One constraint of conducting any empirical analysis of unpaid family work is lack of academic literature in this area. Besides, as family work is more of a South Asian feature, it has not been discussed with sufficient rigor. Besides, the existing literature on unpaid work is primarily related to those of domestic work/household chores due to its lack of recognition. Especially in the context of Bangladesh, to our knowledge, there is almost no analysis focusing particularly on unpaid family work.

From a definitional point of view, in global context, Antonopoulos (2009) categorized unpaid work as noneconomic or non-SNA activities and defined it (unpaid work) as all non-remunerated activities which lack economic recognition. Here, the author defined non-SNA unpaid work as all household works, care works for family member, and all other volunteer work for community services. Latigo and Neijwa (2005) also provided similar definition and according to them, SNA work, which can be both paid and unpaid, is the one which is performed for the market. Non-SNA works, on the other hand, are those which are performed outside the realm of market activities and are not paid.

In the context of developing countries, evidences show that a large proportion of women are working as unpaid labor in family farms and enterprises with no monetary remuneration (Zammit 2010). This percentage is quite high in many of the developing countries and according to (International Labor Organization 2008), in developing countries majority of women are classified either as own account worker or as unpaid family worker where the former type consists of as high as one-quarter of labor force in South Asia. As for unpaid family work, the percentage is 59% where it is only 18% for male. In the context of India, Das (2006) found that as high as 65% of women are constrained to work at home due to their household responsibility and therefore, only a third of the women within working age were able to work outside their home. Another study by Ghosh (2009), however, found slightly different results as their analysis reflected that an increasing portion of women in India is compelled to do unpaid domestic work because of lack of any alternative job.

In the context of Bangladesh, most of the research in the area of unpaid work deals with unpaid domestic work instead of unpaid family work. The only available academic research to our knowledge is that of Raihan et al. (2016), where Labor Force Survey of Bangladesh of 2010 was used to understand the key features of both male and female unpaid family workers of Bangladesh. The research of Khatun et al. (2015) has focused on unpaid domestic work and based on primary survey, they showed that the contribution of the activities of women, which are unaccounted at the national level, was equivalent to 76.8% of gross domestic product according to replacement cost method, whereas it was 87.2% according to willingness to accept method. Similar conclusion was drawn by Efroymson et al. (2007) as they found that the economic value of work performed by housewives was equivalent to US$ 69.8–91 billion per year.

4 Key Features of Unpaid Family Labor in Bangladesh

As discussed, according to the Bangladesh Bureau of Statistics (2013), 16% of the employed workforce is actually working as unpaid family worker. The majority of whom (78%) are, however, women. Therefore, as revealed in Table 1, only around 16% of females above 15 years of age are engaged in mainstream paid economic activities. A significant percentage of female population who are outside of the labor force (as high as 54% of female population) are also involved in unpaid activities but those activities (e.g., cooking, caring of children, washing, cleaning, etc.) are not counted in the national account, and these unpaid females are considered to be out of the labor force. This analysis is, however, focused on (female) unpaid family workers.

Table 1 Distribution of labor force (% of population over 15 years)

Status	All	Male	Female
In labor force	56.89	81.47	33.37
Employed	53.50	78.54	29.55
Unpaid	8.72	3.86	13.38
Paid	44.86	74.80	16.23
Unemployed	3.39	2.93	3.82
Not in labor force	43.11	18.53	66.63
Unpaid domestic	31.23	7.22	54.19

Source Bangladesh Bureau of Statistics (2013)

Table 2 Distribution of female unpaid worker by level of education

Level of education	% Share
No education	21.98
Below primary class I–IV	18.13
Primary class V–VII	35.17
Secondary class VIII–IX	10.44
SSC/HSC	12.21
Tertiary education	1.77
Other education	0.31
Total	100.00

Source Bangladesh Bureau of Statistics (2013)

A closer look at the characteristics of unpaid workers reveals a number of interesting facts. Data of Labor Force Surveys shows that despite the fact that unpaid workers are not being paid and the work is performed mostly within the premise of household, the unpaid laborers possess some degree of education (Table 2). For example, as high as 35% of unpaid laborers are found to have primary education, with another 12% having SSC/HSC degree and another 10% possessing secondary education (LFS 2013). The result therefore indicates that it might not be lack of opportunities or demand-side factors, rather certain inherent factors which have constrained these females to participate in mainstream paid activities.

In terms of regional distribution, the highest concentration of unpaid family workers is in Dhaka and Rajshahi division with concentration of 23% and 16%, respectively (Table 3).

Given that unpaid workers are based on family enterprises/farms, household characteristics are expected to have important implications toward the pattern of unpaid work. In terms of type of occupation, as high as 45% of unpaid workers are based on agriculture-based households (Table 4). In the context of Bangladesh, it therefore indicates the possibility that otherwise unemployed (or involved only in household domestic work) family members of the household are being engaged in farm-based activities performed by household head which helps the household heads to save their wage bills.

Table 3 Geographical distribution of female unpaid worker

Division	% Share
Barisal	9.96
Chittagong	19.82
Dhaka	22.64
Khulna	11.35
Rajshahi	16.24
Rangpur	9.42
Sylhet	10.59
Total	100.00

Source Bangladesh Bureau of Statistics (2013)

Table 4 Distribution of female unpaid labor by major activity of household

Sector	% Share
Agriculture	45.20
Industry	3.85
Service	42.90
Total	100.00

Source Bangladesh Bureau of Statistics (2013)

Table 5 Distribution of unpaid labor by the relationship status with the head

Relationship Status	% Share
Household head	5.13
Spouse	67.36
Daughter	8.45
Sister/sister-in-law	1.96
Granddaughter	0.23
Daughter-in-law	10.24
Mother/mother-in-law	5.27
Other relatives	1.19
Non-relatives	0.17
Total	100.00

Source Bangladesh Bureau of Statistics (2013)

In this connection, the characteristics of household head, in particular, can affect the intensity and type of unpaid work too. For example, in terms of kinship pattern, female unpaid workers are found mostly (67%) to be the wives of the head. In addition, Table 5 also reveals that, in certain cases, the female unpaid workers also work in the enterprise of their in-laws and in 2013 this figure was almost 10%. Unpaid family work for females, therefore, appears to have close connection with the relationships out of marital bonding.

In terms of occupation of household head of female unpaid worker, as high as 63% of household heads are found to be self-employed with another 25% being wage employed (Table 6). Thus, this overwhelmingly large percentage of self-employed households tends to informally employ their wives/daughter-in-laws in their farm/businesses, instead of employing paid laborer from outside.

Table 6 Occupation of household head with unpaid worker

Occupation of head	% Share
Head unpaid	7.19
Head self-employed	62.59
Head wage employed	25.36
Head unemployed	0.5
Head not in labor force	4.36
Total	100.00

Source Bangladesh Bureau of Statistics (2013)

Table 7 Distribution of unpaid labor by the level of education of the heads

Level of education	% Share
No education	25.72
Below primary class I–IV	18.05
Primary class V–VII	20.06
Secondary class VIII–IX	13.86
SSC/HSC	16.99
Tertiary education	4.67
Other education	0.66
Total	100.00

Source Bangladesh Bureau of Statistics (2013)

Table 7 shows that in most of the cases, the head of the household of female unpaid worker have no education or only primary education with negligible percentage having tertiary level of education. Unpaid family work, therefore, tends to be related to low education level of household.

The descriptive data analysis therefore reveals that unpaid workers are primarily involved in farm activities with self-employed household heads and with certain degree of landholding. Besides, a significant percentage of unpaid workers are found to have some degree of education, and therefore they have the potential to get remuneration through mainstream labor market activities. Given the prevalence of kinship, it is quite likely that the factors behind participation in the labor market of unpaid worker might be quite different from those of paid worker.

While analyzing unpaid family work, we should also keep in mind that there is a sizable proportion of working-age women who are not only unpaid but are also outside of the labor market. As shown in Table 8, as high as 65% of working-age women are considered as outside of the labor force but engaged in domestic "noneconomic" activities.

Given an overwhelmingly high percentage of unpaid females not in the labor force but involved in *noneconomic* activities, in Table 9, a comparison of key characteristics of unpaid family labor with those of not in the labor force (but involved in unpaid domestic work) and those engaged in paid employment is shown. As shown in Table 9, although there is no significant difference between the age structure of paid and unpaid family labor, those who are not in the labor force

Table 8 Classification of females according to broad economic categories

Labor force category	% Share
Unpaid and not in labor force	64.67
Unpaid and in labor force	15.96
Paid employment	19.37
Total	100.00

Source Bangladesh Bureau of Statistics (2013)

Table 9 A comparison of key characteristics of females engaged in different modes of labor market status

	Paid employment	Unpaid family (in LF)	Unpaid (not in LF)
Average age (years)	33.37	33.12	37.42
Head self-employed (%)	39.74	62.71	51.25
Head has some education (%)	81.91	74.35	77.26
Have children under 5 in household (%)	34.34	45.65	37.39
Average household income (taka)	22583.93	15236.48	16336.34
Have tertiary education (%)	10.97	1.77	2.56
Have no education (%)	16.16	21.98	27.65
Have SSC/HSC education (%)	25.31	12.21	24.86
Have below primary (class I–IV) education (%)	9.10	18.13	10.54
Have primary (class V–VII) education (%)	24.67	35.17	17.53
Have secondary (class VIII–IX) education (%)	13.36	10.44	16.47

Source Bangladesh Bureau of Statistics (2013)

(but engaged in domestic noneconomic activities) are found to be of slightly older age cohort. As expected, unpaid family work is more prevalent when the household head is self-employed. Besides, households with children under 5 years of age are found to be more common in case of unpaid family labor, indicating the possibility of care responsibility constraining women to confine in unpaid family work. As expected, those engaged in paid work have greater proportion of tertiary education, whereas those outside the labor force are found to have significant women without education. It is, however, interesting that, although about a quarter of females in paid and out of the labor force have SSC/HSC degree where the corresponding figure for the unpaid family labor is only around 12%. On the other hand, as high as 35% of the unpaid family workers have primary degree and another 18% have below primary education. Although it appears that unpaid family workers are more of below primary and primary category with paid workers possessing greater percentage of tertiary educated females and also those with SSC/HSC degree, the effect of education on participation decision of females is therefore quite complex and requires in-depth analysis.

5 What Determines Individual's Decision to Work as an Unpaid Family Worker? Insights from Econometric Analysis

Given that unpaid workers contribute towards the national income of the country without receiving any monetary or job-specific nonmonetary benefit, it is important to understand the factors that affect individual's decision to work as unpaid worker instead of joining the paid mainstream labor market activities. In addition, as discussed, another component of unpaid work, typically performed by females, is that of household activities, which are not considered as labor market activities. From a broader perspective, we can therefore consider three major modes of labor market participation of women: (i) unpaid (and not in labor force); (ii) unpaid family (and in labor force), and (iii) paid.[1] Given the differences in key characteristics of these three groups as suggested in Tables 9 and 10, with the help of Labor Force Survey data of 2013, results of a multinomial logit model have been shown where we have considered three categories of labor market status of a woman: (i) not in labor force but engaged in unpaid domestic work (category 1); (ii) unpaid family worker (category 2); and (iii) paid worker (category 3). Given that a female chooses among all the available labor market outcomes (which are more than two and which not necessarily can be ranked systematically), the most appropriate model to understand the factors affecting the choice of labor market outcome is multinomial logit model under which a decision to choose among more than two alternatives without any natural ordering can be modeled. In particular, the purpose of this exercise is to understand the differences (if any) that different factors might cause to choose unpaid family work as opposed to paid employment and unpaid domestic work.

As explanatory variables, we have included (i) age of the individual and its square; (ii) five education dummies (no education; below primary education, primary education, secondary education, SSC/HSC, and tertiary education with no education being the base); (iii) dummy for education of head (1 if possess some education, 0 otherwise); (iv) dummy for head's occupation (1 if self-employed, 0 if otherwise); (v) amount of land possessed by the household; (vi) log of household income; (vii) dummy of whether the household has any child less than 5 years old (1 if any under 5 child, 0 otherwise); (viii) dummy for rural (1 if rural, 0 otherwise); (ix) 7 divisional dummies with Dhaka being the base.

Estimates of Table 10 reveal the importance of different socioeconomic factors on different labor market outcomes. For example, in comparison to unpaid nonlabor market activity, age of the respondent appears to have negative effect in choosing both unpaid family work and paid work. The impact of education appears to be

[1]It should, however, be kept in mind that a woman who is in labor force and engaged in either paid or unpaid activities can be involved in unpaid domestic work too. But in this analysis we only considered those unpaid categories who are not in labor force but has reported (in the survey) to spend time in household chores, e.g., cooking, washing, cleaning, taking care of children and the elderly, etc.

Table 10 Multinomial logit model estimation (base "unpaid and not in labor force")

Variables	Unpaid and in labor force	Paid employment
Age of the individual	–0.024[b] (0.009)	–0.018[b] (0.007)
Age of the individual (squared)	0.001 (0.001)	–0.001 (0.001)
Log of household income	–0.001 (0.056)	0.828[c] (0.038)
Dummy for head's occupation (1 = self-employed, 0 = otherwise)	0.380[c] (0.058)	0.765[c] (0.044)
Dummy for education of head (1 = some education, 0 = otherwise)	0.083 (0.073)	–0.149[b] (0.01)
Dummy for household member with age under 5 (1 = yes, 0 = otherwise)	0.224[c] (0.054)	–0.167[c] (0.042)
Below primary (class I–IV) education	0.472[c] (0.094)	0.174[b] (0.05)
Primary (class V–VII) Education	0.526[c] (0.086)	0.552[c] (0.072)
Secondary (class VIII–IX) education	–0.565[c] (0.110)	–0.022 (0.082)
SSC/HSC	–0.367[c] (0.099)	0.221[c] (0.074)
Tertiary education	0.135 (0.176)	1.445[c] (0.099)
Amount of land possessed by the household	0.001 (0.001)	–0.001[c] (0.001)
Dummy for rural area (1 = yes, 0 = otherwise)	0.717[c] (0.063)	–0.013 (0.046)
Division: Barisal	0.110 (0.094)	–0.398[c] (0.071)
Division: Chittagong	0.183[b] (0.081)	–0.094 (0.060)
Division: Khulna	–0.091 (0.087)	–0.473[c] (0.66)
Division: Rajshahi	0 (omitted)	0 (omitted)
Division: Rangpur	–0.247[c] (0.094)	–0.367[c] (0.067)
Division: Sylhet	0.125 (0.090)	–0.382[c] (0.069)
Constant	–1.589[c] (0.571)	–8.182[c] (0.405)

Note c, b, and a indicate statistical significance at the 1, 5, and 10% levels, respectively. The figures in parentheses are the standard errors

Table 11 Marginal effects for the category of unpaid family worker

Variables	Marginal effect
Age of the individual	−0.002[a] (0.001)
Age of the individual (squared)	0.001 (0.001)
Log of household income	−0.025[c] (0.005)
Dummy for head's occupation (1 if self-employed, 0 if otherwise)	0.015[c] (0.006)
Dummy for education of head (1 if possess some education, 0 otherwise)	0.013[a] (0.007)
Dummy for household member with age under 5 (1 = yes, 0 = otherwise)	0.027[c] (0.005)
Below Primary (class I–IV) education	0.042[c] (0.009)
Primary (class V–VII) education	0.0356[c] (0.008)
Secondary (class VIII–IX) education	−0.056[c] (0.011)
SSC/HSC	−0.043[c] (0.010)
Tertiary education	−0.031[a] (0.017)
Amount of land possessed by the household	0.001[a] (0.001)
Dummy for rural area (1 = yes, 0 = otherwise)	0.072[c] (0.006)
Division: Barisal	0.023[b] (0.009)
Division: Chittagong	0.021[c] (0.008)
Division: Khulna	0.005 (0.008)
Division: Rajshahi	0 (omitted)
Division: Rongpur	−0.013 (0.009)
Sylhet	0.024[c] (0.009)

Note c, b, and a indicate statistical significance at the 1, 5, and 10% levels, respectively. The figures in parentheses are the standard errors

quite different across different labor market statuses: in comparison to "no education," below primary as well as primary education tend to have positive impact to both unpaid and paid activities in the labor force than to be outside the labor force. However, in comparison to the base category, having secondary as well as higher secondary education have negative impact to work as unpaid family labor as opposed to unpaid domestic activities. Being in rural area, as expected have positive and significant impact on choosing unpaid family work, in comparison to unpaid nonlabor market activities, whereas the coefficient has come as insignificant in case of paid work. Regional factors have found to have important impact on choosing different modes of labor force participation as reflected by the divisional dummies. The choice between paid versus unpaid domestic work and unpaid family versus unpaid domestic work also differs significantly across the economic status of household as the coefficient of household income has been found as positive and highly significant for the former choice only. One of the interesting findings of Table 10 is the effect of care work on labor market status of women and estimates show that, in comparison to be outside of labor force and engaged in domestic activities, having young child (under 5 years of age) in the household increase the probability to work as unpaid family worker but reduces the probability to be in paid work. Family responsibility therefore appears to be a strong constraint for women to participate in mainstream labor market activities.

In terms of the characteristics of household head, multinomial logit estimates show that, if household head has some degree of education, then it acts as a negative factor to choose paid activity as opposed to be unpaid domestic worker. Besides, given an overwhelming percentage of unpaid family worker belonging to self-employed household head, estimates reveal that having a self-employed household head increases the probability to work both as unpaid family worker and as paid worker (as opposed to be outside of labor force and being engaged in domestic work).

In order to supplement the findings of Table 10, in Table 11 the marginal effects of the explanatory variables on the decision to choose unpaid family work are shown. As reflected in Tables 10, 11 reveals the importance of different sociodemographic and household factors in affecting the decision to choose unpaid work. For example, age acts a negative factor for unpaid family work and therefore we see (Table 9) greater proportion of relatively younger women working as unpaid family worker. Education has crucial role to play in terms of choice of unpaid family work and as reflected in Table 10, in comparison to those without any education (no education being the base), having some degree of education (below primary and primary) tend to have positive impact on the choice of unpaid family work but if the women have above primary education that has significant negative effect. Similar finding was reflected in our descriptive as well (Table 9). A number of household factors have been found crucial too. For example, the estimates reveal significant and positive impact of household head's occupational status as well as education on the decision of choosing unpaid family work by the female members of the household. In addition, amount of landholding has found to be a significant positive factor. All of these coefficient estimates, therefore, strengthen our prior belief that the choice of unpaid family labor is mostly driven by the requirement of the household rather than by the individual characteristics of the unpaid family worker. The positive and significant coefficient estimate of child dummy also supports such conclusion.

6 Conclusion

Based on the data of Labor Force Survey, it has been revealed that unpaid work is typically common in the context of Bangladesh where mostly women work without remuneration in the enterprise/farm of their spouses or father/mother-in-law. Our econometric estimation indicated the importance of a number of socioeconomic factors in the decision to choose unpaid work as opposed to paid activities or to remain out of the labor force and to engage in unpaid domestic work. For example, although they do not receive any remuneration for their work, it is interesting to find that a significant percentage of unpaid workers have some degree of education which indicates the possibility of their getting absorbed in the mainstream labor market activities. In addition, a number of household factors are found to play important role in choosing unpaid work. For example, occupation of household head (head being self-employed) along with greater landholding has strong positive effect on the decision to work as unpaid worker. Having children under 5 years of age also increases the probability to get involved in unpaid family work.

From our analysis, it can therefore be deduced that rather than the conventional factors prevailing in the labor market, a number of socioeconomic factors related primarily to households act as crucial determinants toward involvement in unpaid activities and thereby constraining participation in mainstream labor market. As a result, despite their effective contribution in the national income, unpaid family workers do not get any monetary reward and also lacks any ownership or authority over the farm/business in which she contributes. The key challenge in the context of unpaid family work is therefore to ease their burden of work and to help them to eventually move toward the mainstream labor market. To this end, a number of recommendations can be proposed:

- In order to ease the burden of unpaid work, the government can consider a number of policies like those of improving the infrastructure, encouraging agro-business activities, providing credit at low interest for purchasing agricultural equipment, etc.
- With a view to encourage them to engage in mainstream labor market, there should be increasing initiatives like those of establishing information cell regarding training, low-cost credit, etc. In this context, government's skill development programs should encourage greater participation of women.
- Given the significance of care responsibility in women's choice of labor market status, it is crucial to provide childcare facilities at workspace and such strategies can encourage women to switch toward formal wage/self-employment.
- There is no denying the fact that being married at a younger age often forces young girls to stay at home and to work at family farm/business. From a policy point of view, effective implementation of laws preventing child marriage should be given up most priority.

References

Antonopoulos, R. (2009). *Policy integration and statistics department.* Working paper no. 86. Geneva: International Labor Organization.

Bangladesh Bureau of Statistics. (2013). *Labor force survey.* Dhaka: Bangladesh Bureau of Statistics (BBS).

Das, M. B. (2006). *Do traditional axes of exclusion affect labor market outcomes in India?* Social development papers no. 97. Washington, DC: World Bank.

Efroymson, D., Biswas, B., & Ruma, S. (2007). *The economic contribution of women in Bangladesh through their unpaid labor.* Dhaka: Health Bridge and Canadian International Development Agency (CIDA).

Ghosh, J. (2009). Informalization and women's workforce participation: A consideration of recent trends in Asia. In S. Razavi (Ed.), *The gendered impacts of liberalization: Towards 'embedded' liberalism?* London: Routledge.

International Labor Organization. (2008). *Lobal employment trends for women*. Geneva: International Labor Organization.

Khatun, F., Khan, T. I., Pervin, S., & Jahan, H. (2015). *Estimating women's contribution to the economy: The case of Bangladesh*. Dhaka: Centre for Policy Dialogue and Manusher Jonno Foundation.

Latigo, A. A., & Neijwa, M. (2005). *A new round of time-use studies for Africa: Measuring unpaid work for pro-poor development policies*. Global Conference on the Unpaid Work and the Economy Gender, Poverty and the Millennium Development Goals. Addis Ababa, 1–3 Oct.

Raihan, S., Bidisha, S. H., & Jahan, I. (2016). *Unpacking unpaid labor in Bangladesh*. Mimeo, South Asian Network on Economic Modeling (SANEM).

Zammit, A. (2010). *Value chains and decent work for women: What is to be done?* Programme paper no. 88. Geneva: ILO Policy Integration and Statistics Department, International Labor Organization.

Dynamics of Employment in the Urban Informal Sector in Bangladesh

Selim Raihan, K. M. Nafiz Ifteakhar and Mir Tanzim Nur Angkur

1 Introduction

The informal economy refers to activities and income that are partially or fully outside government regulation, taxation, and observation. The main attraction of the undeclared economy is financial. This type of activity allows employers, paid employees, and the self-employed to increase their take-home earnings or reduce their costs by evading taxation and social contributions. On one hand, informal employment can provide a cushion for workers who cannot find a job in the formal sector. But on the other hand, it entails a loss in budget revenues by reducing taxes and social security contributions paid, and therefore the availability of funds to improve infrastructure and other public goods and services. It invariably leads to a high tax burden on registered labor.

Like many developing countries, the urban formal sector in Bangladesh is not able to provide enough job opportunities for its growing labor force. The growing labor forces can easily find themselves in the urban informal sector for their livelihoods. Therefore, urban formal sector has gained much attention to the

This chapter contains excerpts from the authors' previous publication as an op-ed in a newsletter (see: http://sanemnet.org/sanemafeefcontainer/uploads/2015/09/Thinking-Aloud_VII_N4.pdf)

S. Raihan (✉)
Department of Economics, University of Dhaka, Dhaka, Bangladesh
e-mail: selim.raihan@gmail.com

K. M. Nafiz Ifteakhar
Institute of Health Economics, University of Dhaka, Dhaka, Bangladesh

M. T. N. Angkur
Department of Economics, East West University, Dhaka, Bangladesh

S. Raihan · K. M. Nafiz Ifteakhar · M. T. N. Angkur
South Asian Network on Economic Modeling (SANEM), Dhaka, Bangladesh

S. Raihan (ed.), *Structural Change and Dynamics of Labor Markets in Bangladesh*, South Asia Economic and Policy Studies,
https://doi.org/10.1007/978-981-13-2071-2_6

policymakers for its important significance in the economy. In this context, it is very important to understand the dynamics and different issues of this urban informal sector, so that better policies can be designed to address the requirements of the workers engaged in these sectors. Against this background, this study provides a detailed overview of the urban informal sector in Bangladesh and explores the factors that affect the decision of the individuals to enter into the urban informal sector.

2 Literature Review

The concept of informal sector gained much attention over the last few decades. This is especially, true in the contexts of most developing countries where the informal sector has been a major factor behind employment creation, production, and income generation. Hart (1973) was the first to put forward the concept of "informal sector" into the academic literature as part of the urban labor force, which takes place outside of the formal sector.

A number of empirical studies exist on the determinants of labor force participation in the urban informal sector mainly in the context of developing countries. Most of these empirical studies found individual, household, social, and economic characteristics such as age, year of schooling (educational attainment), marital status, number and age of children, size of the households, household headship, region of residence, religion, wage, and gender to be the major factors that may affect an individual's participation to the urban informal sector.

In the context of Kenya, Wamuthenya (2010) found that sex, marital status, age, level of education, and household headship were significant factors in case of labor force participation in the urban informal sector. In the Sri Lankan context, Jayawardena and Arunatilake (2010) found that being male increased the likelihood of participation in the informal sector and being old decreased the chance of being in the informal sector compared to that of the public sector. Furthermore, individuals with the very low level of education and with no training had more chance of being employed in the informal sector as opposed to the public sector.

Marcouiller et al. (1997) and Saavedra and Chong (1999), in the context of Peru, found that young people, individuals who were not household heads and females were more likely to participate in the informal sector. Funkhouser (1996) observed similar results for several Central American countries. Reddy et al. (2001), in the context of Fiji, showed that those who participated in the urban informal sector had on average education less than the primary level. Timalsina (2011), in the context of Nepal, found that people with low level of education and skills were engaged in urban informal activities.

3 Overview of the Urban Informal Employment in Bangladesh

The study has used the Labor Force Survey (LFS) of Bangladesh for 2005 and 2010 to analyze the dynamics of urban informal employment in Bangladesh. Defining informal work was the challenge for this study. Different studies have defined informality based on certain characteristics ranging from ease of entry, low resource base, family ownership, small-scale, labor-intensive, adapted technology, unregulated but competitive markets, and informal processes of acquiring skills. The LFS provides a limited amount of information, which can be used to define informality.

We have defined informality in this paper by using three dimensions. The first dimension relates to the production unit or enterprise in which the workers work. More specifically, if the production units or enterprises are not registered with the concerned authority, then we consider those units fall under the informal sector. The second dimension relates to the existence of contract between the workers and the employers. If there is no contract between workers and employers either in written or verbal form, then we classify those workers as belonging to the informal sector. In addition to the above two criterion, for the wage employed workers, if the workers do not get any kind of pay slips or any kind of documents for their wages, then they are considered to be involved in the informal sector. In other developing countries such as Brazil, Mexico, and India, they consider two indicators—jobs with no social security coverage or written records as means of defining informal wage employment (Hussmans 2004).

Based on the abovementioned definitions, employment in the urban areas in Bangladesh is divided into formal and informal employments. Figure 1 states that in both 2005 and 2010, informal employment accounted for around two-thirds of the total urban employment. However, during 2005 and 2010, there has been a reduction in that share of informal employment from 70% in 2005 to 65% in 2010.

In terms of employment by nature of employment and gender, the share of female workers in both urban formal and informal sectors increased in 2010

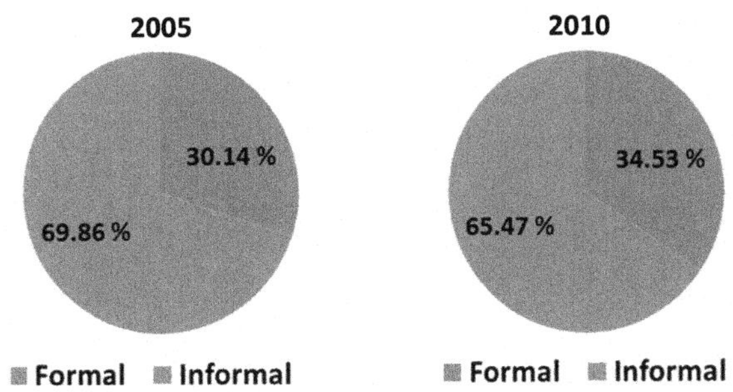

Fig. 1 Relative sizes of urban formal and informal sectors. *Source* LFS, 2005 and 2010

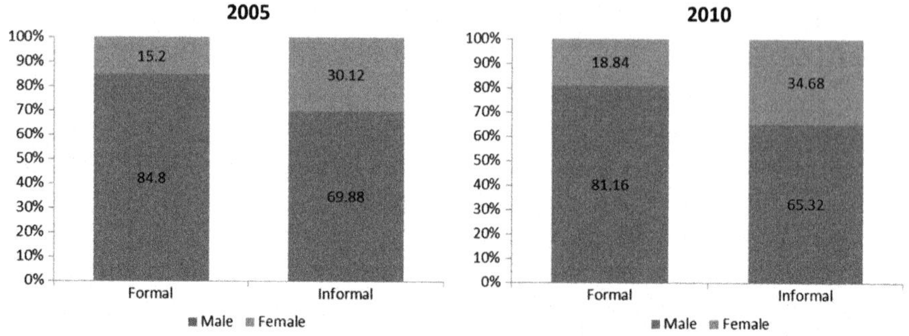

Fig. 2 Urban employment by nature of employment and gender. *Source* LFS, 2005 and 2010

compared to those in 2005. However, for the male workers, the share fell for both formal and informal sectors in 2010 as compared to those in 2005 (Fig. 2).

Figure 3 shows that in terms of age group of workers, the shares of younger age groups in informal sectors decreased in 2010 compared to those in 2005, particularly those belonging to the age groups of 15–19, 20–24, 25–29, and 30–34. Similarly, the shares of older age groups belonging to 50–54, 55–59, 60–64, and 65 + in informal sector declined in 2010. However, the shares for the middle-aged workers belonging to 35–39, 40–44, and 45–49 age groups, increased in 2010 compared to those in 2005.

Figure 4 shows that in the case of only male workers, the younger age groups belonging to 15–19, 20–24, 25–29, and 30–34 age groups participated more in urban formal sector in 2010 as compared to those in 2005. In 2010, the shares of middle-aged group belonging to 40–44, 45–49 in informal sector also decreased. For the older groups belonging to 60–64 and 65+, the shares in urban informal sector fell in 2010 as opposed to 2005.

Considering only female workers, Fig. 5 suggests that the involvement of the younger workers belonging to the age groups 20–24, 25–29, and 30–34 in urban informal sector decreased in 2010 compared to those in 2005 except for the age

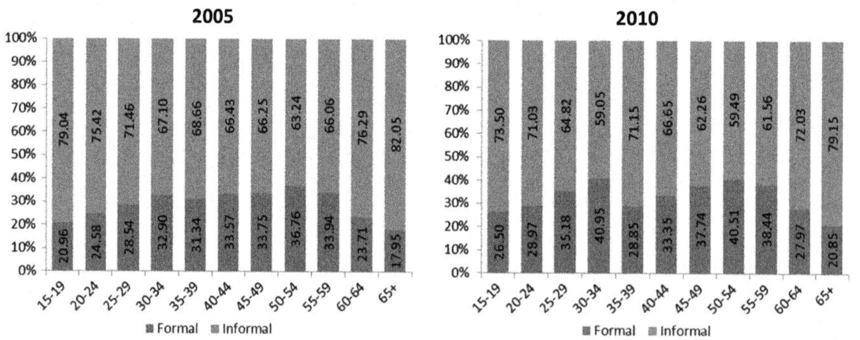

Fig. 3 Urban employment by age and nature of employment (overall). *Source* LFS, 2005 and 2010

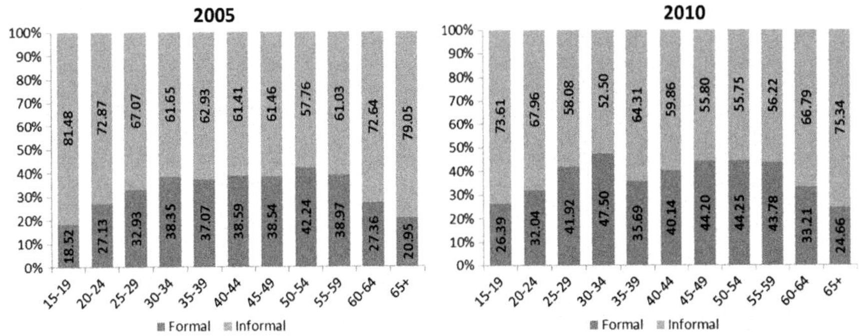

Fig. 4 Urban employment by age and nature of employment (male). *Source* LFS, 2005 and 2010

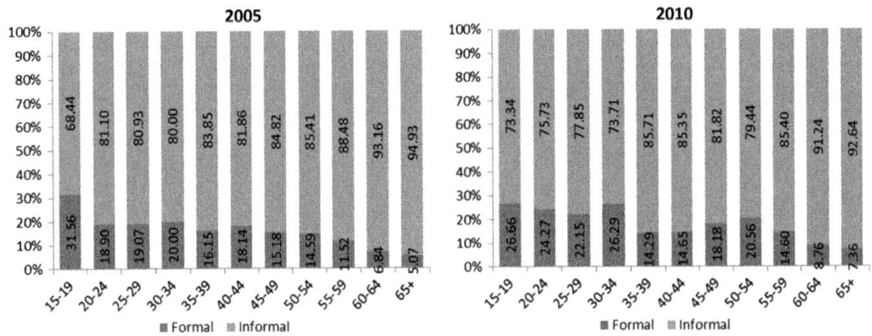

Fig. 5 Urban employment by age and nature of employment (female). *Source* LFS, 2005 and 2010

group belonging to 15–19. For the middle-aged groups, 35–39 and 40–44, their shares in urban informal sector increased in 2010 as opposed to 2005. But for the relatively older age groups belonging to 45–49, 50–54, 55–59, 60–64, and 65+ , the involvement in urban informal sector fell in 2010.

From the above analysis, it can be inferred that in both 2005 and 2010, middle-aged male workers were more likely to be involved in the formal sector employment compared to younger and older aged workers. This may be due to the fact that middle-aged workers tend to be more skillful compared to younger workers and this is justified on the ground that there is a positive relationship between years of education and formal sector participation. Due to the age constraint, older workers may not have that much efficiency to work in the formal sector and in the process, they get employed in the informal sector. For female workers the formal sector participation is less in both 2005 and 2010 compared to their male counterparts. This also may occur because of the fact that female education is still very low compared to their male counterpart.

Figure 6 shows the employment by level of education and nature of employment for workers. It is of no surprise to see that majority of the workers with the lower level of education found themselves involved in the urban informal sector in both

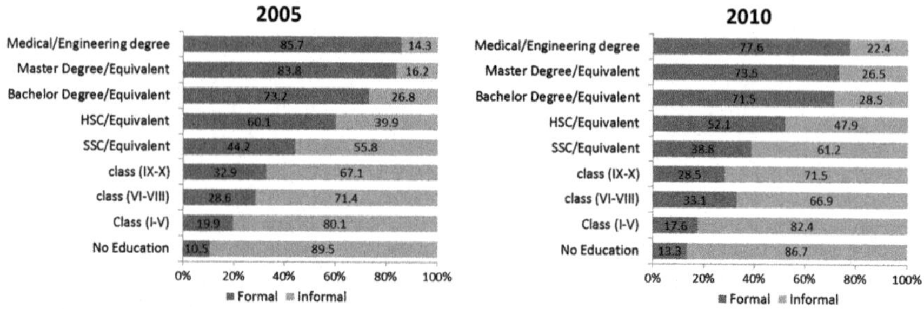

Fig. 6 Urban employment by level of education and nature of employment (overall). *Source* LFS, 2005 and 2010

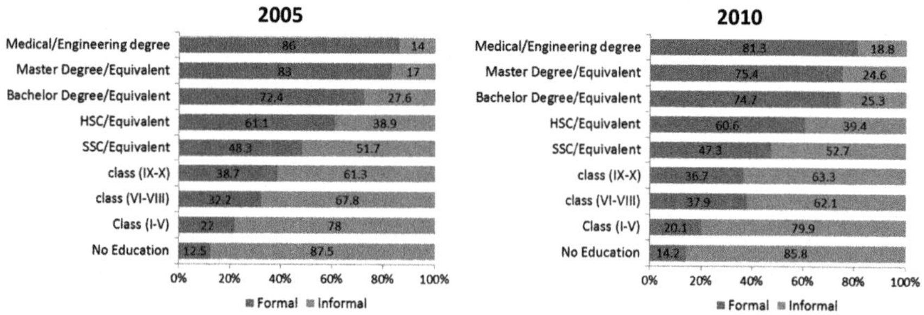

Fig. 7 Urban employment by level of education and nature of employment (male). *Source* LFS, 2005 and 2010

2005 and 2010. It can be seen that the share of formal sector is higher than that of the informal sector for workers attaining higher secondary education and above in both 2005 and 2010. This implies, workers who passed higher secondary education or higher level of education found themselves more in formal sector relative to informal sector in both the years.

From Fig. 7, it is seen that male workers with lower level of education, particularly below HSC education, were more employed in the informal sector in both the years. The figure also suggests that once a male worker passed HSC or higher level of education, he is more likely to get employed in formal sector rather than in the informal sector.

Considering only the female workers, Fig. 8 shows almost the same pattern of employment by level of education and nature of employment for both years as we have seen for male and for the overall situation. However, there lies a difference in the sense that in 2005, female workers were more involved in formal sector compared to informal sector with HSC and above level of education, but this has changed in 2010, where female workers were more involved in formal sector compared to the informal sector after they have passed bachelor's degree. In general, it could be seen that the share of formal employment at very high level of

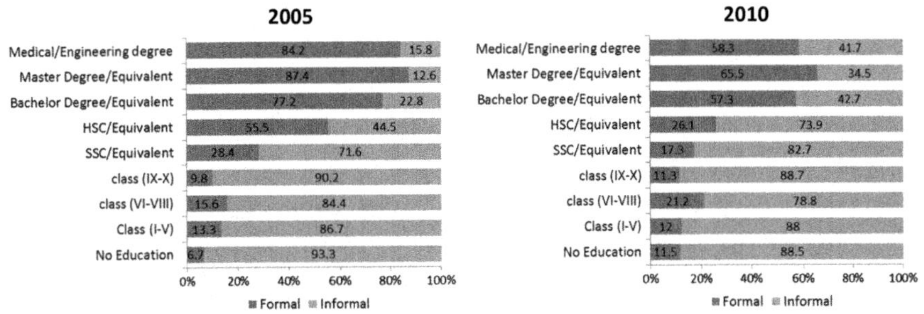

Fig. 8 Urban employment by level of education and nature of employment (Female). *Source* LFS, 2005 and 2010

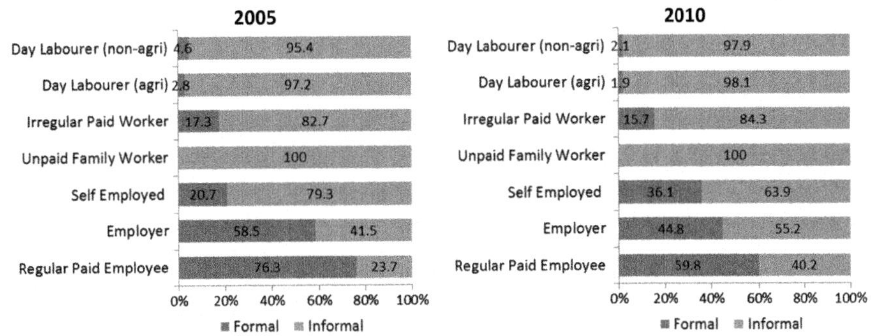

Fig. 9 Urban employment by employment status and nature of employment (overall). *Source* LFS, 2005 and 2010

education had been reduced. Lack of opportunities in the urban formal sector and rise in informal sector wage might be responsible for this.

Figure 9 shows the urban employment by status and nature of employment. It can be seen that for unpaid workers, the nature of employment is fully informal. And for the category of regular paid employee, the share of formal employment is higher in both years, though the share declined in 2010. For the rest of other categories, the share of informal employment is higher except in employer category. For employer, the share of formal employment was higher in 2005 but this changed in 2010 where the share of informal employment became higher. Also, it can be seen that during 2005 and 2010, the share of formal employment increased for self-employed labor only.

Figure 10 represents the status and nature of employment considering only male workers. The “employer” category in both 2005 and 2010, were almost equally involved in formal and informal sector. But for the rest of the categories, informal employment shares were higher except for the regular paid employee. In particular,

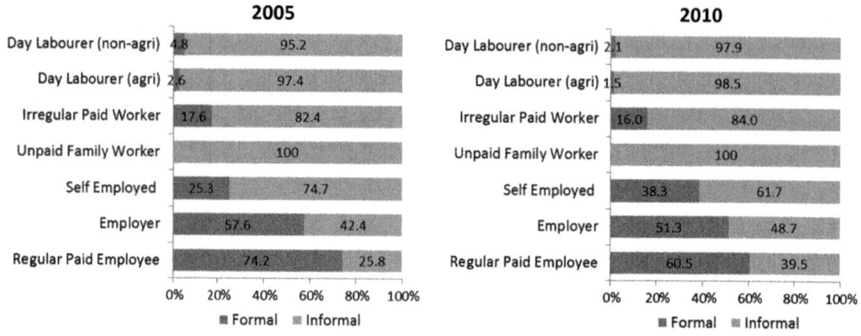

Fig. 10 Urban employment by employment status and nature of employment (male). *Source* LFS, 2005 and 2010

for self-employed labor, the share of formal employment increased during the period.

Considering only the female workers, Fig. 11 shows almost the same pattern of employment by employment status and nature of employment for both years as we have seen for male and for the overall situation. For all categories, informal employment shares were higher except for the employer and regular paid employee in both 2005 and 2010. In particular, for self-employed female labor, the share of formal employment increased remarkably during the period.

The aforementioned overview section provides a bivariate association between the individual determinants of informal sector participation. The possible determinants include the status of employment, age of workers, level of education, and gender. To imply causality further, econometric estimation of urban informal sector participation is required which is covered in the following section.

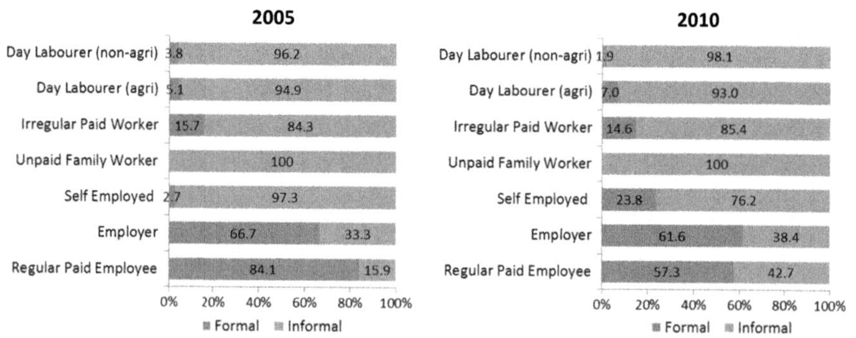

Fig. 11 Urban employment by employment status and nature of employment (female). *Source* LFS, 2005 and 2010

4 What Determines Participation in the Urban Informal Employment?

This study aims to find out the factors affecting the decision of participating in urban informal sector. There may be several unobservable individual factors, which may affect the informal sector participation of the labor belonging to urban areas. This unobserved heterogeneity (i.e., individual ability) might result in the inconsistency of the estimated parameters, which is known as heterogeneity bias. To remove this biasness, fixed effect estimator was used. To apply fixed effect estimator, we needed to have a panel data, which is currently unavailable. For the purpose of the estimation, we developed a pseudo panel by constructing the cohorts (cohorts are the subgroups of the sample) using the "industry types". In our case, the labor from a particular industry type was taken as a cohort of that industry type. That means for each industry type, we will have a cohort. Though there are several industry types in the Labor Force Survey of 2010 and 2005, we have reclassified (i.e., merge comparable industry types into one, recode where necessary) the industry types to make that data of 2005 comparable with the data of 2010. This study has used the following regression model.

$$\begin{aligned} informal_{it} = & \beta_0 + \beta_1 edu_{it} + \beta_2 deprto_{it} + \beta_3 age_{it} + \beta_4 age\_sqr_{it} + \beta_5 land_{it} \\ & + \beta_6 female_{it} + \beta_7 unpaid_{it} + \beta_8 self_{it} + \mu_{it} \end{aligned}$$

In the above regression model, the dependent variable is the informal intensity of any sector, i.e., the percentage of informal participation in a particular industry type out of total employed persons in that industry type. This variable can thus be termed as the informal sector participation. The variables that affect the decision of participation in the informal sector can include both individual and family characteristics. To capture the effect of individual and family characteristics, years of schooling (edu), individual age, dependency ratio (deprto), measured as the ratio of number of dependents in the family to total members of the family, and gender (female dummy) are introduced as explanatory variables. The square term of age (age_sqr) is also included in the regression to capture the nonlinearity in the effect of age on the informal sector participation. The financial condition of the workers' household may also affect the decision to enter in the informal sector. The land holding (land), measured in acres, was used as a proxy of the financial condition of the household. Furthermore, an employed person may be a wage employed (wage), self-employed (self), or may be an unpaid worker (unpaid) as per the LFS (Labor Force Survey) classification. We, therefore, have introduced dummies representing these three groups in the regression to see whether there is any association between informal sector participation and employment types after controlling for other factors. The category of wage employed (wage) is omitted from the regression as we are taking this group as the base category.

By taking the average for each cohort, we are able to construct a pseudo panel where each of the observation represents a particular industry type. The interpretations of the independent variables in the context of the pseudo panel are the following:

- The variable representing education level of the workers is interpreted as average years of schooling of the labor employed in a particular industry type.
- Family dependency is described as the average family dependency ratio of the labor employed in a particular industry type.
- Family landholding is the average landholding of the family of the labor employed in a particular industry type.
- The variable female represents the percentage of female workers out of total workers employed in a particular industry type.
- The variable age is the average age of the labor employed in a particular industry type.
- The effect of employment characteristics, for example, the variable representing self-employed labor (self), is interpreted as the percentage of self-employed labor in a particular industry type out of total employed person in that industry type. Other two independent variables of employment characteristics are interpreted in the same way.

We have applied fixed effect estimator in the pseudo panel, which is basically applying OLS on time demean data and in this process, the unobserved heterogeneity (the industry fixed effect) is removed. We have also applied the random effect estimator, which is basically applying the OLS on quasi-demeaned data. Random effect estimator is used when it is assumed that the unobserved heterogeneity is not correlated with any of the explanatory variables appeared in the regression model.

4.1 Regression Results Considering All Employment Types

Table 1 presents the regression results considering all employment types. In general, the fixed effect and random effect results are similar. From the fixed effect estimation, we have found that 1 year increase in average years of schooling of labor employed in a particular industry code would decrease the informal intensity (the percentage of labor employed in informal type of firm out of total number of labor in the respective industry code) of that industry code on an average by 0.048% points. The estimated coefficients of dependency ratio imply that an increase in average dependency ratio of the families of an industry classification leads to an increase in the informal intensity of that industry classification. The coefficient of age is negative and significant while the coefficient of age squared is positive and significant, which imply a quadratic relationship between age and informal sector participation. More specifically, initially an increase in age reduces the informal sector participation, while after a certain level of age the effect of age on the informal sector participation becomes positive. The estimated coefficient of

Table 1 Pseudo-panel regression on sectoral informal intensity (all employment types)

Explanatory variables	Informal intensity (fixed effect)	Informal intensity (random effect)
Education	-0.048^{a} (0.013)	-0.041^{a} (0.005)
Dependency ratio	0.140^{b} (0.058)	0.085^{b} (0.039)
Landholding	-0.0005^{c} (0.001)	-0.001^{c} (0.001)
Age	-0.058^{a} (0.022)	−0.049a (0.019)
Age squared	0.001^{a} (0.0003)	0.001b (0.0002)
Female	0.034^{c} (0.127)	-0.01^{c} (0.09)
Unpaid labor	0.567^{a} (0.219)	0.555^{a} (0.136)
Self-employment	0.27^{b} (0.12)	0.30^{a} (0.07)
Constant	1.51^{a} (0.41)	1.49^{a} (0.34)
Number of observations	235^{c}	235^{c}
F	8.475^{a}	
chi2		510.23^{a}
R2	0.539^{c}	0.569^{c}

Note a, b and c indicate statistical significance at the 1, 5 and 10% levels respectively. The figures in parentheses are the standard errors

female is not significant, which suggests that gender does not have any effect on informal intensity of an industry type. The estimated coefficients of the unpaid labor suggest that this worker group is likely to be more associated with informal sector than that of the wage employed labor, which is the base category. The estimated coefficients of the other worker group, i.e., self-employed are also found to be positive and significant under both fixed effect and random effect estimator. This implies that self-employed worker is more likely to be associated with urban informal sector compared to the wage employed labor.

4.2 *Regression Results Excluding Unpaid Labor*

Table 2 presents the results of informal intensity regression for the model, which excludes the unpaid labor from the pseudo-panel data set. Similar results are observed for the variables like education, dependency ratio, age, female dummy, etc., as have been found for the overall model. Like the earlier case, wage employed is considered as the base category. The estimated coefficient of the self-employed labor, under both fixed effect and random effect models, is found to be positive and significant, which suggests that compared to the wage employed labor category, self-employed labor is more likely to be involved in the urban informal sector.

Table 2 Pseudo-panel regression on sectoral informal intensity (unpaid labor dropped)

Explanatory variables	Informal intensity (fixed effect)	Informal intensity (random effects)
Education	−0.048[a] (0.012)	−0.043[a] (0.005)
Dependency ratio	0.181[a] (0.057)	0.105[a] (0.041)
Landholding	−0.0012[c] (0.001)	−0.0015[c] (0.001)
Age	−0.06[a] (0.023)	−0.044[b] (0.019)
Age squared	0.001[a] (0.0003)	0.001[b] (0.0002)
Female	−0.005[c] (0.118)	−0.01[c] (0.095)
Self-employed	0.302[a] (0.114)	0.327[a] (0.063)
Constant	1.51[a] (0.412)	1.40[a] (0.35)
Number of observations	235[c]	235[c]
F	8.022[a]	
chi2		485.90[a]
R2	0.511[c]	0.543[c]

Note a, b and c indicate statistical significance at the 1, 5 and 10% levels, respectively. The figures in parentheses are the standard errors

5 Conclusion

This paper has provided a detailed overview of the urban informal sector in Bangladesh and has explored the factors that affect the decision of the individuals to enter into the urban informal sector. The paper has used sophisticated econometric models in exploring such determinants. The regression results suggest that education plays a key role in promoting formal sector participation. Also, certain household and individual characteristics, such as dependency ratio and age of the workers also have important implications for informal sector participation. Workers belonging to younger and older age groups are more inclined to participate in urban informal sector than the workers belonging to the middle-aged groups. Also, workers coming from a family with high dependency ratio have to resort to urban informal sector activities for their livelihood. It is also found that employment types affect the decision to enter in the urban informal sector. While, unpaid workers are fully associated with the informal sector employment, compared to the self-employed labor, wage employed labor are less likely to be associated with the informal sector.

References

Funkhouser, E. (1996). The Urban Informal Sector in Central America: Household Survey Evidence. *World Development, 24*(11), 1737–1751.

Hart, K. (1973). Informal Income Opportunities and Urban Employment in Ghana. *Journal of Modern African Studies, 11*(1), 61–89.

Hussmans, R. (2004). *Measuring the informal economy: From employment in the informal sector to informal employment* (Working Paper No. 53), Policy Integration, Department Geneva: Internation Labor Office, ILO.

Jayawardena, P., & Arunatilake, N. (2010). Why people choose to participate in the informal sector in Sri-Lanka. *The Indian Journal of Labour Economics, 53*(2).

Marcouiller, D., Castilla, V. R., & Woodruff, C. (1997). Formal Measures of the Informal-sector wage gap in Mexico, El Salvador and Peru. *Economic Development and Cultural Change, 45* (2), 367–392.

Reddy, M., Naidu, V., & Mohanty, M. (2001). The urban informal sector in Fiji: Results from a survey. *Fijian Studies, 1*(1), 127–154.

Saavedra, J., & Chong, A. (1999). Structural reform, institutions and earnings: evidence from the formal and informal sectors in urban peru. *The Journal of Developments Studies, 35*(4), 95–116.

Timalsina, K. P. (2011). An Urban Informal Economy: Livelihood Opportunity to Poor or Challenges for Urban Governance, Study of Street Vending Activities of Kathmandu Metropoliton City. *International Journal of Policies and Good Governance*, 2(2.2), Quarter II, 1–13.

Wamuthenya, W. (2010). *Determinants of employment in the formal and informal sectors of the urban areas of kenya* (Research Paper NO. 194). Nairobi: African Economic Research Consortium (AERC).

Some Estimates of First Demographic Dividend in Bangladesh: An Application of the Bangladesh National Transfer Account

Bazlul H. Khondker and Muhammad Moshiur Rahman

1 Introduction

Bangladesh has entered the window of population dividend opportunities from 1991 onward as the dependency ratio decreased. However, the expressed time of the window of opportunities is not bolstered by observational confirmation. The absence of certain proof on the period and extent of the demographic dividend is a gap which policy-makers must address when setting needs for human resource and capital investment to gather the economic advantages of the demographic move. Applying the methodology of National Transfer Account (NTA), this study is an endeavor to fill this gap by indicating so as to evaluate the demographic benefit for Bangladesh. Therefore, the objective of the paper is to evaluate the first demographic dividend in Bangladesh and to explore the conditions to appreciate it.

2 Review of Literature

There is a large pool of literature on demographic patterns and their effects on the economy; however, the evidence on the connection between economic growth and the working-age population is limited. Bloom et al. (2000) and Mason (2001)

This chapter contains excerpts from the authors' previous publication as an op-ed in a newsletter (see: http://sanemnet.org/sanemafeefcontainer/uploads/2016/01/Thinking-Aloud_VII_N8.pdf).

B. H. Khondker (✉)
Department of Economics, University of Dhaka, Dhaka, Bangladesh
e-mail: bazlul.khondker@gmail.com

B. H. Khondker · M. M. Rahman
South Asian Network on Economic Modeling (SANEM), Dhaka, Bangladesh

S. Raihan (ed.), *Structural Change and Dynamics of Labor Markets in Bangladesh*, South Asia Economic and Policy Studies,
https://doi.org/10.1007/978-981-13-2071-2_7

suggested that East Asia's high economic performance was largely associated with the noteworthy move in the age structure of the region; and they found a positive association between high economic performance and the proportion of the working-age population—capturing the transition in the age structure. Applying cross-country panel data from 1965 to 1995, Bloom and Canning (2004) demonstrated a positive and important relationship between the economic growth and growth of the share of the working-age population. Mason and Lee (2006) proposed that every nation in the Asia and Pacific region needed to act to gather the first demographic dividend. Similarly, other papers (i.e., Fry and Mason 1982; Higgins 1998; Kelley and Schmidt 1996; Person 2002; Rajan and Subramanian 2008) also found positive association between national aggregate rates for major economic variables and demographic structure.

3 Overview of Demographic Transition and Employment Structure in Bangladesh

3.1 Demographic Transition in Bangladesh

Demographic transition captures the movement of a society from an equilibrium, portrayed by high fertility and high mortality, to another one depicted by low fertility and low mortality. In the initial phases of the transition, mortality falls first and especially among the children (Bloom et al. 2000). Improved survival among the young cohorts creates a boom in generation and a surge in fertility decisions. Thus, child dependency rate rises and population growth adjusts downward to account for lower mortality, and the mean age of the population begins to increase. As the large cohorts enter the working age, population expands relative to the total population and the child dependency ratios decline. The last stage of this transition is characterized by a surge in the size of the elderly population as large cohorts reach retirement age, compelling up to the old-age dependency ratio.

According to the Census 2011, Bangladesh's population stood at 149.8 million implying an increase of 25.4 million between 2001 and 2011. By 2030, the projected total population of Bangladesh will be 185.1 million due to two factors: (i) an increase in life expectancy at birth for male and female, respectively, from 67.8 and 69.1 years in 2005–2010 to 74.4 and 76.6 in 2025–2030, and (ii) a decline in the total fertility rate (TFR) from 2.40 to 1.83.

Figure 1 shows the demographic and age structure transition in Bangladesh. According to the World Population Prospectus (2015), the implication of the demographic transition on age structure is evident for the population under 15 years of age as the share in the total population of this age group fell from 44.7% in 1970 to 31.7% in 2010; and is projected to decline to 17.3% in 2050. At the same time, the population under the age of 20 years fell from 54.7% in 1970 to 42.2% in 2010 and is projected to decline to 23.5% in 2050. The large decline in the share of the population under 20 years of age has been associated with a substantial rise in the

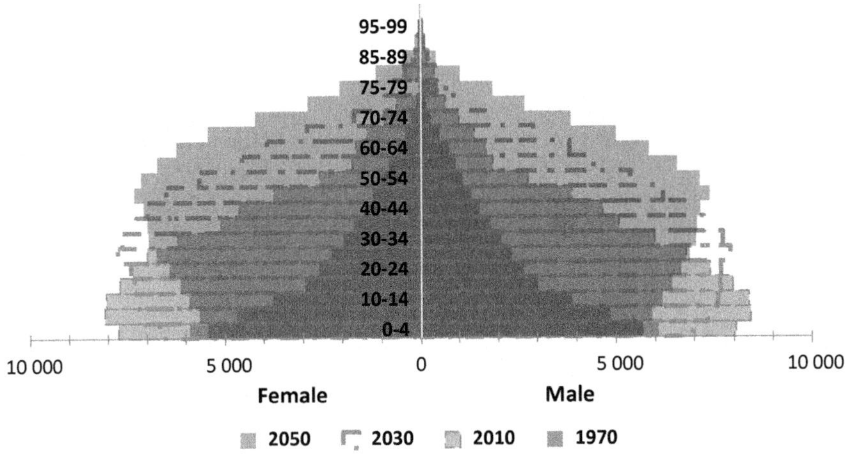

Fig. 1 Demographic and age structure transition in Bangladesh. *Note* population in thousand. *Source* Constructed from United Nations World Population Prospects: The 2015 Revision

proportion of the working-age population (15–64 years) from 41.9 to 53.2% from 1970 to 2010 and is projected to be a maximum of 60.3% in 2050.

According to Fig. 2, the annual exponential population growth rate was above 2% between the late 1970s and the mid-1990s. This period was associated with a birth rate of above 35/1000 population and gradual decline in the death rate. On the other hand, the annual exponential population growth rate was below 2% from late 1990s to the recent years when both the death and birth rates have been gradually declining. Although population growth rates suggest somewhat smooth declining pattern, sudden large drop in the growth between 1970 and 1975 deserves some

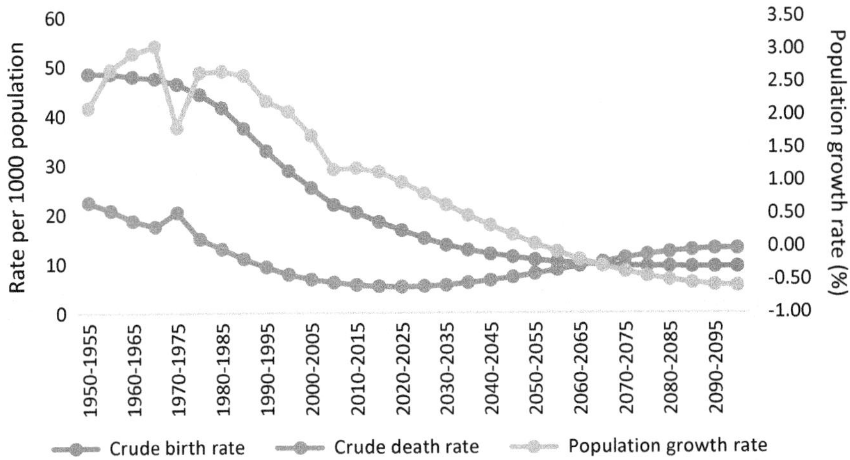

Fig. 2 Crude birth rate, crude death rate population growth in Bangladesh. *Source* Constructed from United Nations World Population Prospects: The 2015 Revision

elaboration. Curlin et al. (1976) related this drop to marked fluctuation in the crude death rate and the liberation war in 1971. In particular, the death rate, during that period, climbed sharply to 210/1000, 37% higher than the 5-year average. By 1972–1973, a significant recovery was noted (i.e., 162 death per 1000), although the rate remained above normal levels. Full recovery to the trend was observed in 1973–1974, 3 years after the liberation war. However, during 1974–1975 period—a period associated with exorbitant increase in price of food grains—mortality rate increased and fertility rate declined (see Chowdhury and Curlin 1978 for details). Both crude death rates and infant mortality (primarily post-neonatal mortality) increased sharply in 1974 and remained high in 1975.

The upshot of the above discussion points to the fact that the age structure of Bangladesh's population is likely to undergo remarkable transitions in near future leading to a decline in the relative share of children and an increase in the share of the elderly and working-age populations.

3.2 Economic Structure, Employment, and Labor Force Participation

In the 1960s, the then East Pakistan's economy grew by an annual average rate of around 4%. About a fifth of that economy was destroyed during the 1971 Liberation War, and severe dislocations caused at that time left Bangladesh on a slower economic growth trajectory for the following two decades. Then, the economic growth accelerated from 1990 to a growth rate over 4% in the first half of 1990s. During the latter half of 1990s, the growth rate exceeded over 5%. In the last decade, it has been hovering around average 6% growth rate.

The sectoral economic growth as well as the structure of the economy has changed significantly over the past two decades. The growth rate of agricultural sector has varied over the last two decades with low to moderate magnitude. The manufacturing sector experienced significant growth. Growth rate of the services sector has been stable at around 5–6% over the last two decades. The share of agriculture in GDP declined from over 50% in 1972 to 16% in 2014, with a decline in employment share from about 75–45%. Since 1980, the share of manufacturing has been on the rise approaching 20% of GDP in 2014. However, services, mostly informal, continued to make up the bulk of economic activity, holding at about 50% in 2014 compared to about 45% in 1972.

Structural transformation has also affected the employment structure, albeit to a lesser extent. Table 1 presents share of employed persons aged 15 years and above by broad economic sectors during 4 consecutive year categories: 1990–2000, 2002–2003, 2005–2006, and 2010. Share of employment in agriculture was 51.1% in 1999–2000. It slightly increased to 52.2% in 2002–2003 but keep on decreasing after that. Despite the declining trend, it still accounts for 47.5% of the total employment in 2010.

A major feature of the labor force participation in Bangladesh is the low level of female labor participation. Figure 3 shows considerable variations with respect to

Table 1 Percentage of employed persons aged 15 years and over by broad economic sector

Broad sector	1999–00	2002–03	2005–06	2010
Agriculture	51.06	52.15	48.21	47.51
Non-agriculture	48.94	47.85	51.79	52.49
Manufacturing	9.53	9.75	10.95	12.34
Other industry	3.09	3.63	3.37	4.97
Services	36.32	34.47	37.47	35.17

Source Labor Force Survey, BBS

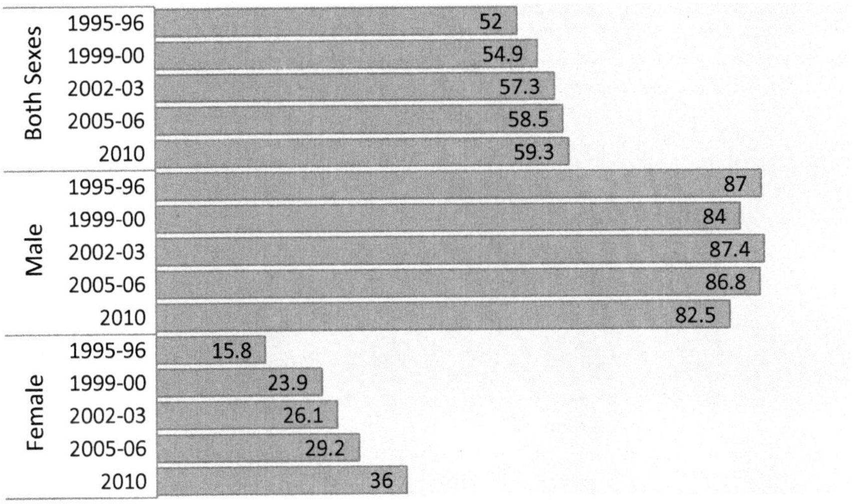

Fig. 3 Labor force participation rate in Bangladesh (%). *Source* Labor Force Survey, BBS

male and female labor force participation. It is found that labor force participation increased from 52% in 1996 to 59.3% in 2010. A structural shift in male and female labor force participation has been observed during this period. More specifically, male labor force participation decreased from 87% in 1996 to 82.5% in 2010, while female labor force participation experienced almost 100% increase, from 15.8% in 1996 to 36% in 2010.

Employment by formal and informal sources is shown in Fig. 4. The share of informal employment has historically been high in Bangladesh. More than 75% of the workers were employed in the informal sector between 2002–2003 and 2005–2006. The share of informal employment increased to around 87% in 2010 from 79% reported for 2005–2006.

Figure 5 shows employment by formal and informal sector and by gender for selected years. In year 2002–2003, shares of employment for male and female were similar in both informal and formal sectors. More specifically, 78.8% of male employment was in the informal sector while the corresponding figure for female

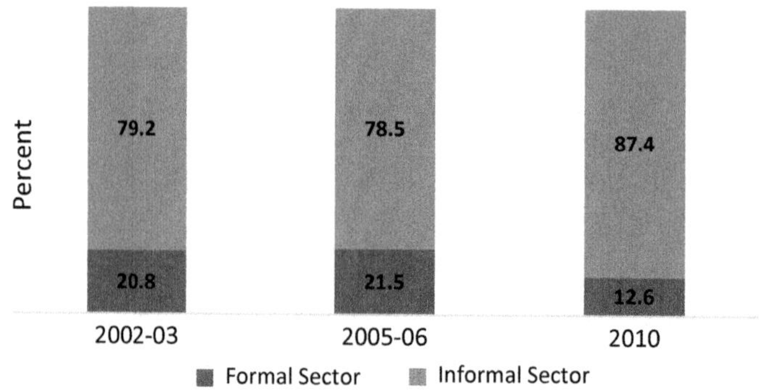

Fig. 4 Percentage of employed persons aged 15 years and over by formal and informal sector (%). *Source* Labor Force Survey, BBS

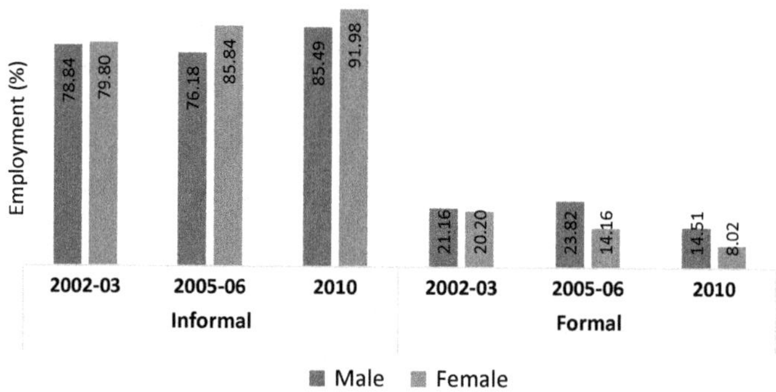

Fig. 5 Percentage of employed persons aged 15 years and over by sector and gender. *Source* Labor Force Survey, BBS

employment was slightly higher at 79.8%. Thereafter, the share of female employment in the informal sector increased—by about 6% age points between 2002–2003 and 2005–2006; and by about 12% points between 2002–2003 and 2010. The share of female employment in formal sector thus decreased.

4 National Transfer Accounts Analysis for Estimating the First Demographic Dividend in Bangladesh

National transfer accounts provide an accounting of economic flows to and from residents of a country classified by their age. The accounts are comprehensive in that all economic flows that arise as a consequence of the production of goods and services during the year are incorporated into the accounts. The aggregate values are broadly consistent with those found in national accounts, as detailed in the

System of National Accounts (SNA) methodology maintained by the United Nations. National transfer accounts are structured to emphasize the generational economy and its key features: the economic life cycle and age reallocations realized by relying on intergenerational transfers and assets. NTA is an analytical framework for accounting for the life cycle deficit. The life cycle deficit equals consumption less labor income with the introduction of age into the national accounts. The consumption in an economy from an individual perspective includes publicly (government) sponsored targeted programs for health care, education, poverty alleviation, social assistance, and other goods either in kind or in cash and private (household) consumption for, among other things, education, health care, housing, food, and non-food goods.

The demographic transition can enhance economic growth in *two broad ways*. First, as the dependency ratio declines and the share of working-age population grows relative to the total population, the average number of children per working-age adult also falls. Assuming, this is associated with a freeing up of resources that previously would have been consumed by additional children—allowing living standards to rise. *This is the first demographic dividend.* Second, a *second demographic dividend* may also arise to positively affect economic growth and overall development. More specifically, the second dividend results in when the faster growth of first dividend (i.e., rise in working-age population) leads to larger savings in the short run and higher investment in the human capital and investment per worker in the long run. Important question with regard to the first demographic dividend is the impact of age structure on economic growth. More specifically, how, why, and at which extent age structure influences economic growth? The total dependency ratio is purely a composite indicator to capture the change in age structure and it does not reflect the variations of earnings and the consumption according to the age. This limitation is overcome in the NTA based on the economic life cycle approach (Mason and Lee 2006) which is applied in the current paper.

The datasets for Bangladesh NTA include (i) Household Income and Expenditure Survey (HIES) 2010 from the Bangladesh Bureau of Statistics (BBS); Labor Force Survey (LFS) 2010 from the Bangladesh Bureau of Statistics (BBS); (iv) UNFPA population prospectus data; and (iv) National Accounts Statistics (SNA) from the Bangladesh Bureau of Statistics (BBS).

According to the NTA methodology, the life cycle deficit (LCD) at each age is the superfluous of consumption over labor income. In order to derive the monetary value of LCD by age, it is essential to measure labor income, which, in this paper, is the aggregate of wage of employees (including both in kind and cash) and a fixed part of mixed income (income from own business enterprise). Data of LFS has been used in this purpose. In order to derive age patterns of public and private consumption for education, health and other expenditures and labor income, member level and unit level data with public (government), and private (household) distinctions are required which is collected from the HIES 2010 data. Results from the Bangladesh NTAs 2010 have been reported under two broad headings:

(i) economic lifecycle and lifecycle deficit; and (ii) economic support ration and first demographic dividend.

4.1 Economic Life cycle and Life cycle Deficit

Figure 6 shows the consumption profile by age. This is the combined profiles of per capita consumption of education, health care, and other consumptions separated by public and private contributions. The consumption profile suggests a sharp rise in consumption alongside increasing the age, particularly for school-age consumers. Per capita yearly consumption increases sharply from about 4 years of age till it attains an early peak at about 19 year, indicating investment in education and it continues up to 25 years.

Figure 7 shows distribution of the per capita labor income according to the age profile. This reflects a number of distinctive features. It is an inverse U-shaped curve suggesting low earning potential at early ages. The labor income increases steeply till about 34 years of age, and then steadily increases between 35 and 49 years of age. Thereafter, income starts declining, and after 54, it declines rapidly with advancing age. The presence of child labor is obvious with the early age of entry into the labor force with share of labor income of young persons. The tapering income profile of the elderly is indicative of their low wages as many are self-employed, or work in the informal sector.

Figure 8 shows the deficit for each age group. Three distinct age groups are found in terms of LCD. As expected, two deficit groups are children (age 0 to 19)

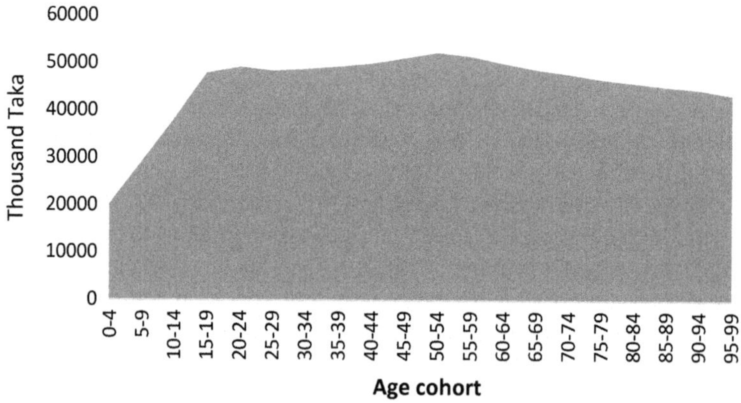

Fig. 6 Per capita consumption profile, 2010. *Source* Authors' calculation, Bangladesh National Transfer Accounts of 2010

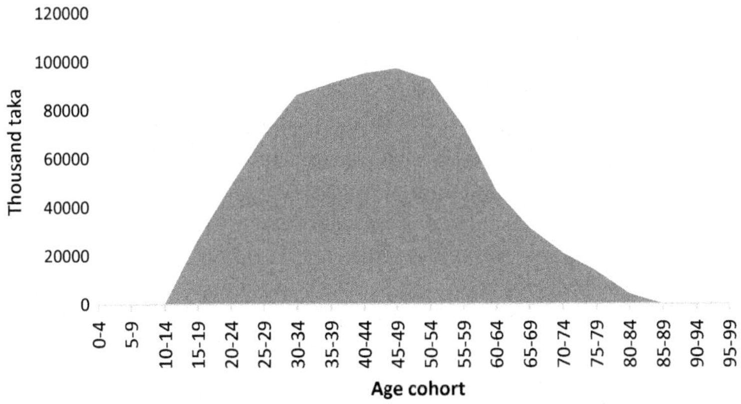

Fig. 7 Per capita labor income profile, 2010. *Source* Authors' calculation, Bangladesh National Transfer Accounts of 2010

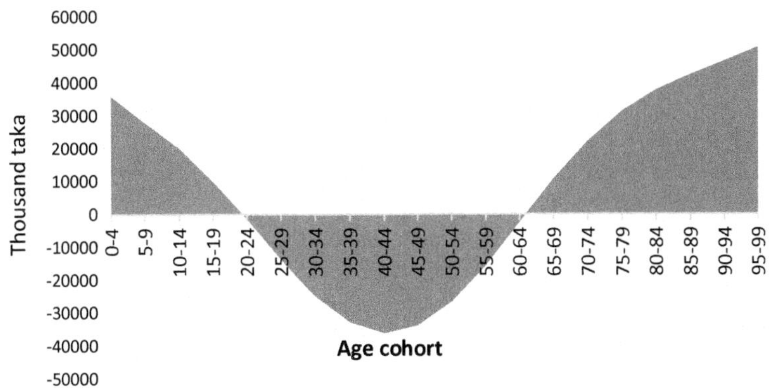

Fig. 8 Per capita life cycle deficit profile, 2010. *Source* Authors' calculation, Bangladesh National Transfer Accounts of 2010

and the elderly (65+). However, the deficit for elderly group is higher than the children perhaps indicates that low levels of income as well as higher poverty among households with children compared to household with elderly.[1] The group encompassing age 20 and 64 is generating surplus in Bangladesh.

[1]According to HIES 2010, head count poverty rates among households with children (age 0–18) has found to be 1.7% points higher than the national average of 31.5%. On the other hand, head count poverty rate among households with elderly (age 60+) has found to be 3.3% points lower than the national average (Khondker 2014).

4.2 *The Economic Support Ratio (ESR) and the First Demographic Dividend*

According to the 2006 revision, several assumptions have been used by UN to project the population. Following that, eight variants underlying the fertility, mortality, constant fertility, and mortality and also with international migration assumptions have been used in this paper to observe the first demographic dividend. These variants are used to observe the probable year of highest ESR with the range of the first demographic dividend. We also use it to estimate the maximum year left to harvest the benefits of the first demographic dividend.

Figure 9 shows that ESR is varying according to the various variants of the population growth rate. In particular, with high variant population growth, ESR increases positively till 2030. On the other hand, with the medium variant population growth, it increases till 2035 and with low variant it increases positively up to 2040. Thus, according to these three variants of population growth—high, medium, and low—the first demographic dividend in Bangladesh will likely to stay, respectively, till 2030, 2035, and 2040.

Figure 10 captures the ESR variations with respect to constant fertility, constant mortality, and instant replacement rate. It is found that ESR will increase positively till 2030 with both the instant replacement and constant fertility. This suggests that the first demographic dividend will exist up to year 2030. On the other hand, with the constant mortality rate, the ESR will rise positively till 2040 and the first demographic dividend will exist up to year 2040.

Patterns of out-migration may also affect the first demographic dividend. Figure 11 shows ESR patterns under zero migration. With no change in fertility–mortality, it will rise positively till 2030 suggesting that the first demographic

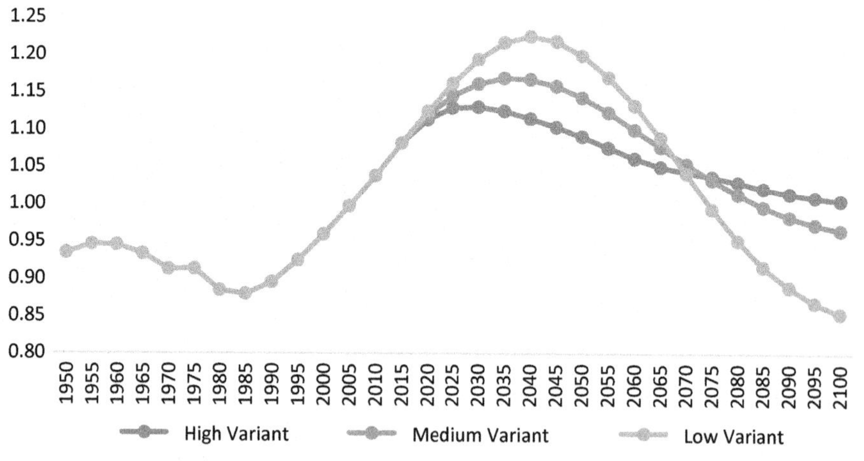

Fig. 9 Economic support ratio in 2010 for different variants of the population growth rate. *Source* Authors' calculation, Bangladesh National Transfer Accounts of 2010

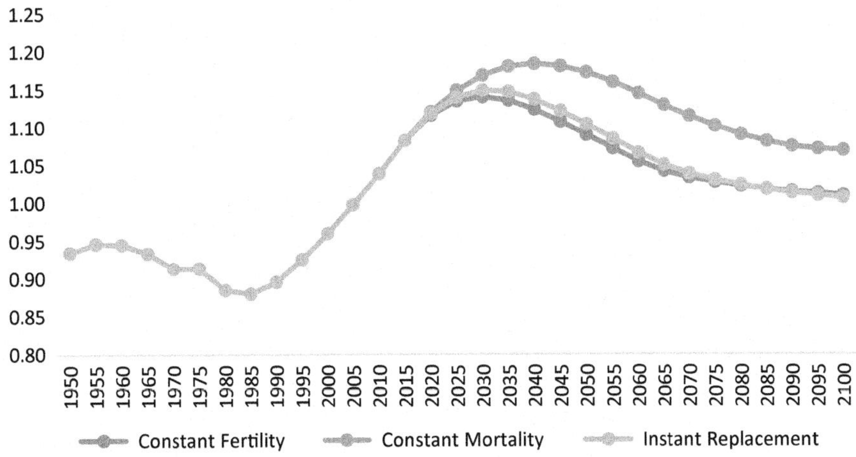

Fig.10 Economic support ratio in 2010 for constant fertility, constant mortality, and instant replacement rate. *Source* Authors' Calculation, Bangladesh National Transfer Accounts of 2010

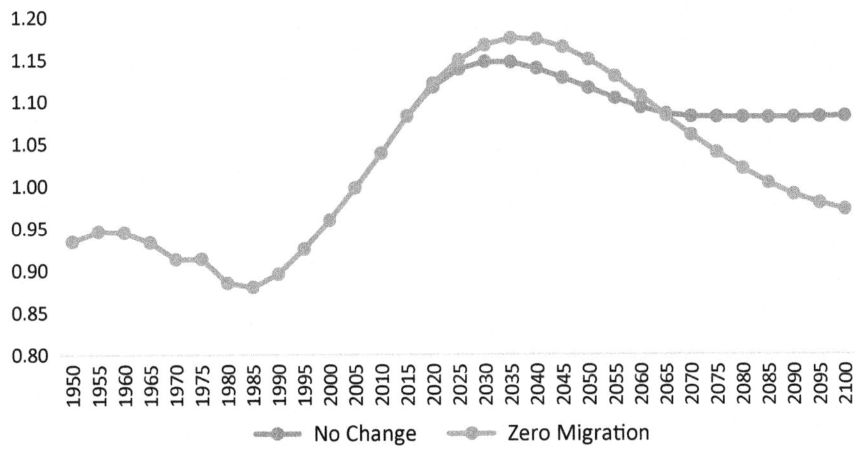

Fig. 11 Economic support ratio in 2010 under zero migration. *Source* Authors' Calculation, Bangladesh National Transfer Accounts of 2010

dividend will exist up to year 2030. While with the zero migration rate, the ESR will increase positively till 2040 and the first demographic dividend will exist up to year 2040.

Table 2 summarizes the estimates of first demographic dividends under various assumptions of population growth, fertility–morality rate, and rate of migration. According to these estimates, it may be argued that the first demographic dividend in Bangladesh will continue to a point somewhere between 2030 and 2040. After that, it will approach toward further change in the demographic situation.

Table 2 Estimated first demographic dividend under various assumptions of population projection

Population with various assumptions	*Year of highest ESR*	*Range of first demographic dividend*	*Years left from 2015*
Fertility assumptions: convergence toward total fertility below replacement level			
High variant	2030	1990–2030	15
Medium variant	2035	1990–2035	20
Low variant	2040	1990–2040	25
Constant fertility	2030	1990–2030	15
Instant replacement	2030	1990–2030	15
Mortality assumptions			
Constant mortality	2040	1990–2040	25
Constant fertility and mortality assumption			
No change	2035	1990–2035	20
International migration assumptions			
Zero migration	2040	1990–2040	25

Source Authors calculation, based on Bangladesh National Transfer Accounts of 2010

5 Conclusion

Utilizing the NTA system, this paper estimates the extent of first demographic dividend using ESR. According to the estimates, the first demographic dividend predominates from 2020 to 2045 according to several population projection variants. The connection between the demographic dividends and income growth is policy dependent. The first demographic dividend is in part of the result of the growing working-age population and can be admitted if employment opportunities grow to keep pace. In order to reap the economic gains of the potential first demographic dividend, nonetheless, adequate job opportunities need to be created.

World Bank (2016) provides a list of policy priorities for leveraging demographic dividend at the country level (Table 3). The analysis in the previous sections suggests that Bangladesh is inching toward the phase of late-dividend (i.e., phase 3). Accordingly, Bangladesh should have implemented policies those were relevant for the early phase of demographic dividend during 1990s. However, review of policies in Bangladesh suggests that country could not make adequate investment for creating employment (i.e., investment as percent of GDP has remained short by about 3–4% points) and in human capital including vocational and technical training. Bangladesh could manage only 2% investment of her GDP in education—the figure seems inadequate given much higher levels of educational investment found in other countries. Very low female labor force participation (i.e., 36% in 2010 compared to 82% male participation) envisaged existence of barriers to female labor force participation. Moreover, efforts to strengthen conditions

Table 3 Policy priority for leveraging demographic change

Phase	Issues	Recommended policies and strategies
1. Pre-dividend	*Sparking demographic transition* Improving human development outcomes to reduce fertility rates	• Improve maternal and child health by strengthening provision of basic health care services
		• Expand education without letting girls fall behind
		• Empower women and give them access to comprehensive family planning services
2. Early-dividend	*Accelerating job creation* Creating productive jobs for the growing share of the population in working age to reap the first demographic dividend	• Invest in human capital, including vocational and technical training
		• Enhance labor market mobility
		• Reduce barriers to female labor force participation
		• Strengthen conditions conducive to savings and job creation (public services underpinning private sector activity, contract enforcement, financial inclusion, and protection of labor rights)
3.Late-dividend	*Sustaining productivity growth* Creating conditions necessary to reap the second demographic dividend and beginning to prepare for aging	• Continue mobilization of savings for productive investment
		• Ensure that public policies across the board encourage labor force participation of both sexes
		• Design cost-effective and sustainable systems for welfare and human development that address current needs (including health, child care, education, and support to vulnerable elderly) and that can be adapted to meet the needs that emerge as aging proceeds
4. Post-dividend	*Post-dividend adapting to aging* Maintaining and improving welfare in the context of a declining working-age share and growing old-age share	• Complete reforms of welfare systems—including pensions, health care, and long-term care—that ensure fiscal sustainability and, as part of integrated approaches, protection of the vulnerable, elderly and others, and encouragement of work among those who are able
		• Raise labor force participation and productivity (including incentives for participation targeted at women and older cohorts; and life long
		• Pursue policies that encourage a rebound of fertility, among other things by making it easier for men and women to combine child rearing and participation in the labor market

Source Based on Table 6.1, World Bank (2016)

conducive to savings and job creation are found to be insufficient considering a national saving rate in the vicinity of 30% and underemployment rate of more than 20%. Since Bangladesh did not take appropriate policies in the right time, Bangladesh may fail to exploit the benefit of the first demographic dividend.

Against these backdrops, the Seventh Five-Year Plan proposes some ambitious goals with respect to investment, employment generation, and skill creation. More specifically, the plan aims to increase investment by about 3–4% of GDP from the current level of 28% over the next 5 years and to increase investment in education, training, and human development. Along with these, vocational training and skills development should get priority and adequate allocation. In the case of female labor force participation, Seventh Five-Year Plan raised the importance of increasing female labor participation, though the plan did not elaborate the strategies. The relevant strategies may include releasing women from domestic care activities, prohibiting child marriage, ensuring secured working condition, etc. Another positive development has been the formulation and subsequent approval of National Social Security Strategy (NSSS). The NSSS is inclusive of all population irrespective of race, religion, profession, location, or ethnicity. It seeks to modernize the Bangladesh social security by combining tax-funded safety net programs with contributory social insurance and employment regulations to protect the workers.

References

Bloom, D., & Canning, D. (2004). *Global Demographic Change: Dimensions and Economic Significance.* NBER (Working Paper No. 10817). NBER.

Bloom, D., Canning, D., & Malaney, P. (2000). Demographic change and economic growth in Asia. *Population and Development Review, 26.*

Chowdhury, A. K., & Curlin, G. T. (1978, Jan). *Recent trends in fertility and mortality in rural Bangladesh 1966–1975* (Working paper No. 03), Cholera Research Laboratory, Dhaka: ICDDRB.

Curlin, G. T., Chen, L. C., & Hussain, S. B. (1976). Demographic crisis: The impact of the Bangladesh Civil War (1971) on births and deaths in a rural area of Bangladesh. *Population Studies: A Journal of Demography, 30*(1).

Fry, M., & Mason, A. (1982). The variable rate of growth effect in the life-cycle model. *Economic Enquiry, 20.*

Higgins, M. (1998). Demography, national savings, and international capital flows. *International Economic Review, 39.*

Kelley, A., & Schmidt, R. (1996). Saving, dependency, and development. *Journal of Population Economic, 9.*

Khondker, B. H. (2014). *Poverty, Vulnerability and Inequality in Bangladesh.* Dhaka: Paper 01, NSPS Background Paper Series, Ministry of Planning, Government of Bangladesh.

Mason, A. (2001). *Population Change and Economic Development in East Asia: Challenges Met, Opportunities Seized.* California: Stanford University Press.

Mason, A., & Lee, R. (2006). Reform and support systems for the elderly in developing countries: Capturing the second demographic dividend. *Genus LXII*(2), 11–35.

Person, J. (2002). *Demographics, Human Capital, and Economic Growth: A Study of US States 1930-2000.* FIEF working paper.
Rajan, R., & Subramanian, A. (2008). Aid and growth: what does the cross country evidence really show? *Review of Economics and Statistics, 90*(4), 643–665.
World Bank. (2016). *Global Monitoring Report 2015/2016—Development Goals in an Era of Demographic Change*. Washington DC: The World Bank.

How Does Social Protection Affect Labor Force Participation in Bangladesh?

Selim Raihan and Israt Jahan

1 Introduction

Social protection programs in Bangladesh have primarily targeted at reduction of poverty in the country. Various social protection programs address the issues related to basic needs of the people. There are some programs which are directly linked to the recipient of social protection and his or her participation in the labor force. However, experiences from different countries shows that different social protection programs, even if they are not directly linked to any employment activities, can have important implications for labor force participation of the individuals of the households under the coverage of any of those programs.

In context of labor force participation (LFP), the scenarios for male individuals are different than that of female ones. Over the last few decades, the male labor force participation has been observed well above 80%. Along with the economic growth, female labor force participation has also increased to around 36% in 2010 (Labor Force Survey). However, the growth in female LFP is still very low. The study allows the scope to find the potential for the rise in female LFP in Bangladesh. Increased LFP can have significant implications for economic growth and poverty alleviation. Among different policies, programs, and economic activities that can improve female LFP, association with any social protection programs is a significant factor.

S. Raihan (✉)
Department of Economics, University of Dhaka, Dhaka, Bangladesh
e-mail: selim.raihan@gmail.com

S. Raihan · I. Jahan
South Asian Network on Economic Modeling (SANEM), Dhaka, Bangladesh

S. Raihan (ed.), *Structural Change and Dynamics of Labor Markets in Bangladesh*, South Asia Economic and Policy Studies,
https://doi.org/10.1007/978-981-13-2071-2_8

2 Literature Review

Ntuli (2007), in the context of South Africa, estimated labor force participation functions and the results show that participation of women in the labor market is influenced positively by nonlabor income (which includes social security funds like disability grants, childcare grants and pension). The results from the study by Cipollone et al. (2013), in the contexts of European countries, suggests that a high degree of labor market flexibility together with a high level of social protection leads to significant gains in terms of women's labor market participation. International Labor Organization (2012) showed a clear relationship between labor force participation and social security coverage. Gilligan et al. (2008) evaluated the impact of productive safety net program in Ethiopia and found that both female and male, from beneficiary households of public works transfers, were less likely to undertake wage work. However, when public works transfers came together with other food security programs, such impacts were reversed.

In South Asia, nearly half a billion poor people are with limited coverage of social protection. There are about 90% workers who work in the informal sector. It makes social protection more challenging. Countries like Bangladesh, India, and Pakistan have considerable spread of social protection programs but others have very little coverage (Banerji and Rawlings 2012). Justino (2007) observed that, in India, overall expenditure on social protection had a significant positive impact on economic development as social security policies boosted the productive capacities of the poor, increased incomes and promoted employment. In Bangladesh, there are a large number of people who are self-employed both in the formal and informal sector. However, seasonality has a large impact on the labor market in Bangladesh, as in the lean season, unemployment increases and migration occurs. Social protection program during the lean season can have a significant effect on the labor market stability in Bangladesh (Bangladesh Bank 2008).

3 Methodology

A cross section econometric model is used to see the effects of social protection on labor force participation behavior at the individual level that uses the Household Income Expenditure Survey (HIES) data of 2005 and 2010. Instead of Labor Force Survey (LFS), the study uses HIES data for the reason that it includes household and individual information about social protection and the gain from each social protection scheme. It is to mention that the labor force participations for both male and female are observed lower than that of LFS. In the context of the study, these discrepancies have less impact on it as the study aims at finding the impact of social protection on labor force participation.

To analyze the impact more efficiently, two variables regarding social protection have been generated. The *participation variable* is a dummy variable showing the individual had been covered with any social protection scheme or not. The *coverage variable* represents the share of income from social protection in the total income of the household. As individual income is not well represented in the data, it has been assumed that the income from social protection is shared with all the member of the household. The total income of the household is taken as the mirror of total expenditure of the household.

Along with the conventional definition of labor force participation, another definition (adjusted labor force participation) has also been considered in the study. ILO-OECD definition of LFP has been considered for generating conventional LFP that includes all currently active population who fulfills the requirement of being employed or unemployed in the given period of time and in the given age category. All the individuals who are 15 years or older were considered. People who were ready to work or was working or looking for work for the last 7 days of the survey data have been included in the conventional LFP.

The reason for introducing adjusted LFP was to address some issues regarding LFP. Individuals who were active in the labor force but surveyed as unemployed or out of labor force but active and would join the labor force shortly were included in the adjusted LFP. Individuals who reported reasons like working as unpaid worker at household, temporary sickness, waiting for joining in a new job, job was not available or was on leave from the work for not working, or searching the job were included in this definition. Both the definitions have excluded individuals who are household workers or students. It also excluded people who are too old, handicapped, retired or physically unable to work.

4 Social Protection and Labor Force Participation: Insights from the Analysis of Data

4.1 Overview of Social Protection Programs in Bangladesh

In four major categories (employment generation programs, programs to cope with natural disasters and other shocks, incentives provided to parents for their children's education, and incentives provided to families to improve their health status), the Government of Bangladesh has been maintaining a number of social protection programs (Table 1). Vulnerable group feeding (VGF), open market sales (OPS), cash for work (CFW), food-for-work (FFW), vulnerable group development (VGD), gratuitous relief (GR), and a 100-day employment guarantee scheme are the major programs among them.

Cash transfer and emergency or seasonal relief are the most common social protection provided in Bangladesh. It has to be mentioned that, the allocation and the coverage of social protection have increased significantly during 2005 and 2010. By 2009–2010, social protection became 1.95% of the GDP (Table 2).

Table 1 Major social protection programs in Bangladesh

Type	Program examples
Cash transfers	Old age allowance, widowed and distressed women allowance, disabled allowance
Conditional cash transfers	Primary education stipend program, stipends for female secondary students
Public works or training based cash or in kind transfer	Rural maintenance program, food-for-work, Vulnerable Group Development (VGD), Employment Generation Program (EGP)
Emergency or seasonal relief	Vulnerable Group Feeding (VGF), Gratuitous Relief (GR), Test Relief (TR), Open Market Sale (OMS)

Source Ministry of Finance, Bangladesh

Table 2 Social protection in the national budget: expense and coverage

	2009–10
Social protection amount (million taka)	1,344,431
Social protection (% of budget)	12.16
Social protection (% of GDP)	1.95

Source Budget Documents

4.2 Overall LFP Rates and Participation in the Social Protection by Male and Female

HIES data shows that the overall labor force participation rate did not change from 2005 to 2010 if we take the conventional estimation. However, there is an increase in the adjusted labor force participation. Male adjusted labor force participation for 2005 and 2010 are observed to be 79.21% and 79.7%, respectively, which are close to the rates reflected in the LFS (86.8% and 82.5%, respectively). The female labor force participation rates according to conventional definition are 9.4% in 2005 and 10.45% in 2010, which are significantly lower than LFS data (29.2% in 2005 and 36% in 2010). However, if we consider the adjusted definition, the female LFP rises to 12.56 percent in 2005 and 15.71% in 2010 (Table 3).

Table 3 Labor force participation rates as per the HIES (%)

	2005	2010
Total adult (conventional definition)	44.35	44.14
Total adult (adjusted definition)	45.68	51.43
Male adult (conventional definition)	79.21	79.7
Male adult (adjusted definition)	84.24	88.05
Female adult (conventional definition)	9.40	10.45
Female adult (adjusted definition)	12.56	15.71

Source Data from HIES 2005 and 2010

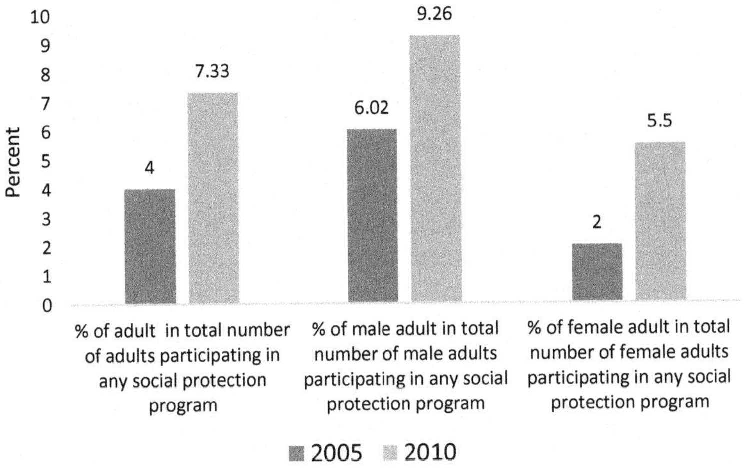

Fig. 1 Participation in the social protection programs as per the HIES. *Source* Data from HIES 2005 and 2010

Figure 1 suggests that the total percentage of adults participating in any social protection program has increased from 4% (2005) to 7.33% (2010). Adult male individuals are more likely to participate in social protection program than female ones. In 2005, 6.02% of total adult male participated in social protection program in contrast to only 2% for female. In 2010, the percentages rose to 9.26% and 5.5% for male and female adults respectively.

4.3 Education and Social Protection

Table 4 shows the percentage of people (adult and child) under social protection programs by years of education. With no education, 7.38% of males were under social protection programs in 2005, and that rose to 9.94% in 2010. 2.74% of females with no education were under social protection programs in 2005, and that rose to 6.69% in 2010. With 5 years of education, 3.78% and 6.07% of males were under social protection programs in 2005 and 2010, respectively. For such education level, 0.97% of females were under social protection programs in 2005, which rose to 3.25% in 2010.

Table 5 shows the percentage of only adults under social protection programs by years of education. 11.94% adult males, who did not have education were under social protection coverage in 2005. For females, it was 3.78%. The percentage rose to 16.24% for males and 9.03 for females in 2010. With 5 years of education, 4.83% of adult males were under social protection programs in 2005, which rose to 7.09% in 2010. 0.98% of adult females were under social protection programs in 2005, which rose to 2.68% in 2010.

Table 4 Percentage of people (adult and child) under social protection programs by years of education

Years of education	Male		Female	
	2005	2010	2005	2010
0	7.38	9.94	2.74	6.69
1	0.87	4.24	0.00	2.76
2	1.52	8.25	0.32	9.53
3	2.39	11.43	0.81	7.91
4	3.14	7.89	0.56	7.03
5	3.78	6.07	0.97	3.25
6	1.64	6.40	0.23	7.69
7	2.24	5.85	0.71	5.83
8	3.12	5.39	0.41	3.72
9	1.55	4.25	0.07	2.90
10	1.34	4.66	0.17	2.63
12	0.46	0	0.20	0
16	0.70	4.61	0.75	0.65
17	0.28	0	0.00	0

Source Data from HIES 2005 and 2010

Table 5 Percentage of adult population under social protection programs by years of education

Years of education	Male		Female	
	2005	2010	2005	2010
0	11.94	16.24	3.78	9.03
1	7.69	5.45	0.00	4.17
2	6.32	12.82	2.13	9.09
3	6.22	14.98	2.41	3.13
4	5.78	10.49	1.21	4.01
5	4.83	7.09	0.98	2.68
6	2.56	9.28	0.40	1.09
7	3.01	6.64	0.70	2.51
8	3.54	5.84	0.29	2.67
9	1.64	4.37	0.07	2.16
10	1.35	4.68	0.17	2.59
12	0.46	0	0.20	0
16	0.70	4.61	0.75	0.65
17	0.28	0	0.00	0

Source Data from HIES 2005 and 2010

4.4 *Land Ownership and Social Protection*

Table 6 suggests that 6.81% of adult males who were landless were under social protection in 2005, the share decreased to 6.56% in 2010. 4.75% of landless adult females were under social protection in 2005, which rose to 7.52% in 2010.

Table 6 Percentage of adult population under social protection programs by land (total) ownership

Land size (in acre)	Male		Female	
	2005	2010	2005	2010
Landless	6.81	6.56	4.75	7.52
0.01–0.49	7.21	8.37	2.49	6.07
0.50–0.99	6.76	13.94	0.90	4.98
1.00–2.49	3.89	14.02	0.52	3.71
2.50–7.49	1.86	12.47	0.16	3.77
7.50+	1.19	6.29	0.92	5.37

Source Data from HIES 2005 and 2010

With ownership of 0.01–0.49 acres of land, 7.21% of adult males were included in social protection in 2005. In 2010, it rose 8.37%. For the adult females of that group, the percentage was 2.49% in 2005 and 6.07% in 2010.

4.5 Age, Location, and Social Protection

Table 7 shows that, for both male and female, the coverage of social protection programs is higher in rural areas than in urban area. Also, the coverage is higher for the older age groups. In general, the coverage increased for all age groups in 2010 compared to that in 2005.

4.6 Employment Category and Social Protection

The distribution of males and females in different employment categories shows dynamics of the coverage of social protection coverage (Table 8). The coverage for

Table 7 Percentage of male and female under social protection programs by region and age

Age category	Male				Female			
	Rural		Urban		Rural		Urban	
	2005	2010	2005	2010	2005	2010	2005	2010
5–14	0.29	6.13	0.14	1.26	0.37	10.16	0.14	3.59
15–25	1.02	2.18	0.39	1.18	0.36	3.27	0.22	1.65
26–35	7.24	11.26	3.14	4.13	1.48	3.80	0.56	1.54
36–45	12.22	16.14	3.94	6.91	2.83	5.96	2.34	2.94
46–55	13.38	16.80	6.00	8.20	4.46	9.27	2.07	4.77
56–65	14.27	23.97	4.06	11.01	6.34	14.64	1.42	9.57
66–75	12.78	28.30	9.34	16.46	6.76	24.33	7.77	13.90
75+	12.02	25	2.35	22.55	8.38	18	7.14	17

Source Data from HIES 2005 and 2010

Table 8 Percentage of people under social protection programs by employment category

Employment category	2005	2010
Male self-employed	5.32	12.61
Male wage employed	8.04	9.53
Male unemployed	1.76	2.65
Female self-employed	8.83	13.93
Female wage employed	6.47	12.21
Female unemployed	4.76	2.73

Source Data from HIES 2005 and 2010

Table 9 Percentage of people under social protection programs by sector and employment category

Employment category	Farm		Nonfarm	
	2005	2010	2005	2010
Male self-employed	5.26	7.95	5.37	17.15
Male wage employed	15.47	6.19	5.21	17.33
Female self-employed	7.22	8.33	9.45	20.71
Female wage employed	13.40	9.15	5.16	28.39

Source Data from HIES 2005 and 2010

self-employed and wage employed, both for male and female, increased in 2010 compared to those in 2005; however, such rise is very prominent for male self-employed and female wage employed. The coverage of the social protection for unemployed people was poor, both for male and female, both in 2005 and 2010.

Segregation of employment categories by farm and nonfarm activities shows that while in 2005, there was a mixed picture, nonfarm activities were more targeted by social protection programs than the farm activities in 2010 (Table 9).

5 Remittance and Social Protection

Table 10 shows that, despite some mixed patterns in 2005, in 2010, compared to the remittance-receiving households, males and females from non-remittance receiving households were under larger coverage of social protection.

6 Social Protection and Labor Force Participation: Insights from Econometric Analysis

Results of the cross section logistic models (Tables 11, 12, 13 and 14), indicates that females' labor force participation increases with the rise in social protection participation. Also, with the rise in the coverage of social protection, labor force participations of both male and female increase.

Table 10 Remittance and coverage of social protection

Status of remittance receipt	Male		Female	
	2005	2010	2005	2010
Remittance non-receiving household	6.45	10.43	1.76	6.06
Remittance receiving household	4.84	7.96	2.55	2.97
Remittance non-receiving household (internal)	6.12	10.01	1.70	5.57
Remittance receiving household (internal)	5.66	14.54	3.07	5.58
Remittance non-receiving household (international)	6.39	10.60	2.10	6.05
Remittance receiving household (international)	2.21	4.64	1.11	1.76

Source Data from HIES 2005 and 2010

Table 11 Cross section logistic regression results on adult female labor force participation (conventional)

Explanatory variables	Dependent variable: adult female labor force participation			
	2005 (1)	2005 (2)	2010 (1)	2010 (2)
Age	−0.008[a] (0.002)	−0.007[a] (0.002)	−0.024[a] (0.002)	−0.022[a] (0.002)
Average years of schooling	0.058[a] (0.011)	0.057[a] (0.013)	0.096[a] (0.012)	0.096[a] (0.012)
Dummy for literacy (1 = yes, 0 = otherwise)	−0.709[a] (0.109)	−0.703[a] (0.118)	−0.972[a] (0.109)	−0.980[a] (0.109)
Dummy for present enrollment in education (1 = yes, 0 = otherwise)	−0.194[a] (0.071)	−0.194[a] (0.071)	−2.736[a] (0.186)	−2.685[a] (0.185)
Dummy for marriage (1 = yes, 0 = otherwise)	−0.152[b] (0.066)	−0.172[a] (0.062)	−0.705[a] (0.063)	−0.729[a] (0.063)
Dummy for female headed households (1 = yes, 0 = otherwise)	1.258[a] (0.075)	1.316[a] (0.067)	0.546[a] (0.062)	0.533[a] (0.062)
Number of ill members in household	−0.066[b] (0.030)	−0.067[b] (0.033)	−0.039 (0.031)	−0.042 (0.031)
Number of household members with age 65 plus	−0.166[b] (0.069)	−0.175[b] (0.074)	−0.234[a] (0.069)	−0.261[a] (0.070)
Number of household members with age under 5	−0.271[a] (0.049)	−0.268[a] (0.052)	−0.348[a] (0.048)	−0.336[a] (0.048)
Dummy for rural area (1 = yes, 0 = otherwise)	−0.413[a] (0.063)	−0.412[a] (0.063)	−0.319[a] (0.055)	−0.310[a] (0.055)
Household size	−0.101[a] (0.016)	−0.105[a] (0.018)	−0.106[a] (0.016)	−0.111[a] (0.016)
Per capita landholding	−0.136[a] (0.012)	−0.137[a] (0.012)	−0.088[a] (0.009)	−0.089[a] (0.009)
Dummy for social protection participation (1 = yes, 0 = otherwise)	0.687[a] (0.140)		0.811[a] (0.091)	
Social protection coverage		0.025[b] (0.011)		0.079[a] (0.013)

(continued)

Table 11 (continued)

Explanatory variables	Dependent variable: adult female labor force participation			
	2005 (1)	2005 (2)	2010 (1)	2010 (2)
Constant	−1.512[a] (0.147)	−1.245[a] (0.181)	−0.163 (0.153)	0.712[a] (0.206)
Number of observation	16,086	16,086	18,656	18,656
Wald chi^2 (13)	1162.35	1058.43	1106.52	1074.1
Prob > chi^2	0	0	0	0
Pseudo R^2	0.1137	0.1119	0.1031	0.1003

Note a, b, and c indicate statistical significance at the 1, 5, and 10% levels, respectively. The figures in parentheses are the standard errors

Table 12 Cross section logistic regression results on adult female labor force participation (adjusted)

Explanatory variables	Dependent variable: adult female labor force participation			
	2005 (1)	2005 (2)	2010 (1)	2010 (2)
Age	0.007[a] (0.002)	0.007[a] (0.002)	−0.017[a] (0.002)	−0.016[a] (0.002)
Average years of schooling	0.038[a] (0.010)	0.038[a] (0.010)	0.070[a] (0.011)	0.071[a] (0.011)
Dummy for literacy (1 = yes, 0 = otherwise)	−0.493[a] (0.098)	−0.492[a] (0.098)	−0.720[a] (0.097)	−0.726[a] (0.097)
Dummy for present enrollment in education (1 = yes, 0 = otherwise)	−0.255[a] (0.065)	−0.254[a] (0.065)	−3.566[a] (0.177)	−3.532[a] (0.176)
Dummy for marriage (1 = yes, 0 = otherwise)	−0.749[a] (0.059)	−0.747[a] (0.059)	−1.536[a] (0.057)	−1.550[a] (0.056)
Dummy for female headed households (1 = yes, 0 = otherwise)	0.976[a] (0.071)	0.973[a](0.071)	0.207[a] (0.064)	0.204[a] (0.064)
Number of ill members in household	−0.027 (0.026)	−0.027 (0.026)	−0.018 (0.028)	−0.021 (0.028)
Number of household members with age 65 plus	−0.022 (0.061)	−0.023 (0.061)	−0.072 (0.056)	−0.088 (0.056)
Number of household members with age under 5	−0.185[a] (0.044)	−0.186[a] (0.044)	-0.329[a] (0.042)	−0.322[a] (0.042)
Dummy for rural area (1 = yes, 0 = otherwise)	−0.333[a] (0.059)	−0.335[a] (0.059)	−0.159[a] (0.050)	−0.154[a] (0.050)
Household size	−0.050[a] (0.014)	−0.049[a] (0.014)	−0.041[a] (0.013)	−0.044[a] (0.013)
Per capita landholding	−0.111[a] (0.012)	−0.111[a] (0.012)	−0.084[a] (0.009)	−0.085[a] (0.009)
Dummy for social protection participation (1 = yes, 0 = otherwise)	0.321[a] (0.010)		0.571[a] (0.099)	
Social protection coverage		0.018[c] (0.011)		0.055[a] (0.013)

(continued)

Table 12 (continued)

Explanatory variables	Dependent variable: adult female labor force participation			
	2005 (1)	2005 (2)	2010 (1)	2010 (2)
Constant	−1.531[a] (0.135)	−1.331[a] (0.178)	0.350[b] (0.135)	0.955[a] (0.198)
Number of observation	14,968	14,968	17,138	17,138
Wald chi^2 (13)	1060.37	1061.33	1578.93	1572.81
Prob > chi^2	0	0	0	0
Pseudo R^2	0.0937	0.0938	0.1275	0.1264

Note a, b, and c indicate statistical significance at the 1, 5, and 10% levels, respectively. The figures in parentheses are the standard errors

Table 13 Cross section logistic regression results on adult male labor force participation (conventional)

Explanatory variables	Dependent variable: adult male labor force participation			
	2005 (1)	2005 (2)	2010 (1)	2010 (2)
Age	−0.039[a] (0.002)	−0.038[a] (0.002)	−0.069[a] (0.003)	−0.069[a] (0.003)
Average years of schooling	−0.072[a] (0.009)	−0.070[a] (0.008)	−0.025[b] (0.011)	−0.024[b] (0.011)
Dummy for literacy (1 = yes, 0 = otherwise)	0.072 (0.082)	0.071 (0.081)	0.105 (0.102)	0.109 (0.102)
Dummy for present enrollment in education (1 = yes, 0 = otherwise)	−0.455[a] (0.051)	−0.452[a] (0.050)	−4.539[a] (0.119)	−4.537[a] (0.119)
Dummy for marriage (1 = yes, 0 = otherwise)	3.020[a] (0.074)	3.027[a] (0.083)	2.805[a] (0.095)	2.809[a] (0.095)
Dummy for female headed households (1 = yes, 0 = otherwise)	−0.136 (0.095)	−0.150 (0.101)	−0.441[a] (0.114)	−0.437[a] (0.114)
Number of ill members in household	−0.067[a] (0.018)	−0.068[a] (0.019)	−0.059[b] (0.028)	−0.057[b] (0.028)
Number of household members with age 65 plus	−0.513[a] (0.047)	−0.518[a] (0.050)	−0.328[a] (0.052)	−0.328[a] (0.052)
Number of household members with age under 5	0.122[a] (0.039)	0.122[a] (0.041)	0.024 (0.047)	0.019 (0.047)
Dummy for rural area (1 = yes, 0 = otherwise)	0.240[a] (0.052)	0.229[a] (0.053)	0.167[a] (0.059)	0.164[a] (0.059)
Household size	−0.053[a] (0.011)	−0.052[a] (0.011)	−0.064[a] (0.014)	−0.059[a] (0.014)
Per capita landholding	−0.007 (0.012)	−0.006 (0.011)	0.041[a] (0.010)	0.042[a] (0.010)
Dummy for social protection participation (1 = yes, 0 = otherwise)	0.178 (0.126)		0.068 (0.089)	

(continued)

Table 13 (continued)

Explanatory variables	Dependent variable: adult male labor force participation			
	2005 (1)	2005 (2)	2010 (1)	2010 (2)
Social protection coverage		0.035[a] (0.012)		0.037[b] (0.018)
Constant	1.720[a] (0.105)	2.105[a] (0.174)	3.573[a] (0.137)	3.687[a] (0.147)
Number of observation	16,002	16,002	17,680	17,680
Wald chi^2 (13)	3780.34	2669.19	3012.62	3013.48
Prob > chi^2	0	0	0	0
Pseudo R^2	0.2300	0.2303	0.4247	0.4249

Note a, b, and c indicate statistical significance at the 1, 5, and 10% levels, respectively. The figures in parentheses are the standard errors

Table 14 Cross section logistic regression results on adult male labor force participation (adjusted)

Explanatory variables	Dependent variable: adult male labor force participation			
	2005 (1)	2005 (2)	2010 (1)	2010 (2)
Age	0.039[a] (0.004)	0.039[a] (0.004)	−0.011c (0.006)	−0.009 (0.006)
Average years of schooling	−0.091[a] (0.010)	−0.091[a] (0.010)	0.025 (0.018)	0.023 (0.018)
Dummy for literacy (1 = yes, 0 = otherwise)	0.033 (0.096)	0.032 (0.096)	−0.175 (0.173)	−0.179 (0.174)
Dummy for present enrollment in education (1 = yes, 0 = otherwise)	−0.676[a] (0.059)	−0.675[a] (0.059)	−5.485[a] (0.141)	−5.459[a] (0.141)
Dummy for marriage (1 = yes, 0 = otherwise)	2.030[a] (0.090)	2.029[a] (0.090)	1.897[a] (0.162)	1.909[a] (0.162)
Dummy for female headed households (1 = yes, 0 = otherwise)	−0.010 (0.102)	−0.014 (0.102)	0.504[a] (0.185)	0.500[a] (0.186)
Number of ill members in household	−0.052[b] (0.021)	−0.052[b] (0.021)	0.038 (0.053)	0.043 (0.053)
Number of household members with age 65 plus	−0.281[a] (0.060)	−0.283[a] (0.060)	−0.137 (0.109)	−0.136 (0.108)
Number of household members with age under 5	0.152[a] (0.047)	0.152[a] (0.047)	0.064 (0.088)	0.065 (0.088)
Dummy for rural area (1 = yes, 0 = otherwise)	0.293[a] (0.061)	0.291[a] (0.061)	0.183[c] (0.105)	0.191[c] (0.105)
Household size	−0.046[a] (0.013)	−0.046[a] (0.013)	−0.046[c] (0.026)	−0.047[c] (0.026)
Per capita landholding	−0.057[a] (0.014)	−0.057[a] (0.014)	0.016 (0.019)	0.018 (0.019)
Dummy for social protection participation (1 = yes, 0 = otherwise)	0.253[b] (0.103)		0.753[b] (0.308)	

(continued)

Table 14 (continued)

Explanatory variables	Dependent variable: adult male labor force participation			
	2005 (1)	2005 (2)	2010 (1)	2010 (2)
Social protection coverage		0.041[a] (0.015)		0.023[c] (0.008)
Constant	0.167 (0.134)	0.632 (0.214)	2.968[a] (0.259)	3.045[a] (0.266)
Number of observation	15,132	15,132	16,716	16,716
Wald chi^2 (13)	3893.77	3895.09	3244.05	3244.85
Prob > chi^2	0	0	0	0
Pseudo R^2	0.2953	0.2954	0.6612	0.6606

Note a, b, and c indicate statistical significance at the 1, 5, and 10% levels, respectively. The figures in parentheses are the standard errors

Table 11 shows that a female adult, who gets any social protection, is 1.99 times in 2005 and 2.25 times in 2010 more likely to participate in labor force, other things remaining the same. Similarly, one percent increase in social protection coverage in total expenditure of the household leads a female 1.02 times in 2005 and 1.08 times in 2010 times more likely to participate in the labor force, other things remains the same. Variables like age, years of education, present enrollment in education, marital status, location, gender of the head, number of ill members, household size, per capita land holding, number of household members with age 65 plus, and number of household members with age under 5, were controlled in these logistic models. In general, age, marriage, being in the rural area, larger household size, presence of ill household members, and household members aged lower than 5, have statistically significant negative impacts on the female labor force participation. On the other hand, education has a strong positive statistically significant impact.

The results are almost similar for the regression involving female labor force participation with the adjusted definition (Table 12). It shows that, an adult female under any social protection program is 1.38 times in 2005 and 1.77 times in 2010 more likely to participate in labor force, other things remaining the same. Similarly, one percent increase in social protection coverage in total expenditure of the household leads a female 1.20 times in 2005 and 1.06 times in 2010 more likely to participate in labor force, other things remains the same.

The labor force participation (under the conventional definition) for male cannot be defined by the involvement in social protection program for both for 2005 and 2010 (Table 13). The coverage of social protection, however, has a positive effect on male adult's labor force participation. One percent increase in social protection coverage in expenditure makes an adult male 1.03 times more likely to participate in labor force, other things remains the same. The coefficients are almost the same for 2005 and 2010, which suggests that social protection coverage had almost an unchanged effect on adult male labor force participation during these two years.

The dummy variable for the marital status has a significant effect on both adult male and adult female labor force participations, other things remains the same. It suggests that while married women are less likely to participate in the labor force, married men are more likely to participate. The relationships of male labor force participation with other variables are similar to those under the regression results for female labor force participation.

The results using adjusted labor force participation for male are presented in Table 14. Now, an adult male under any social protection program is 1.28 times in 2005 and 2.12 times in 2010 more likely to participate in labor force, other things remains the same. Also, one percent increase in social protection coverage in total expenditure of the household leads a male 1.04 times in 2005 and 1.02 times in 2010 more likely to participate in labor force, other things remains the same.

7 Conclusion

This study finds that female labor force participation in Bangladesh increases if either she has a direct provision to the social protection program or her household is under the coverage of any social protection programs, so that the income from which can support a part of her household expenditures. Therefore, to promote female labor force participation, social protection programs can be very instrumental. The policy implications are very clear. Providing social protection directly to the female can bring them to participate in the labor force. Also, supporting other members of the household with any type of social protection can also facilitate the female labor force participation. It is also found that males' access to social protection programs also have some positive significant impact on their labor force participation. Hence, social protection is a good instrument in expanding labor force participation of both male and female. Male's income from social protection increases the coverage of social protection in terms of household's total expenditure, which can facilitate a rise in the female labor force participation too. Furthermore, the provision of social protection programs for the dependent members of the households (both young and elderly dependents) helps females of the households as it reduces their burden of care works, which can also act as a stimulator for their labor force participation.

References

Banerji, A., & Rawlings, L. (2012). *The World Bank 2012–2022 social protection and labor strategy—Resilience, equity and opportunity*. Washington D.C.: World Bank.

Bangladesh Bank. (2008). *Recent employment situation and labor market developments in Bangladesh*. Policy Paper 0807. Dhaka: Bangladesh Bank.

Cipollone, A., Patacchini, E., & Vallanti, G. (2013). *Women labor market participation in Europe: Novel evidence on trends and shaping factors.* IZA Discussion Paper No. 7710. Bonn: Institute for the Study of Labor.

Gilligan, D.O., Hoddinott, J., & Taffesse, A.S. (2008). *The impact of Ethiopia's productive safety net programme and its linkage*. IFPRI Discussion Paper 00839, Washington. DC: International Food Policy Research Institute.

International Labor Organization. (2012). *Employment and social protection in the new demographic context.* in *International Labor Conference*, ILO. Geneva: 102nd Session.

Justino, P. (2007). Social security in developing countries: Myth or necessity? Evidence from India. *Journal of International Development, 19*(3), 367–382.

Ntuli, M. (2007). *Determinants of South African Women's labor force participation 1995–2004.* Discussion Paper No. 3119, Bonn: Institute for the Study of Labor.

How Do Education and Skill Development Affect the Transition from "Good-Enough" Job to "Decent" Job?

Selim Raihan and Mahtab Uddin

1 Introduction

In the arena of economic literature, it is now well established that economic growth is a necessary but insufficient condition for development (Sen 1999). In addition, increasingly, there is a consensus among academicians that employment creation as such does not guarantee social, economic, and political inclusion or basic human rights as chartered by the UN system. Within this context, the focus of the policy exercise has shifted from mere economic growth approach toward a broader approach of inclusive growth. The International Labor Office's "Decent Work" agenda replicates the importance of such a context. Although the decent work agenda has been initiated since 1999, the ongoing current literatures are highly concentrated either on policy implications or depict the decent work agenda from a macro point of view. Majority of the studies conducted on decent job primarily focused on the demand-side issues. However, there is a need to explore the supply-side issues as the composition of labor supply itself can be a determining factor for the status of the decent job. This article follows the definitions of "good-enough" job, "good" job, and "decent" job from Raihan (2014) where it is argued that there could be three stages for moving toward "decent" job. The first stage is the "good-enough" job which shows the transition from no job to job or from unpaid family job to paid job. The second stage is the "good" job which shows the transition from "good-enough" job to job with better return, formal job security,

S. Raihan (✉) · M. Uddin
Department of Economics, University of Dhaka, Dhaka, Bangladesh
e-mail: selim.raihan@gmail.com

S. Raihan · M. Uddin
South Asian Network on Economic Modeling (SANEM), Dhaka, Bangladesh

S. Raihan (ed.), *Structural Change and Dynamics of Labor Markets in Bangladesh*, South Asia Economic and Policy Studies,
https://doi.org/10.1007/978-981-13-2071-2_9

and enhanced workers' rights. The third stage is the "decent" job, which is the transition from "good" job to a state of productive employment in compliance with agreed international standards of working environment and workers' rights.

2 Literature Review

Most of the studies on decent work, using country-level macro data, primarily focused on demand-side issues. Ghai (2003) examined different indicators for measuring and comparing decent work status of the OECD countries, using the country-level aggregate data, and formulated an index to measure the performances and patterns of decent work in the industrial countries in the 1990s, and found that some countries like Sweden, Denmark, and Norway performed better than other OECD countries. Analogous to Ghai (2003), Anker et al. (2002) identified various statistical indicators to measure decent work in a cross-country perspective. In the context of Bangladesh, Mujeri (2004) assessed the availability of the decent work statistical indicators for the country and constructed an aggregate scenario of the decent work environment, and identified that the quality, coverage of the data, as well as comparability and consistency of the data over time were the major challenges.

A number of papers identified the informal sector as the major vulnerable and challenging sector for the implementation of the decent job agenda. Cohen and Moodley (2012), in the case of South Africa, found that the major challenges for decent work were the poor working conditions, workers' exploitation in the growing informal sector, and implementation of social protection and social dialog which included the informal sectors. Amin (2002) argued for an integral approach for ensuring decent work for the workers in the informal sector in the Asian countries. Ahn (2008) discussed the challenges of growing informal employment in South Asia and analyzed measurable indicators of decent work in the informal economy. The author argued that in order to introduce an environment conducive to promoting decent work, it would be inevitable to organize and mobilize workers in need through the promotion of social dialog. In line with this argument, Servais (2004) proposed that the states should give the workers more significant part to play in the regulatory process, and suggested that the key role of the national, regional, and local authorities should include identification and recognition of the social actors, promotion of access to information by eliminating hindrances such as anti-union practices and by taking part in their establishments.

Some studies stressed the importance of the enhancement of global value chains and broader trade arrangements to promote compliance with labor standards. Trade agreements and supply chain relationship can put pressures on governments and businesses to improve conditions for workers (Polaski 2009). Pressure from civil society campaigns, and in light of increasingly aware consumers, quality now includes social and environmental issues (Barrientos 2007). This is putting pressure on producers to improve employment conditions and ensure labor standards are met.

Although the aforementioned papers looked primarily at the demand-side issues, there is a need to consider the supply-side effects too as far as the promotion of decent job is concerned. Indeed, for a sustainable improvement in the working condition as well as the lives of the workers there is no other alternative but to enhance the productivity of the workers through skill development, i.e., through education and training. The objective of the current study is to explore on how education and training can play the role in improving the quality of employment.

3 The Labor Market in Bangladesh: How Does It Stand in Terms of Quality of Employment?

3.1 Classification of the Quality of Employment

We have used the Labor Force Survey data of 2010 (BBS 2010) for Bangladesh and the available indicators in that survey to classify the jobs as per the definitions suggested by Raihan (2014). As the data and questions in the questionnaire of LFS, 2010 are different for wage employed and self-employed, we had to set different definitions for these categories.

Following Raihan (2014), in the case of wage employment, we have defined a decent job as a job which is permanent, has a written job contract, decent working hours, decent and adequate earnings, leave, pension, and termination notice. On the contrary, a job is "good-enough" if he/she has at least a paid job. In between "decent" job and "good-enough" job, there is a "good" job which is defined as having a permanent employment along with a decent earning. Following ILO (2012), decent earning is defined as earnings which are higher than two-thirds of the median income. The decent working hour is defined as working hour which is neither low nor excessive and lies in between 35–48 h per week.

Following Raihan (2014), in the case of self-employment, we consider "decent job" as a job with decent earnings, permanent employment, and decent working hours, while the definitions of "good" job and "good-enough" job remain the same. A challenge that we faced in case of self-employment was the missing data problem of the income of the self-employed. We applied the technique of multiple imputations by chained equations (MICE) for determining the missing incomes from the available observable characteristics.[1]

[1]For details on MICE please see Schafer (1999), Royston (2009), Royston and White (2011), Marchenko (2011), Azur et al. (2011) and Bouhlila and Sellaouti (2013).

3.2 Employment Categories and Quality of Job

Figure 1 suggests that in 2010 in the case of wage employed, while the decent job appeared to be only 10%, good job and good-enough job constituted 36% and 54%, respectively. For self-employed, decent job comprised of 9%, while good job and good-enough job constituted 39% and 52%, respectively.

Figure 2 shows that the proportion of decent job is the highest among the regular paid employee constituting 27.1% of total regular paid employees. The significance of a good job is also the highest for this employment category. However, in all other cases, more than three-fourths of employment is good-enough, whereas the proportion on decent job is very insignificant.

As shown in Fig. 3, in the case of self-employment, around 20% of the employers appear to be with decent jobs, whereas decent job is less than 10% in both agricultural and nonagricultural self-employment. More than 50% of the jobs in the employer category are good jobs, whereas around 50% of the jobs in both agricultural and nonagricultural self-employment categories are good-enough.

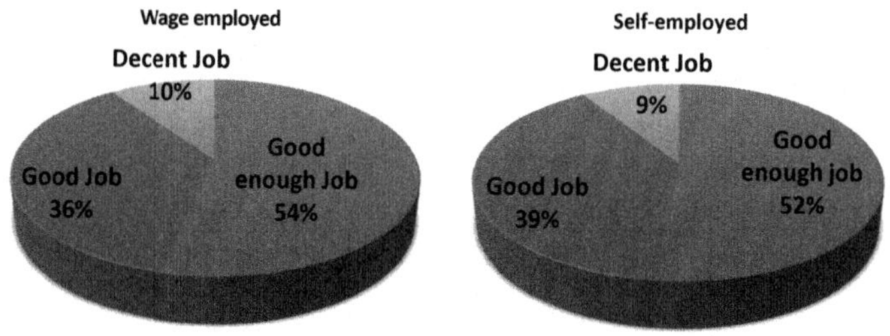

Fig. 1 Distribution of quality of job. *Source* Authors' calculation from the LFS, 2010

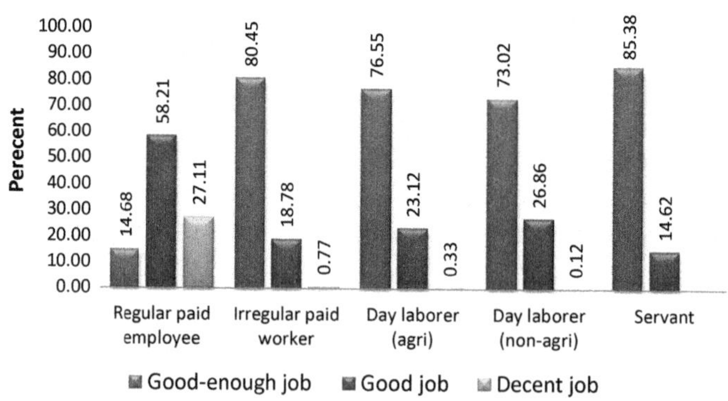

Fig. 2 Distribution of wage employed by type and quality of job. *Source* Authors' calculation from the LFS, 2010

Fig. 3 Distribution of self-employed by type and quality of job. *Source* Authors' calculation from the LFS, 2010

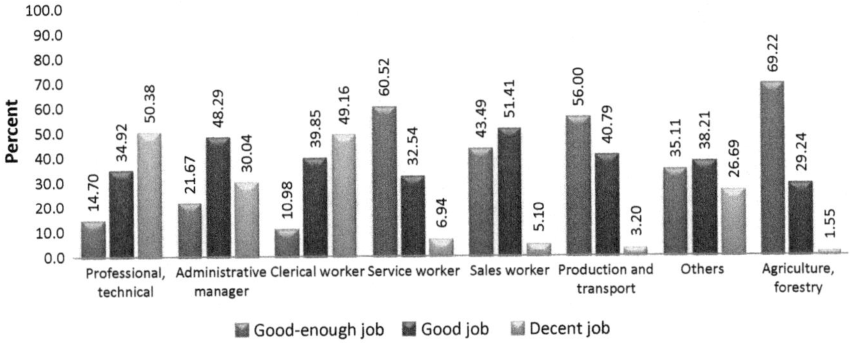

Fig. 4 Distribution of wage employed by job quality and source of employment. *Source* Authors' calculation from the LFS, 2010

Figures 4 and 5 show the proportion of job qualities among various occupations that are wage employed and self-employed, respectively. For the wage employed (Fig. 4), the highest share of a decent job is being generated in the "professional, technical" occupation as 50.4% of total wage employed in "professional, technical" are in decent jobs. The share of a decent job is also high among "administrative manager" (30%) and "clerical workers" (49.2%). The share of "good" job is also high for these categories. The figure thus points out that the professions those tend to be highly productive by nature are more likely to have greater shares of a decent job. In contrast, wage labor in service work, sales work, production and transport work, and agriculture are predominantly good-enough with a very small share of the decent job.

However, for the self-employed category, as shown in Fig. 5, we do not see such variations in job quality. Among the clerical workers and professional—technical workers, the share of a good job comprises of 49.2% and 36.5%, respectively. Although not as high as the wage employed category, decent job accounts for the

Fig. 5 Distribution of self-employed by job quality and source of employment. *Source* Authors' calculation from the LFS, 2010

highest percentage in the professional–technical, administrative manager, and clerical worker occupational categories. Although weak, it resembles the link between productivity and the quality of jobs.

3.3 Age Distribution and Quality of Job

Table 1 shows that for the wage employed, more than 50% of the good-enough job as well as good job are mostly concentrated among the age-groups between 15 and 34. In contrast, more than 50% of the decent job is concentrated among the age-group between 25 and 44.

On the contrary, Table 2 shows that when considering self-employed, more than 58% comes from the age-groups between 25 and 44 in the case of "good-enough" job. In the cases of "good" job and "decent" job, more than 50% is comprised of the age-groups between 35 and 44. A sharp contrast between Tables 1 and 2 is related to the share of youth employment in total "good-enough" job or "good" job—while

Table 1 Age distribution and quality of job for wage employed

Age category	Good-enough job	Good job	Decent job
15–24	27.7	24.4	9.6
25–34	26.6	31.1	28.0
35–44	21.7	23.2	26.2
45–54	12.9	12.7	26.8
55–64	7.5	6.0	8.1
65+	3.8	2.6	1.3
Total	**100**	**100**	**100**

Source Author's calculation from the LFS, 2010

Table 2 Age distribution and quality of job for self-employed

Age category	Good-enough job	Good job	Decent job
15–24	9.8	6.5	9.5
25–34	23.1	21.3	19.5
35–44	35.1	26.1	26.0
45–54	20.3	24.0	23.3
55–64	7.8	13.8	13.2
65+	3.9	8.4	8.4
Total	**100**	**100**	**100**

Source Author's calculation from the LFS, 2010

Table 3 Age distribution and quality of job for wage employed

Age category	Good-enough job	Good job	Decent job	Total
15–24	60.09	36.00	3.92	100
25–34	50.11	39.92	9.97	100
35–44	51.10	37.21	11.69	100
45–54	48.50	32.46	19.05	100
55–64	57.12	31.24	11.64	100
65+	64.96	30.89	4.15	100

Source Author's calculation from the LFS, 2010

youth employment (for the wage employed category), in total "good-enough" job or "good" job, comprises of more than 24%, in case of self-employed this share is less than 10%.

To see the distribution of age and quality of job from a different perspective, we intend to look at the quality of the job with respect to segregated age-group. Table 3 shows that most of the youth employment is concentrated in good-enough job (about 60.1%). It is also evident from Table 3 that employment in decent job steadily rises from only 3.9% for the age-group of 15–24 to 19.1% for the age-group of 45–54. Thereafter, the share of decent job among the later two age-groups continues to fall again. A similar pattern is noticed (in Table 4) when

Table 4 Age distribution and quality of job for self-employed

Age category	Good-enough job	Good job	Decent job	Total
15–24	59.64	30.02	10.33	100
25–34	53.93	37.89	8.18	100
35–44	58.90	33.29	7.81	100
45–54	47.51	42.71	9.78	100
55–64	37.78	50.72	11.50	100
65+	33.37	53.85	12.77	100

Source Author's calculation from the LFS, 2010

observing the youth employment profile of the self-employed category apart from the fact that we do not observe any kind of trend between decent job and age distribution like we have seen in the case of wage employed.

3.4 Education and Quality of Job

The strong relationship between education and quality of job can be depicted from the Fig. 6 (for the wage employed) and Fig. 7 (for the self-employed). In the case of wage employed, workers with no education or primary education are mostly prevailing in the "good-enough" job (comprising more than 60%). On the contrary, workers with secondary or higher than secondary education are mostly engaged in the "good" job or "decent" job (comprising more than 50%). For example, while 30.7% of the workers with SSC/HSC education availed "decent" job, 55.8% of the workers with university education got employed in "decent" job.

In case of self-employed (Fig. 7), persons with education equivalent to secondary education or lower are concentrated in good-enough jobs while persons with SSC/HSC or higher level of education are primarily concentrated in good jobs. A contrasting feature of Fig. 7 with respect to Fig. 6 is that, while, in the case of wage employed, we found the large pool of university graduates are employed in the "decent" job, we see only 12% of the university graduates engaged in "decent" self-employment. In concurrence, about 47% of the university graduates are found to be self-employed in the "good" job.

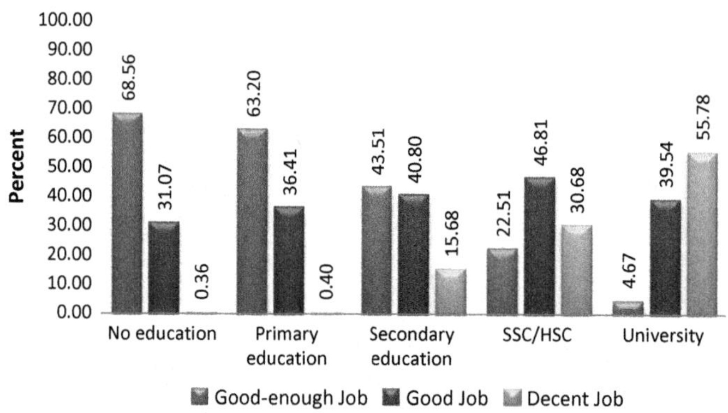

Fig. 6 Education and quality of job for wage employed. *Source* Authors' calculation from the LFS, 2010

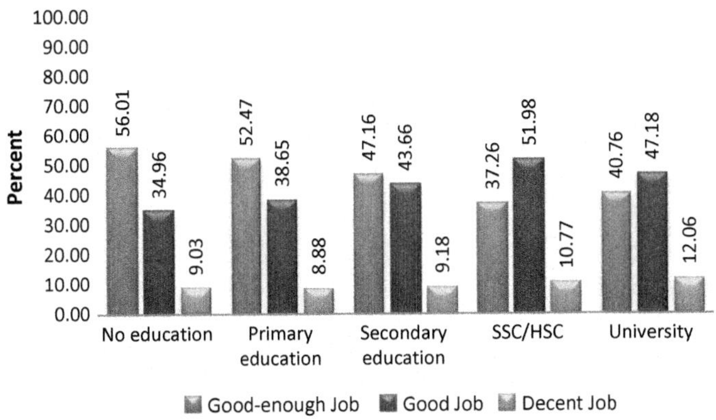

Fig. 7 Education and quality of job for self-employed. *Source* Authors' calculation from the LFS, 2010

3.5 *Training and Quality of Job*

Figure 8 shows that for the wage employed, while only 5.2% of the persons in good-enough job received training, the rate is 11.7% and 32.8% for persons in good job and decent job, respectively. In contrast, Fig. 9 shows that the percent of people received training in case of self-employment is about only 5% which remains invariably the same for all three job qualities.

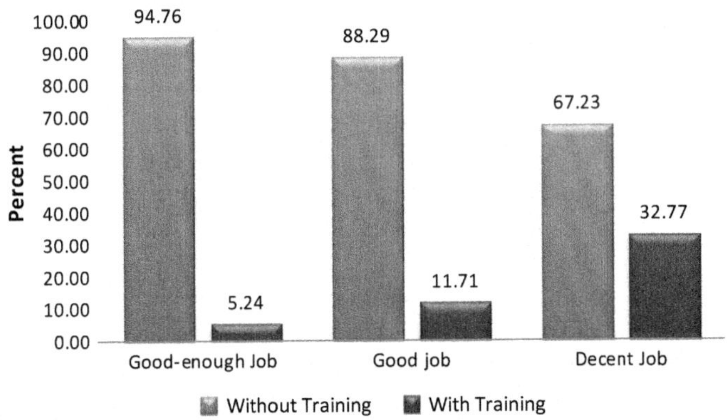

Fig. 8 Training and quality of job for wage employed. *Source* Authors' calculation from the LFS, 2010

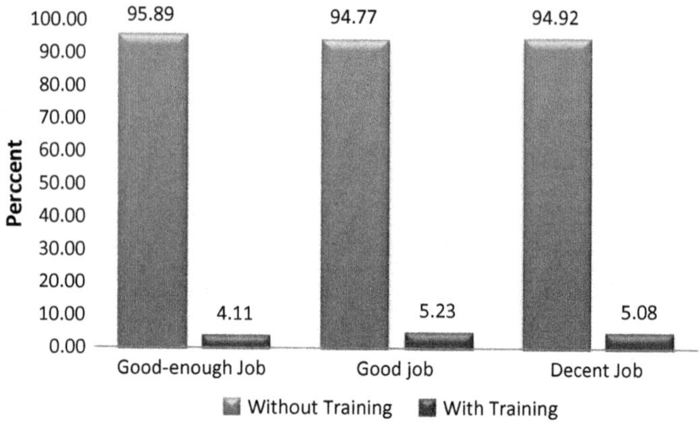

Fig. 9 Training and quality of job for self-employed. *Source* Authors' calculation from the LFS, 2010

4 How Do Education and Skill Matter for a Better Job? Insights from Econometric Exercises

In order to see the impacts of education and training over the quality of employment, we have run two separate multinomial logistic regressions—one, considering only the wage employed category, and the other considering only the self-employed category. In both of the cases, our base category is a good-enough job.

In case of the first set of regression where we considered only the wage employed, we find that education and training have a highly significant impact on moving from good-enough job to good job and decent job (Table 5). The results from average marginal effect reported in Table 5 suggest that, though primary education is found to be insignificant in changing the quality of job, persons with secondary and higher secondary education have almost 20% points higher probability to be in a decent job compared to persons with no education. The impact of education is found to be the highest for university education, as being educated in a university increases the probability to be in a good job by 18% points while it increases the probability to be in a decent job by 26% points compared to the persons with no education. Moreover, education of the household head has a statistically significant and positive trans-generational impact if the household head has more than primary education. Household heads with secondary or higher secondary education increase the probability of a worker to be in a good job by more than 5% points and to be in a decent job by around 3% points compared to the household heads with no education. The magnitude is the same in case of a decent job if the household head possesses a university degree. The results also indicate that training helps to move people up from good-enough job to good job or decent job. Compared to persons without training, a trained worker has more than 6% points higher probability to be in a good job or a decent job.

Table 5 Average marginal effects (for wage employed category)

Explanatory variables	Marginal effects for good-enough job (category 1)	Marginal effects for good job (category 2)	Marginal effects for decent job (category 3)
Primary education	0.005 (0.010)	0.020 (0.014)	−0.025 (0.016)
Secondary education	−0.079[a] (0.011)	−0.110[a] (0.012)	0.191[a] (0.009)
SSC/HSC	−0.160[a] (0.011)	−0.032[b] (0.013)	0.193[a] (0.009)
University education	−0.433[a] (0.033)	0.174[a] (0.032)	0.258[a] (0.011)
Age	−0.020[a] (0.001)	0.011[a] (0.001)	0.0094[a] (0.001)
Age squared	0.0002[a] (0.000)	−0.0001[a] (0.000)	−0.0001[a] (0.000)
Family income	−0.219[a] (0.003)	0.185[a] (0.004)	0.034[a] (0.002)
Female dummy	0.083[a] (0.007)	−0.117[a] (0.008)	0.033[a] (0.004)
Training dummy	−0.066[a] (0.010)	0.034[a] (0.010)	0.032[a] (0.003)
Household head with primary education	−0.023[b] (0.009)	0.023[b] (0.010)	0.0001 (0.008)
Household head with secondary education	−0.082[a] (0.011)	0.054[a] (0.012)	0.028[a] (0.006)
Household head with SSC/HSC	−0.091[a] (0.012)	0.064[a] (0.013)	0.027[a] (0.006)
Household head with university education	−0.028 (0.031)	−0.003 (0.029)	0.031[a] (0.008)
Land holding	−0.0004[a] (0.000)	0.0002[c] (0.0001)	0.0002[a] (0.000)

Note a, b, and c indicate statistical significance at the 1, 5, and 10% levels, respectively. The figures in parentheses are the standard errors

Table 5 also suggests that there is a concave relationship between age and the probability of having good job or decent job, i.e., the probability of having a better job increases at a decreasing rate with the increase in age. The gender dummy (female) shows that females have 8.3% higher probability to be in a good-enough job compared to the male category. The coefficients of family income further suggest that with the rise in family income—the probability of a person to be in good job or decent job increases significantly. Although to a lesser extent, the implication of per capita household land is analogous to the impact of family income.

To understand how and to what extent education and training shift the quality of job, we have also calculated the relative risk ratio (RRR) of the corresponding variables for each category compared to the base category (Table 6). We find that RRR is significant for all other levels of education except primary education. For a person with secondary education relative to no education, the relative risk (RR) for a decent job compared to good-enough job would be expected to increase by a

Table 6 The result of multinomial logit regression in case of wage employment (in terms of RRR)

Explanatory variables	Category (base category: good-enough job)	
	Category 2 (good job)	Category 3 (decent job)
Primary education	1.016 (0.052)	0.667 (0.174)
Secondary education	1.105 (0.067)	23.245[a] (3.628)
SSC/HSC	1.722[a] (0.113)	32.701[a] (5.229)
University education	6.959[a] (1.278)	241.06[a] (57.132)
Age	1.100[a] (0.006)	1.241[a] (0.016)
Age squared	0.998[a] (0.0001)	0.997[a] (0.0001)
Family income	3.182ac (0.078)	3.791[a] (0.162)
Female dummy	0.592[a] (0.026)	1.204[b] (0.092)
Training dummy	1.364[a] (0.075)	2.076[a] (0.149)
Household head with primary education	1.138[a] (0.057)	1.093 (0.147)
Household head with secondary education	1.501[a] (0.097)	2.078[a] (0.236)
Household head with SSC/HSC	1.580[a] (0.109)	2.128[a] (0.247)
Household head with university education	1.105 (0.187)	1.788[a] (0.353)
Land holding	1.001[a] (0.001)	1.004[a] (0.001)
Constant	0.00001[a] (3.11e−06)	2.71e−09[a] (1.27e−09)
Number of observations	26,417	
LR chi^2 (28)	11373.92	
Prob > chi^2	0.0000	
Pseudo R^2	0.2305	

Note a, b, and c indicate statistical significance at the 1, 5, and 10% levels, respectively. The figures in parentheses are the standard errors

factor of 23.2. The RR for decent job relative to good-enough job would increase by a factor of 32.7 and 241.1 for the attainment of higher secondary and university education, respectively, compared to the no education category holding all other things constant. These results indicate the strong capability of higher education in lifting up the quality of employment generation as opposed to no education. Although small in magnitude, training does have a highly significant impact. For persons with training in comparison to persons without training, the relative risk for having a decent job compared to good-enough job would increase by a factor of 2.1 holding all other variables constant.

In the second regression, reported in Table 7, we have considered the self-employed category while our base category remains the same ("good-enough" job). However, in this case, we have dropped variables related to household head, as self-employed persons are predominantly household heads (about 72%). Average marginal effects, reported in Table 7, show that level of education has a statistically significant impact on moving from good-enough job to good job or decent job.

Table 7 Average marginal effects (for self-employed category)

Explanatory variables	Marginal effects for good-enough job (category 1)	Marginal effects for good job (category 2)	Marginal effects for decent job (category 3)
Primary education	−0.012[c] (0.006)	0.02[b] (0.006)	−0.008[c] (0.004)
Secondary education	−0.028[a] (0.008)	0.038[a] (0.008)	−0.01[c] (0.005)
SSC/HSC	−0.065[a] (0.008)	0.070[a] (0.008)	−0.0053 (0.005)
University education	−0.002 (0.018)	0.002 (0.018)	0.0002 (0.010)
Age	−0.006[a] (0.001)	0.007[a] (0.001)	−0.0011[c] (0.001)
Age squared	0.00003[b] (0.00001)	−0.0001[a] (0.000)	0.0000[b] (0.000)
Family income	−0.136[a] (0.004)	0.112[a] (0.004)	0.0240[a] (0.002)
Female dummy	0.496[a] (0.007)	−0.393[a] (0.009)	−0.1038[a] (0.007)
Training dummy	0.0003 (0.012)	−0.001 (0.012)	0.001 (0.007)
Land holding	−0.0007[a] (0.000)	0.001[a] (0.000)	0.0001[a] (0.000)

Note a, b, and c indicate statistical significance at the 1, 5, and 10% levels, respectively. The figures in parentheses are the standard errors

While persons with primary education have around 2% points higher probability to be in good job compared to the no education category, it has almost negligible but negative influence over the probability of attaining a decent job. Persons with secondary or higher secondary education have more than 4% points higher probability of having a good job compared to no education category. The data suggests no significant impact of university education over the attainment of good job or decent job. Moreover, impacts of training are also found to be insignificant in cases of such transitions. A possible explanation of the insignificance of these major variables could be that only a very low percentage of people in the self-employed category participated in any training program (only about 4%) or had a university degree (2.24%) in the LFS 2010 data. This finding stylizes nothing but the fact that the majority of the self-employed sector comprises of unskilled labor who lack higher education and/or proper training.

Table 7 also suggests that compared to males, females have 39% points and 10% points lower probability to be in a good job and decent job, respectively. Just like the previous case, in case of self-employment, we find a highly significant influence of family income over the probability of availing a good job or decent job. Per capita land holding has also a significant effect on the quality of employment that a person may avail. Combined, these two show that the socioeconomic context of a household may play an important role in assuring better quality employment to its

Table 8 The result of multinomial logit regression in case of self-employment (in terms of RRR)

Explanatory variables	Category (base category: good-enough job)	
	Category 2 (good job)	Category 3 (decent job)
Primary education	1.089[b] (0.037)	0.950 (0.052)
Secondary education	1.192[a] (0.053)	0.974 (0.070)
SSC/HSC	1.435[a] (0.059)	1.128[c] (0.073)
University education	1.010 (0.096)	1.007 (0.141)
Age	1.037[a] (0.005)	1.005 (0.008)
Age squared	0.999[a] (0.000)	1.000 (0.000)
Family income	1.947[a] (0.043)	1.886[a] (0.064)
Female dummy	0.0921[a] (0.004)	0.083[a] (0.007)
Training dummy	0.996 (0.065)	1.008 (0.103)
Land holding	1.003[a] (0.000)	1.003[a] (0.000)
Constant	0.002[a] (0.000)	0.001[a] (0.000)
Number of observations	29,196	
LR chi^2 (20)	5576.89	
Prob > chi^2	0.0000	
Pseudo R^2	0.1028	

Note a, b, and c indicate statistical significance at the 1, 5, and 10% levels, respectively. The figures in parentheses are the standard errors

members. Hence, skill development programs may have a multiplier effect through the spillover benefits accrued to its members.

In terms of RRR, reported in Table 8, we find that having primary education compared to no education improves the Relative Risk (RR) to be in a good job compared to good-enough job. However, it does not have any significance with respect to decent job. On top of that, having secondary or higher secondary education compared to no education increases the RR for good job compared to good-enough job by more than a factor of 1.2. However, impacts of university education and training were found to be insignificant in case of RRR.

5 Conclusion

There is no denying the fact that the world of today is equally concerned, if not more, with the quality of employment rather than improvement in numbers. The dominant paradigm in the discussion on the quality of employment focuses on the improvements in the demand side of labor, i.e., issues related to the working condition. In this chapter, we have suggested that although if we initiate improvements at the demand side, there could be a supply-side mismatch intermitting the overall effectiveness of the demand-side policies. From the analysis part of the chapter, we see that education and training have highly significant impacts over the quality of employment that a person may avail. The transition takes place in the form of productivity enhancement. The importance of the productivity enhancement is that even if we can generate terms and conditions for employing "decent work" agenda, in practice, the workers may themselves lack the quality to be absorbed in the transformation process due to their lower productivity. Productivity enhancement will not only create "decent job" benefits to the households at the individual level but will also accelerate the process of transformation at the social level.

Hence, supply-side policies like spreading education and skill development programs to the mass population, removing socioeconomic barriers those have converse impacts over education attainment, and enhancing the diversity of training programs taking into consideration of the domestic as well as global labor market demands should be adapted. Most importantly, to ensure the proper escalation of labor productivity—emphasis must be put on the improvement of the quality of education and training as well. A prompt response from the government incorporating various development agencies and international donors will fasten the process of recognition of the problems, identification of the strategies, and implementation of the policies.

References

Ahn, P. (2008). Organizing as a catalyst for promoting decent work in the informal economy in South Asia. *The Indian Journal of Labour Economics, 51*(4).

Amin, A. N. (2002). *The informal sector in Asia from the decent work perspective*. Geneva: International Labour Office.

Anker, R., Chernyshev, I., Egger, P., Mehran, F., & Ritter, J. (2002). *Measuring decent work with statistical indicators*. Geneva: International Labour Office (Policy Integration Department).

Azur, M., Stuart, E., Frangakis, C., & Leaf, P. (20 March 2011). US National Library of Medicine. Retrieved 20 Nov, 2015, from http://www.ncbi.nlm.nih.gov/pubmed/21499542.

Barrientos, S. (2007). *Global production systems and decent work*. Geneva: Policy Integration Department, International Labour Office.

Bangladesh Bureau of Statistics. (2010). *Labor Force Survey*. Dhaka: Bangladesh Bureau of Statistics (BBS).

Bouhlila, D. S., & Sellaouti, F. (2013). Multiple imputation using chained equations for missing data in TIMSS: a case study. *Large-scale Assessments in Education, 1*, 4.

Cohen, T., & Moodley, L. (2012). Achieving "decent work" in South Africa? *Potchefstroomse Elektroniese Regsblad (P.E.R), 15*(2).

Ghai, D. (2003). Decent work: concept and indicators. *International Labour Review, 142*(2).

International Labor Organization. (2012). Employment and social protection in the new demographic context. In *Geneva: 102nd Session: International Labor Conference, ILO*.

Marchenko, Y. (2011). Retrieved January 5, 2016, from www.stata.com: http://www.stata.com/meeting/sweden11/abstracts/marchenko_nordic11.pdf. Retrieved from Stata Official Website.

Mujeri, M. K. (2004). *Bangladesh decent work statistical indicators: a fact-finding study*. Geneva: International Labour Office.

Polaski, S. (2009). *Harnessing global forces to create decent work in Cambodia*. Geneva: International Labour Organization (International Institute for Laboir Studies).

Raihan, S. (2014). From 'good-enough' job to 'decent' job: inclusive growth in transition in Bangladesh. *Thniking Aloud,* 1.

Royston, P. (2009). Multiple Imputation of missing values: further update of ice, with an emphasis on categorical variables. *The Stata Journal*, *9*(3), 466–477.

Royston, P., & White, I. R. (2011). Multiple imputation by chained equations (MICE): implementation in stata. *Journal of Statistical Software*, *45*(4).

Schafer, J. L. (1999). Multiple imputation: a primer. *Statistical Methods in Medical Research, 8,* 3–15.

Sen, A. (1999). *Development as Freedom*. New York: Alfred A. Knopf.

Servais, J. M. (2004). Globalization and decent work policy: reflections upon a new legal approach. *International Labour Review*, *143*(1–2).

Does Participation in Vocational Training Differ on Agricultural Seasonality?

Israt Jahan and Abu S. Shonchoy

1 Introduction

Skilled workforce is the fundamental requirement for the growth and development of an economy. Hence, training programs are considered to be a potential solution to address the problem of lack of a skilled workforce. For a country like Bangladesh, skill development programs are of top policy importance; and adequately planning for such programs are crucial policy concerns. The country is currently enjoying the youth bulge or popularly known as demographic dividend—a large youth workforce (especially workforce aged 15–24) compared to its dependent population. The age dependency ratio (percentage of working-age population) of Bangladesh is higher than Sri Lanka, India, and Bhutan in South Asia.

However, the 2010 Labour Force Survey (LFS) of Bangladesh noted a worrisome fact that 39.22% of these workforces are uneducated. Given the education level and resulted lack of skill of this particular workforce, training programs need to emphasis more on the proper planning and targeting issues to address the demand and supply nexus of the skill-shortage, to make the youth labor contributing more to the development of the economy.

To address this immediate need of skill-shortage, many private sector interventions—along with public sector—have been conducting various training programs. However, these training programs (even when offered free-of-cost) face a

I. Jahan
South Asian Network on Economic Modeling(SANEM), Dhaka, Bangladesh

A. S. Shonchoy (✉)
Institute of Developing Economies (IDE) JETRO, Chiba, Japan
e-mail: parves.shonchoy@gmail.com

A. S. Shonchoy
University of Tokyo, Tokyo, Japan

S. Raihan (ed.), *Structural Change and Dynamics of Labor Markets in Bangladesh*, South Asia Economic and Policy Studies,
https://doi.org/10.1007/978-981-13-2071-2_10

large attrition rate-many of those who sign-up, do not show-up for the actual training sessions. Various studies have pointed out issues like distance, lack of information, backwardness, social taboo, and lack of networking as important impediments for training program take-up rate. However, there is hardly any study to address the importance of the training program schedule with local agrarian seasonal patterns, which have important targeting issues for the implementing authorities. However, training programs—both public and private—do not typically pay attention to this seasonality and as a result suffer from issues like attrition, discontinuation, and dropout.

To address this important topic systematically, we focus on the northern part of Bangladesh where agriculture is the main source of earning. Distinct seasonal patterns exist in the northern Bangladesh. In this study, using survey data on the sample selection for a training, we focus on the timing of the specific type of training to examine how seasonality makes a difference in participation. To the best of our knowledge, there exists no rigorous study to understand the seasonality impact on the sample selection of a training program.

2 Literature Review

There are demands for skilled workers in different industries of Bangladesh. But the supply of such skilled workers is low. Maclean et al. (2013), in their study, explained the importance and need for technical and vocational education and training to meet this huge labor demand. Maclean et al. (2013) noticed the employment dependence on agricultural work in the South Asian region which they argued to minimize by the technical and targeted education and training. Rahman and Islam (2013) have also emphasized on women's education and skill training for the economic development.

While Bangladesh is having a consistent growth over the economy, certain regions of it are still lagging behind in terms of economic opportunities and development. Different studies have discussed about the seasonal unemployment and its remedy. In Bangladesh, the seasonality is a very common phenomenon as it is mostly based on agriculture. During the seasonal famine, 50–60% of the income falls for the individuals affected for this seasonality (Mobarak et al. 2011).

A particular problem concerns the pre-harvest 'lean' seasons that are more prevalent in the agriculture based economies such as countries in South Asia and sub-Saharan Africa. This period of annual famine, known as 'Monga' in Bangladesh (Shonchoy and Kurosaki 2014). Government, NGOs, and other private organizations provide different programs to accommodate this seasonal impact. Food/cash for work, microcredit, and giving trainings are common among the interventions for consumption smoothing (Mobarak et al. 2011).

Diverse training programs have heterogeneous impact on employment and earnings. Attanasio et al. (2011) (Colombia) and Hicks et al. (2011) (Kenya) have found greater impact on females' well-being than that of male ones. Despite providing the evidence of the impact of training, this study focuses on how training programs should address the seasonality and the agriculturally important time period to pave a long-term pathway to employment and development.

Jahan (2015) has provided the reasoning on how training programs should be designed on the perspective of age, gender, educational and occupational categories. She discussed on what type of people can generate higher incentives from different type of training. Hence, this study bridges the gap in the policy suggestion of a proper and scientific analysis of the seasonality on training programs.

3 Background of the Program

The particular program that we evaluate in this project does a targeted intervention. It is a skill training program for RMG sector operated by Gana Unnayan Kendra (GUK) a local NGO working at the Gaibandha, a vulnerable district of northern Bangladesh. In this program, GUK provides skill training to interested young women and men of extreme poor families on woven garments. Initially, GUK provided 1-month-long residential training on sewing machine operation for the selected candidates from their targeted beneficiary households. The project officially started in July 2013. Gaibandha district was selected for several reasons. Agricultural activities are the main source of income in this region and most of the population of Gaibandha lives a vulnerable life with poverty. Mostly, Aman and Boro paddies are cultivated in this area and during the months of April, July, September, October, and November the availability of agricultural work is very limited.

To understand the demand for such a training program, we conducted a survey to document the socioeconomic condition of the participants based on the eligibility. Table 1 provides the detailed eligibility criterion.

The program aims at training 1600 participants for the RMG sector, however, due to the capacity constraint program authority could not run this program in one go. As a result, we had to divide the program into different quarters (we termed these quarters as "blocks") and continue to hire interested individuals for the training program at different time of the year. We divide all the targeted population into four blocks. Our target was to select eligible candidates from moderate and ultra-poor households. In this survey we asked interested candidates about their age, land holding, household living standards and education, occupation, and employment-related information. Other information includes household amenities (tube-well or latrine), livestock, productive asset that generates income, type of

Table 1 Eligibility criterion

Individual Level
1. *Age*: within 18–35 years of age (verified by national ID card or Birth certificate)
2. *Education*: At least can read and write (checked by signature test)
3. *Employment*: Currently unemployed (In case of women who are not actively engaged in economic activity, ignore this point)
4. *Marital status*: Any status is allowed. (However, in case of unmarried women: ask the parents if they are OK with her decision. In case of married women with children, ask her family or husband about the arrangement of her children in case she goes to Dhaka for a job)
5. *Willingness*: Should be willing to learn additional skills to change his/her profession preferably for the garments industries mostly located in Dhaka
Family Level (only choose between these two groups)
1. Individuals belonging to **Ultra-poor** family *if any of the following four matches*,
• Less than 50 decimals of land (including agricultural, homestead and fallow)
• Does not have household amenities like tube-well or latrine
• Does not have any livestock
• Does not have any productive asset at home that generates income
• House is mostly built with straw and mud
• Does not have any regular source of income and remain completely unemployed during the MONGA (September to December)
2. Individuals belonging to **Moderate poor** family *if any of the following four matches*,
• Less than 100 decimals of land (including agricultural, homestead, and fallow)
• Does own only one of the household amenities among tube-well or latrine
• Does have only one livestock (either own or Adhi)
• Does have only one productive asset at home that generates income
• Whole house is not made with corrugate iron (TIN), partial tin-made house is OK
• Does not have any limited source of income and remain partially unemployed during the MONGA (September to December)

house, and income during the MONGA season have been taken into consideration to define the poverty criteria.

For this study, we received a total of 4123 eligible candidates interested to participate in the training program. The survey was undertaken in four blocks as mentioned before. The number of survey participants and timing of the survey is given in the Table 2. Each of the blocks is implemented in different time of the year. Thus, each block represents one particular time of the year which captures the local seasonality. The survey started in August 2013 for the first block.

Table 2 Details of the survey

Block	Samples	Survey time	Season
First block	1,099	August–October '13	Planting time (Aman), *Monga* time
Second block	1,492	November–December '13	*Monga* time, harvesting time (Aman)
Third block	744	March–April '14	Harvesting time (Boro)
Fourth block	788	June '14	–

Source Survey data

Table 3 Distribution of total sample by Upazila.

Upazila	Samples
Fulchari	776
Gobendagonj	548
Palashbari	471
Sadullahpur	367
Shaghata	730
Sundargonj	1,231
Total	4,123

Source Survey data

We surveyed 1099 samples for the first block. Survey started for the second block in November 2013 and ended in December of the same year. Surveyed for the third and fourth block was done in March–April and June 2014, respectively. Table 2 illustrates the seasonality attached to each block.

The entire survey accumulates six Upazilas (sub-district) of Gaibandha district (Table 3). In these 6 Upazilas, there are 52 unions and 255 villages that were covered by the survey. From the total 4123 samples, the highest share was found from Shundargonj Upazila with 1231 samples and the lowest share was from Sadullahpur with 367 samples.

4 Socioeconomic Condition of the Eligible Candidates

In the section, we analyze the distribution of the samples in different categories based on social economic characteristics. We have categorized the total sample into separate individualistic and household characteristics. Most of them were eligible for the interventions. Almost all are either "Ultra-Poor" or "moderate Poor".

4.1 Individual Characteristics of the Candidates

The average age of the eligible candidates who applied for such a training program is 22.84. It appears that relatively younger youth population is more interested in such a training program. Age-specific categorization, as shown in Fig. 1, suggests that the maximum percentage (43.44%) of the total sample is aged between 18 and 20. 28.16% were in the age category of 21–25 and 19.62% were in the age group of 26–30. A very small percentage of the total sample was aged over 30. There were also some samples, who were invalid under the eligibility criteria of age. Those who were below the required age or above; 0.32% were aged under 18, and 0.24% sample were over the age of 35.

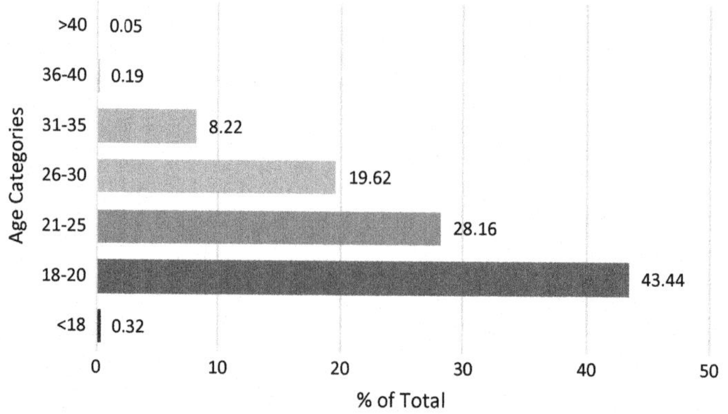

Fig. 1 Distribution of total sample by age category. *Source* Survey data

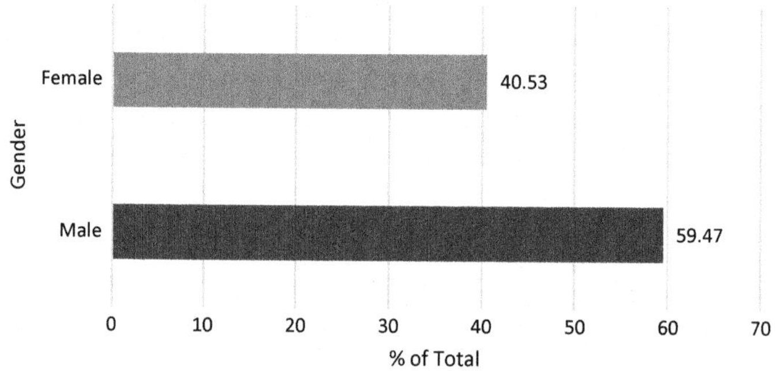

Fig. 2 Distribution of total sample by sex. *Source* Survey data

Figure 2 shows the gender distribution of the sample. Male showed relatively considerable interest in such a training program (59.47%) compared with female (40.53%). Given the remoteness of the location and conservative as well as a patriarchal social system, this statistics is not surprising.

The eligibility criteria on education for the training program were to have at least primary level of education (Fig. 3). About 2.13% of total sample became ineligible for the program due to low educational qualifications. Those who were eligible, 35% had a primary education where another 36% had a secondary level of schooling. The percentages of sample having SSC and HSC are 17.88 and 7.47%, respectively. The portion of the sample having graduate level of study was very small, only 1.58% reported having such a qualification.

In case of marital status, in the total sample, about 50% of those who applied were unmarried (see Fig. 4). About 43.51% reported being married during the time of application and the other 5.92% were either divorced, widowed or separated.

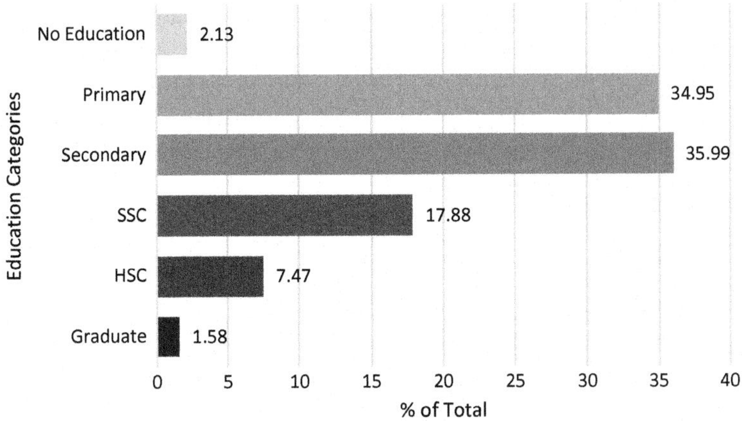

Fig. 3 Distribution of total sample by education. *Source* Survey data

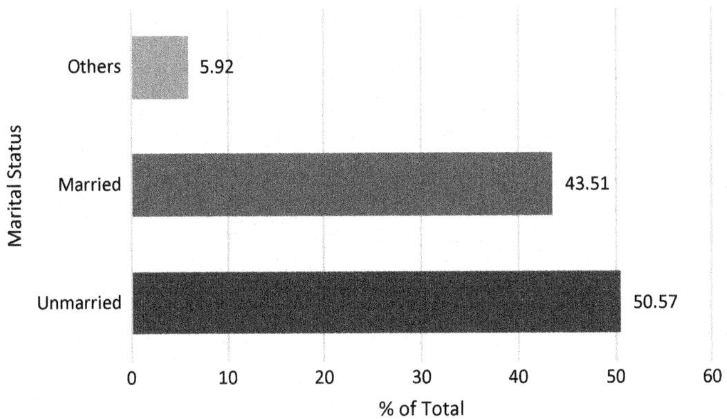

Fig. 4 Distribution of total sample by marital status. *Source* Survey data

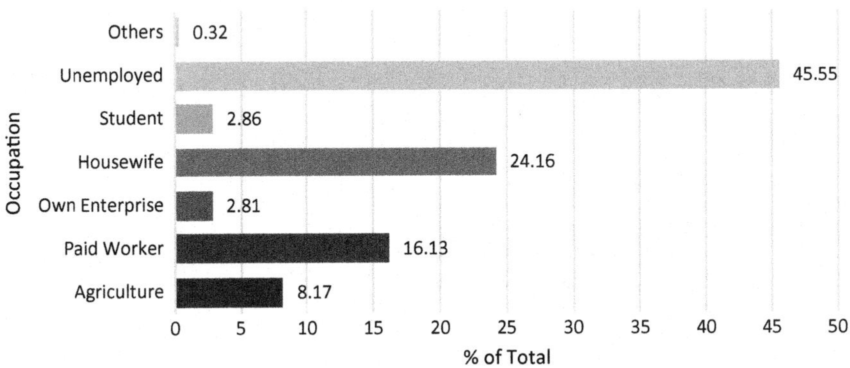

Fig. 5 Occupational distribution of the sample. *Source* Survey data

Figure 5 shows the occupational distribution of the candidates. As the diagram depicts, most applicants (45.55%) were unemployed during the time of the survey. 24.16% were housewives who reported being engaged on daily domestic household work or unpaid family work. Only a relatively small percentage of the sample (16.13%) mentioned being engaged in paid work and 8.17% were involved in agriculture. A very small percentage reported having a small enterprise and having entrepreneurial income.

4.2 *Household Characteristics of the Applicants*

Average household size of our sample was 5. About 34.97% households have no member aged below 12 and 97.67% households do not have any disable member in the household.

As the study targeted the ultra-poor and moderate poor of Gaibandha, the land size was part of the eligibility criteria of the sample and an indicator of poverty. Having no land holding (including agricultural, homestead and fallow) was considered to be ultra-poor and having less than 50 decimals of lands were considered to be moderately poor. In our survey, 15.86% of the sample did not hold any land which shows the extent of poverty in that region (Fig. 6). Maximum percentage (52.8%) was holding land within the range of 0.5–10 decimals. Figure 6 shows the distribution of the total sample in total land holdings.

The agricultural land holding by our sample was on an average very low. 71.67% of the total sample did not hold any type of agricultural land. Very small percentage of the sample had some agricultural land (Fig. 7). Moreover, 99.56% of the household did not have any productive asset like tractor, power tiller, etc., also,

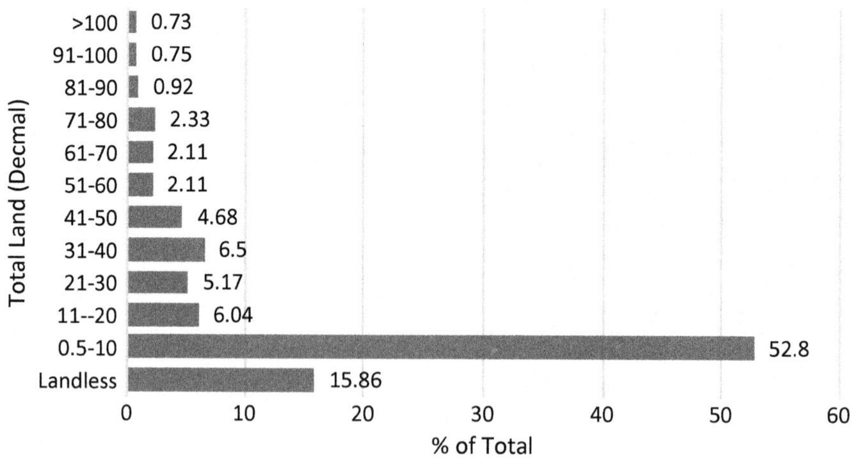

Fig. 6 Total land holding by the samples. *Source* Survey data

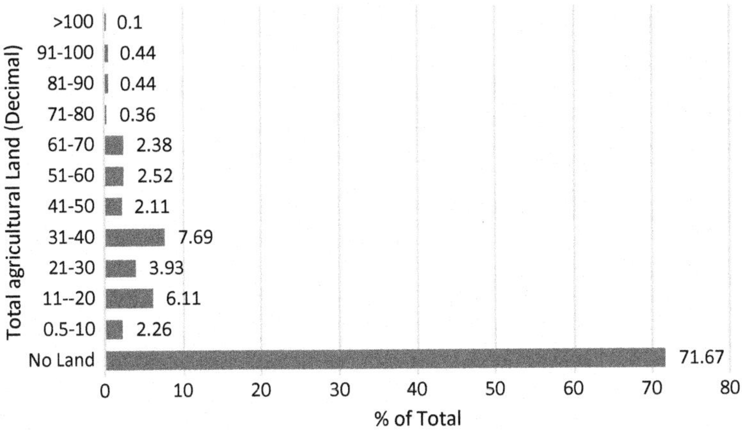

Fig. 7 Agricultural land holding by the samples. *Source* Survey data

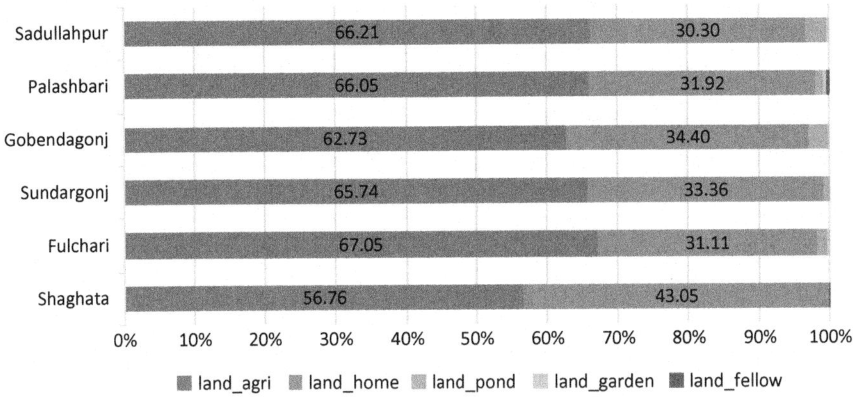

Fig. 8 Distribution of total land by different categories of land. *Source* Survey data

the study found that 43.64% have their own livestock in their household where 6.43% have shared livestock (locally known as "adhi") in their household. Adhi is similar as share cropping contract but instead of crop one shares a livestock.

The distribution of total land holdings based on types of land at Upazila level is presented in Fig. 8. A significant majority used their land for agriculture purpose, followed by land for resident. Interestingly this pattern is quite similar across six Upazilas showing consistency.

Now, focusing our attention to seasonal deprivation or *Monga*, Fig. 9 shows that 79.75% of our survey respondent reported not to have any job or employment in the past *Monga* season (September to November). Those who worked in that season, the average number of days they had an employment is 35, which is about 28% of the time based on the total duration of the *Monga* (Fig. 9).

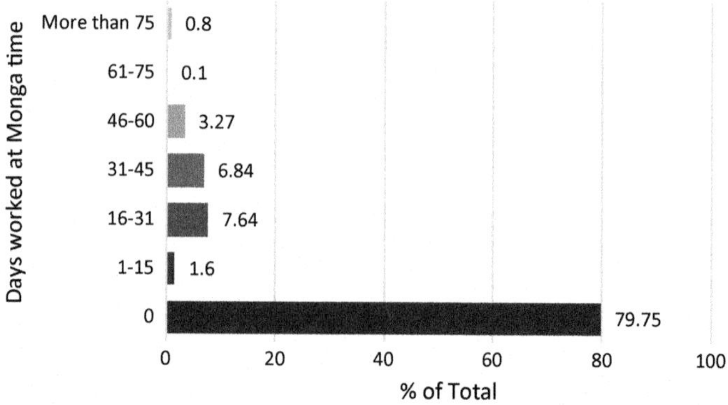

Fig. 9 Days of employment during the last *Monga* season. *Source* Survey data

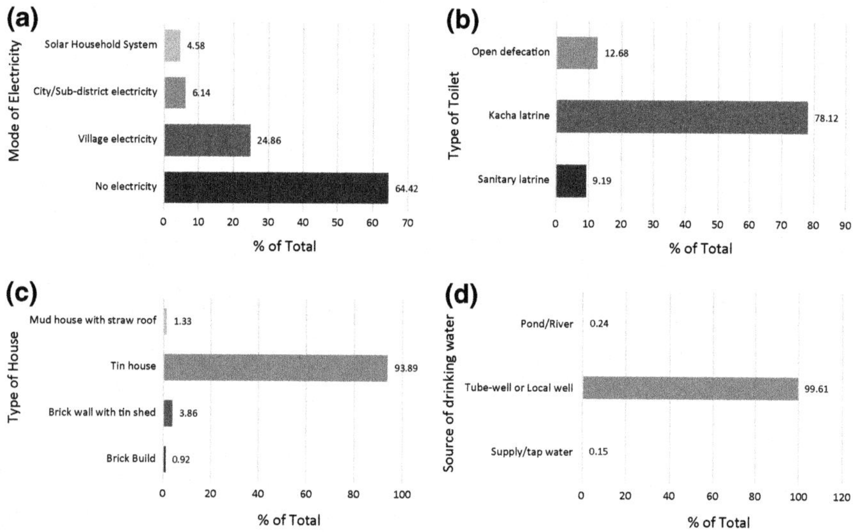

Fig. 10 Utilities available to the samples. *Source* Survey data

Figure 10 shows the percentage of samples having different types of utilities. 64.42% did not get any electricity in their house. 24.86% survey respondents have village-level electricity. Very smaller percentage of the sample had city district electricity or solar system. Moreover, 78.12% of the samples had "kacha" latrine that is made of raw materials available locally. 93.89% of the samples mentioned living in a house that is made of tin (corrugated iron) and almost hundred percent of sample uses tube-well or local well to collect drinking water.

5 Impact of Seasonality on the Sample Survey

Bangladesh is predominantly an agrarian economy and local agrarian seasonality is an important concern for many rural youths, who have direct or indirect interaction with agriculture. Since agricultural day laborers remain unemployed during the off-harvesting and off-plantation period, it is very important for them to gain the maximum income during the peak labor demand season for the agriculture sector. The opportunity cost of participating and continuing a training program during the peak agricultural season is very high for poor rural youth. Hence, intuitively it is costly for them to take part in the training program if the training program coincides with the planting or harvesting season.

In order to see the impact of seasonality on interested training participants, we will now focus our discussion on socioeconomic conditions based on the timing of the survey. In particular, we would like to see whether the socioeconomic characteristics of the participants systematically vary if they are surveyed in a specific season, which is the main question of interest in this section.

In the northern area of Bangladesh, seasonality of lean season (*Monga*) is very pronounced when the agricultural day laborers are job less between the plantation and harvesting time (see Khandker 2012). In Gaibandha, *Monga* time starts typically in September and continues until the end of November. The planting and harvesting time of the mostly grown paddy in northern Bangladesh is Aman and Boro, which are presented in the Table 4.

Only 5.38% of the total sample was surveyed in *Monga* (Table 5). The percentage of people surveyed in planting time (Aman and Boro) and harvesting time (Aman and Boro) are 24.79, 32.69, 36.19, and 1.55, respectively. We see that the share of participants in the harvesting time of Boro is much less than the others. The categories are not mutually exclusive. So the total sum is not equal to 100%.

Table 4 Seasonality in the survey

Category of seasonality	Time
Job-less time: *Monga* time	September–November
Planting time (Aman)	July–August
Planting time (Boro)	January–February
Harvesting time (Aman)	November–December
Harvesting time (Boro)	April–May

Table 5 Survey share based on seasonality

Survey Time	% of survey in the specific time
Monga time	5.38
Planting time (Aman)	24.79
Planting time (Boro)	32.69
Harvesting time (Aman)	36.19
Harvesting time (Boro)	1.55

To understand the systematic socioeconomic pattern of the applicants, we categorized the seasonality into four groups—(i) Normal Time with no seasonal impact (The month of March and June), (ii) *Monga* Time, (iii) Harvesting Time, and (vi) Planting Time. We have merged two plantations and two harvesting seasons into two groups. Then, we created dummies for each group to note the significant difference on socioeconomic situations of the eligible participants compared to that of normal time.

We have conducted several independent group t-test to assess the differences. Here, in all cases, we considered the null hypothesis as, Ho: Difference = mean (0) − mean(1) = 0. Here, mean(0) is the average output of the normal type and mean(1) is the average output in the concerned season. The positive difference shows the higher weight on the average on the normal type, and the negative value of the difference shows the otherwise. The results are reported in Table 6.

Table 6 T-test comparing seasonality

	Monga versus Normal time		Harvesting versus Normal time		Planting versus Normal time	
Category	Difference	t-stat	Difference	t-stat	Difference	t-stat
Gender						
Female	−0.071	−2.089**	−0.065	−3.692***	−0.200	−10.247***
Age category						
Aged 18–20	0.202	5.650***	0.101	5.536***	0.200	10.139***
Aged 21–25	−0.070	−2.199**	−0.030	−1.831**	−0.039	−2.144**
Aged 26–30	−0.082	−2.999***	−0.016	−1.189	−0.109	−6.656***
Aged 31–35	−0.050	−2.931***	−0.055	−5.450***	−0.031	−3.074***
Education category						
Graduate	0.025	2.399**	0.021	4.977***	0.004	0.604
HSC completed	0.088	4.281***	0.036	3.607***	0.043	3.866***
SSC complete	0.177	6.121***	0.117	8.575***	0.017	1.026
Secondary	−0.029	−0.813	0.028	1.607*	0.066	3.402***
Primary	−0.262	−8.126***	−0.203	−11.774***	−0.047	−2.620***
No education	0.000				−0.083	−11.311***
Marital status						
Unmarried	0.247	7.064***	0.151	8.381***	0.209	10.586***
Married	−0.233	−6.858***	−0.144	−8.119***	−0.237	−12.181***
Others	−0.015	−0.835	−0.008	−0.832	0.027	3.072***
Occupation						
Agriculture	−0.118	−6.504***	−0.054	−5.395***	−0.024	−2.383**
Housewife	−0.120	−4.324***	−0.094	−6.271***	−0.154	−9.116***
Self-employed	−0.032	−3.347***	−0.021	−3.773***	−0.020	−3.436***
Paid work	−0.030	−1.171	−0.021	−1.579*	−0.012	−0.796
Student	0.001	0.395	−0.003	−1.776*	−0.103	−12.705***
Unemployed	0.300	8.578***	0.194	10.780***	0.325	16.964***

Note Difference = mean(0) − mean(1). Significance code: ***$p < 0.01$, **$p < 0.05$, *$p < 0.1$

We see that, for female category, the differences are all negative. That means that females also get affected with seasonality compared to the normal time, which shows that seasonality is an important concern for female as well.

Now, comparing different age categories we see that within the age range of 21–35, all the differences are negative and significantly different from zero. As we know, a large share (56%, see Fig. 1) of applicants came from the age range of 20–35, hence our results suggest that if one runs the training program during the period of seasonality, we will plausibly attract a different population. If programs want to target improving the family welfare and poverty status, and targets 20–35 age groups, then they must consider the local agricultural patterns, especially seasonality. In Table 6, we see that younger age range—those who are in the age bracket of 18–20—who are most likely financially dependent and unemployed, uptake the program systematically more during the time of seasonality.

We found that, people with more than 10 years of education (SSC, HSC, or Graduate) are more prevalent in participating in training during the time of seasonality. It demonstrates that those who are more educated than average population, is more interested in taking this training opportunity and would like to enroll more in the period of seasonality as they are less connected with agricultural sector. On the contrary, low educated people, who are mostly involved in agrarian sector, will be less likely to join during the period of agricultural seasonality. In our sample, a large portion of poor people are from this category, about 34% of the entire sample.

Occupation-wise analysis is also consistent with our earlier findings. Interestingly, other than agricultural professional, self-employed professionals are also affected by seasonality and will not likely to enroll in the training program, for reasons described above. Unmarried persons are found to be participating more in the period of seasonality, while married people are less prevalent to participate in the time or *Monga*, harvesting or planting time. Married people have more family responsibilities hence income based pull-factors are more important, hence their opportunity cost of attending a training during the period of seasonality is very high. In our sample married people consist of 43% of the sample.

6 Conclusion

This study sheds light on the critical issue of targeting and local agricultural seasonality for typical skill development training program. We see that organizations those run program for a target population (say ultra-poor) need to be careful about designing the program schedule and timing according to the local seasonality. Otherwise such a program will not be able to achieve the targeted beneficiaries. We see that ultra-poor are the ones who are generally illiterate, low-skilled, asset-less, and typically work as a day-laborer. However, opportunity cost of attending training of this target group during the local agricultural seasonality is very high, as they need to maximize the local opportunity to earn which they can use for consumption smoothing during the period of the lean season. Our analysis show that the socioeconomic attributes of applicants systematically vary during the period of seasonality than normal time. Hence, understanding the seasonality and adequately addressing this into the design of the program is warranted to achieve a target population. Otherwise programs will face issues like mis-targeting, attrition and drop-outs.

References

Attanasio, O., Genicot, G., Barr, A., J., C., & Meghir, C. (2011). *Risk pooling, risk preferences, and social networks*. Working papers gueconwpa 11-11-05, Department of Economics, Georgetown University.

Hicks, J., Kremer, M., Mbiti, I., & Miguel, E. (2011). *Vocational Education vouchers delivery and labor market returns: A randomized evaluation among Kenyan youth* (Unpublished).

Jahan, I. (2015). Analyzing impact of skill training on labour force participation in Bangladesh. In *Mimeo published at SARNET conference of young south Asian scholars of labor economics*. New Delhi: Institute of Human Development.

Khandker, S. R., 2012. Seasonality of income and poverty in Bangladesh. *Journal of Development Economics, Elsevier, 97*(2), 244–256.

Maclean, R., Jagannathan, S., & Sarvi, J. (2013). *Skills development for inclusive and sustainable growth in developing Asia-Pacific*. Dordrecht, Heidelberg, New York, London: Springer.

Mobarak, M., Bryan, G., & Chowdhury, S. (2011). *Encouraging seasonal migration to mitigate the consequences of a seasonal famine in rural Bangladesh*. Policy brief 3014. International Growth Centre.

Rahman, R. I., & Islam, R. (2013). *Female labour force participation in Bangladesh: Trends, drivers and barriers*. ILO Asia-Pacific Working Paper Series, International Labor Organization.

Shonchoy, A. S., & Kurosaki, T. (2014). *Impact of seasonality-adjusted flexible microcredit on repayment and food consumption: Experimental evidence from rural Bangladesh*. Institute of Developing Economies (IDE), JETRO: Tokyo.

How Does Remittance Affect Labor Force Participation Behavior and Employment Choice in Bangladesh?

Selim Raihan, Muhammad Moshiur Rahman, Andilip Afroze and Mahtab Uddin

1 Introduction

In Bangladesh, remittance plays an important role in terms of its contribution to the gross national income and foreign exchange earnings, as well as its significant positive impact in reducing poverty both in the rural and urban areas (Raihan et al. 2009, 2014; Raihan and Sugiyarto 2012; Raihan and Uddin 2011; Khondker and Raihan 2009). Bangladesh is a major exporter of labor, and remittance is the second highest foreign exchange earning sector in this country. Not only international remittance, domestic remittance too has its own contribution to national income. In 2014, personal remittances received (which includes both domestic and international remittance) as a percentage of GDP was 8.7% (World Bank 2016). Though remittance is an asset for the country and it can further be transmitted to the development of the socioeconomic infrastructures of the country, members from the remittance recipient households can have a disparate preference towards the labor market participation decision compared to the non-recipient households. Hence, remittance could be one of the major drivers behind the labor market dynamics in Bangladesh. Against this backdrop, this paper examines the influence of remittances (both international and internal) over the labor market participation behavior of the recipients in agricultural and nonagricultural sectors of Bangladesh. In this study, we have used the Household Income and Expenditure Survey (HIES) 2010 data for our analysis and relevant econometric exercises, as HIES 2010 is the latest available nationwide household-level data that has a separate section on household migration and remittance information.

S. Raihan (✉) · M. Uddin
Department of Economics, University of Dhaka, Dhaka, Bangladesh
e-mail: selim.raihan@gmail.com

S. Raihan · M. M. Rahman · A. Afroze · M. Uddin
South Asian Network on Economic Modeling (SANEM), Dhaka, Bangladesh

S. Raihan (ed.), *Structural Change and Dynamics of Labor Markets in Bangladesh*, South Asia Economic and Policy Studies,
https://doi.org/10.1007/978-981-13-2071-2_11

2 Literature Review

In the literature of migration and remittances, there is no consensus among the scholars regarding the impacts of migration and remittances on labor market participation. The disputed conclusion on the impacts of remittances arises from the fact that, this impact varies with gender, nature of remittances and sometimes on the methodologies being applied. Ndiaye et al. (2015) analyzed the impact of migration and remittances on labor market participation in Senegal and found significant decline in labor market participation of household members with migrants due to remittances. The study also identified less incentive for the remaining household members to create their own businesses. Acosta (2006) and Görlich et al. (2007), in the contexts of El Salvador and Moldova respectively, found gender-specific implication of remittances over the employment status: although, on average, adult male labor force participation as well as activity choice remained unaffected, labor force participation of adult female decreased in the remittance-receiving households. Funkhouser (1992) found a similar result on female labor force participation in Nicaragua However, unlike the previous studies, he found a significant positive impact on males' entrepreneurial activities. In the contrary, Rodriguez and Tiongson (2001) concluded that remittances reduced not only the labor force participation but also overall employment in Manila. Evidence of Albania by contrast showed that only salaried non-migrant employees substituted income for leisure once they received a substantial amount of remittances (Narazani 2009). However, Jadotte (2009) found evidence in support of a declining labor supply with respect to increasing remittances in the Republic of Haiti. A similar result is drawn by Justino and Shemyakina (2012) where they evidenced an inverse relationship between hours of work and remittances for the remittance-receiving households in conflict-prone area in Tajikistan. On the other hand, Schuman (2013) showed that the impact of remittances could be considerably different based on the level of education or skill of the recipient. His findings, in the context of Senegal, showed that highly educated men were more likely to be self-employed and less likely to be wage-employed if they received remittances, whereas there was no evidence on the labor supply responses for the low educated individuals.

In the context of Cameroon, Epo and Baye (2013) found that remittances had a role over the remittance-receiving households in investing more in farm sectors compared to nonfarm activities, and thus led to a switch in employment in favor of the farm sector. This is also supported by the study by De Hass (2006), which in the context of Southern Morocco found that, households, having a rise in remittance income, invested more in housing and agriculture. Böhme (2013) found a positive effect of international migration on the accumulation agricultural assets in Mexico, suggesting the use of capital obtained from international migration mainly for overcoming liquidity constraints for subsistence production.

Therefore, the ongoing literature suffices the existence of relationship between the remittance recipient households and its impacts over the labor market. However, the point of distinction in the literature is that, although the relationship is established, its direction is not. This is due to the fact that, countries differ in terms of socioeconomic diversities, level of education, scope of entrepreneurial ventures, and social and political commitment towards women empowerment.

3 Remittance and Labor Market: How Do They Interact?

3.1 Trends and Patterns of Remittance Flow

The flow of international remittances in Bangladesh rose from less than USD 2 billion in 2000 to more than USD 15 billion in 2015 (Fig. 1). This has placed Bangladesh among the top 10 remittance-receiving countries in the World (World Bank 2016).

The distribution of households in terms of the status of remittance receipt is shown in Fig. 2. It is evident that, in 2010, about 13% of the households received remittances, either from home or abroad.

In accordance with Fig. 2, Fig. 3 shows the distribution of the remittance-receiving households according to the types of remittances. About two-third of the remittance-receiving households received international remittance, while about 30% of the households received internal remittance. Thus, Fig. 3 depicts the relative importance of international remittance over internal remittance.

3.2 Region and Remittance Status

To serve our objective, we have analyzed specific statistics of working age population considering individuals living in remittance-receiving households as the

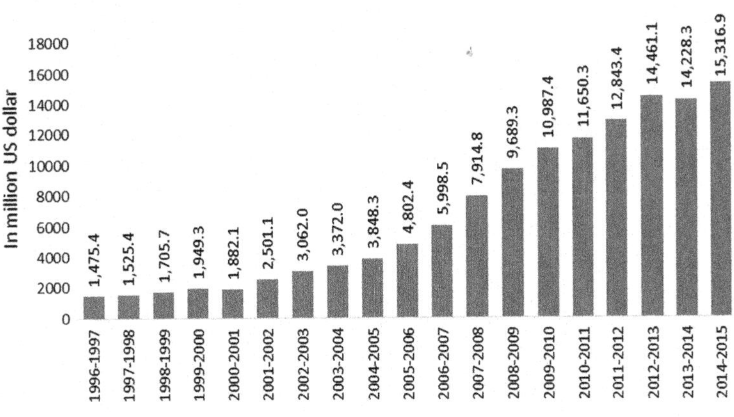

Fig. 1 Remittance sent by expatriate Bangladeshis. *Source* Bangladesh Bank

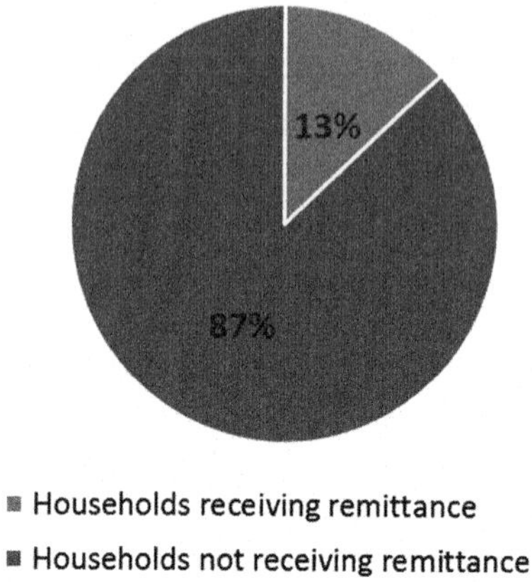

Fig. 2 Remittance status of households. *Source* HIES data, 2010

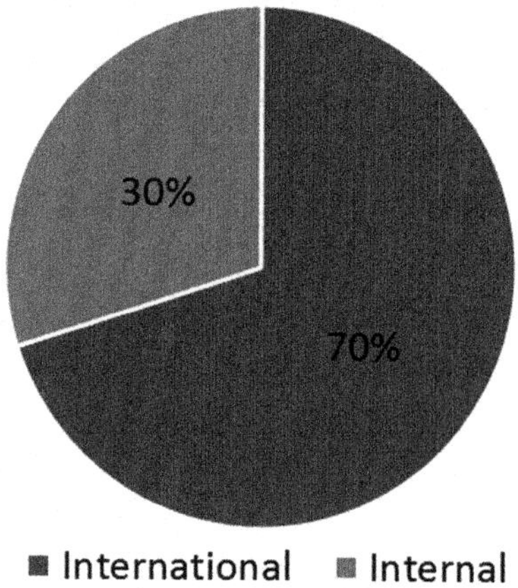

Fig. 3 Households by sources of remittance. *Source* HIES data, 2010

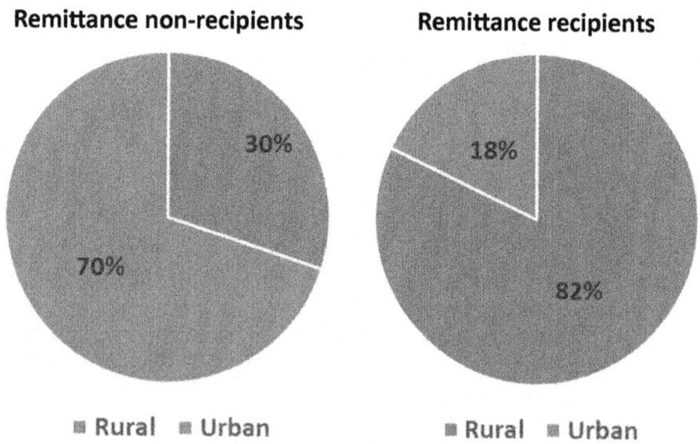

Fig. 4 Rural–urban scenario by remittance status. *Source* HIES data, 2010

remittance recipients. An important feature of remittances is that (Fig. 4) individuals from recipient households were predominantly geographically concentrated in the rural areas (about 82%) while other group was concentrated in the urban areas (about 70%).

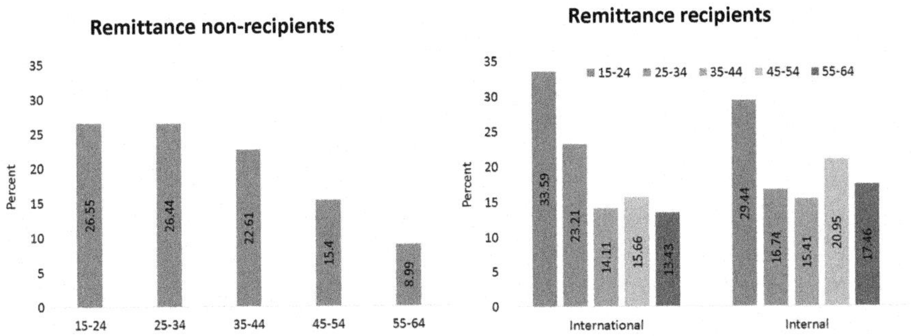

Fig. 5 Age distribution by remittance status and sources of remittance. *Source* HIES data, 2010

3.3 *Age Composition and Remittance Status*

Figure 5 shows that, in the case of individuals belonging to households not receiving remittance, a major portion was from the younger age categories. International remittance also shows a similar pattern with a higher concentration among younger age categories. However, internal remittance shows slightly different pattern. Individuals from internal remittance-receiving households were concentrated at both ends of age category; age groups between 25 and 44 had the lowest concentration.

3.4 *Labor Force Participation and Employment Type by Remittance Status*

Figure 6 represents labor force participation of the individuals from recipient households compared to non-recipient households. It is apparent that the labor force participation of the individuals from the remittance-receiving households was

Fig. 6 Participation in the labor force by remittance status. *Source* HIES data, 2010

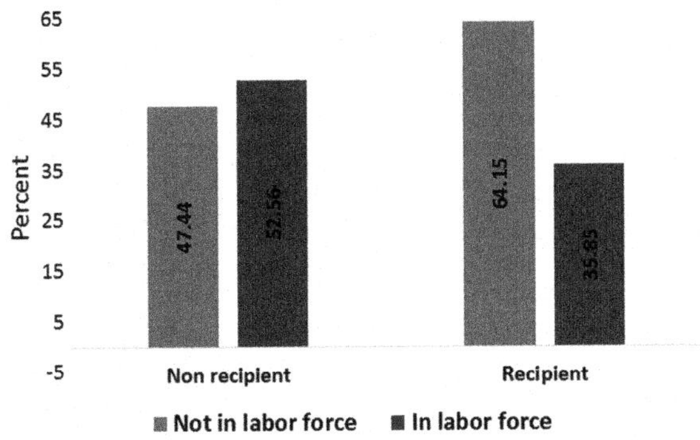

significantly lower than those from the non-remittance-receiving households in 2010. This drop in labor force participation can be explained as a resultant of income effect due to the inflow of remittance income that exceeds the out-migration effect of remittance-receiving households (Amuedo-Dorantes and Pozo 2006).

In Fig. 7, a similar comparison is made between international and internal remittances. About 65% of the individuals from international remittance-receiving households were out of the labor force, whereas this rate was about 60% in case of individuals who belonged to internal remittance recipient households.

Figure 8 shows a sharp contrast between labor market participations in agricultural and nonagricultural sectors. About 85% of the total individuals from remittance-receiving households were engaged in agricultural sector, whereas this rate is about 69% for individuals from the non-recipient households. It clearly shows that individuals from remittance-receiving households were more integrately occupied in the agricultural sector.

Figure 9 shows the labor force participation of the remittance-receiving households by the source of remittance. It is vibrantly evident that more than 80% of the individuals from the remittance-receiving households, for both internal and international remittances, were engaged in agricultural sector.

Figure 10 shows a sharp contrast in the employment status of recipient and non-recipient households. In 2010, agricultural sector was predominantly driven by

Fig. 7 Participation in the labor force by sources of remittance. *Source* HIES data, 2010

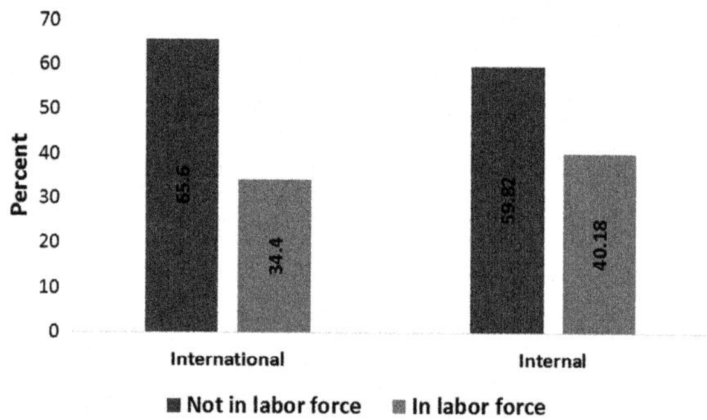

Fig. 8 Participation in agricultural and nonagricultural sectors by remittance status. *Source* HIES data, 2010

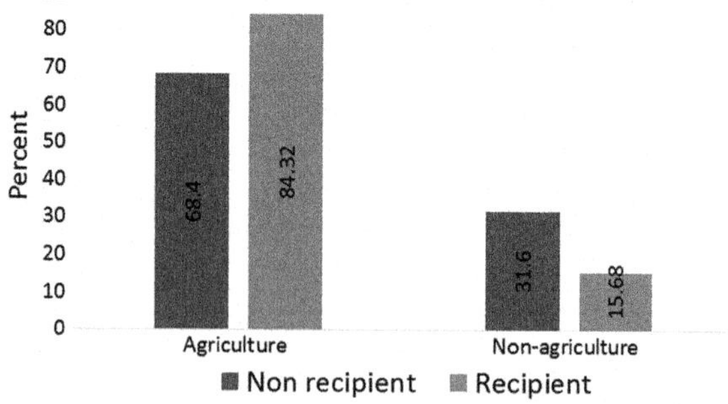

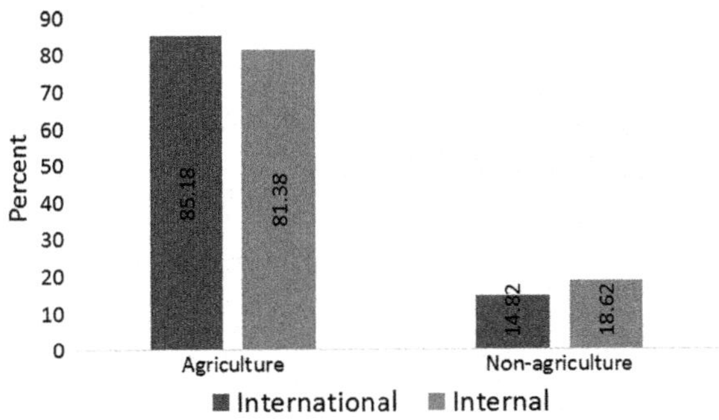

Fig. 9 Participation in agricultural and nonagricultural sectors by sources of remittance. *Source* HIES data, 2010

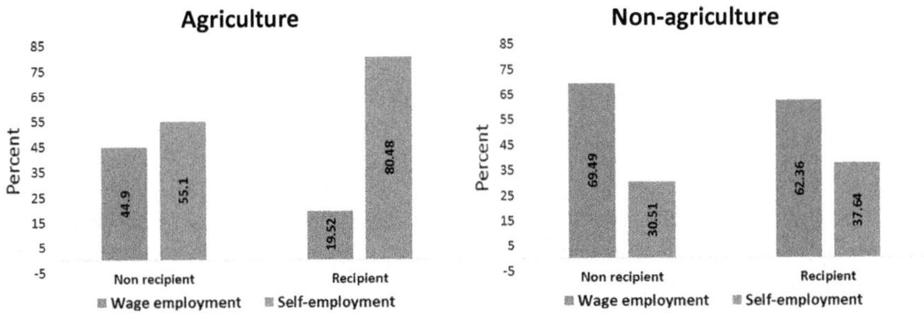

Fig. 10 Status of employment (self vs. wage) by remittance status. *Source* HIES data, 2010

self-employment whether or not participants belonged to remittance-receiving households. In contrast, nonagricultural sector was predominantly driven by wage employment irrespective of remittance status. However, the much larger predominance of self-employment in agriculture among the remittance recipients over their counterparts resembles the fact that, with additional income from remittance, individuals tend to purchase land and move towards self-employment. Similarly, in the case of nonagriculture, remittance helps to mobilize the required capital for self-employment. Therefore, it is seen from Fig. 10 that the ratio of self-employed to wage-employed among the remittance recipients is higher than that observed for the non-recipients.

Figure 11 suggests that if we consider international and internal remittances separately and compare between wage and self-employment, we find somewhat similar pattern of what is observed in Fig. 10. However, even with the predominance of self-employment, the relative importance of wage employment appears to be higher in the case of internal remittance than that of international remittance in agricultural sector. In nonagriculture, the relative importance of self-employment is greater in the case of international remittance than the internal one. This is primarily due to the fact that the amount of international remittance is much higher than the

Fig. 11 Employment status (self vs. wage) by sources of remittance. *Source* HIES data, 2010

internal one, and thus international remittance has a larger capital generating effect for self-employment.

3.5 *Education and Remittance Status*

Figure 12 depicts the differences in educational attainments between the individuals from remittance recipient and non-recipient households. No-education was more prevalent among individuals from non-recipient households compared to individuals belonging to remittance recipient households (both international and internal). 55% of the individuals belonging to international remittance recipient households had education level equivalent to secondary education or above. In case of internal remittance, this rate was 50%, whereas in case of individuals from non-recipient households, this rate was 45.5%. This suggests nothing but the fact that remittance

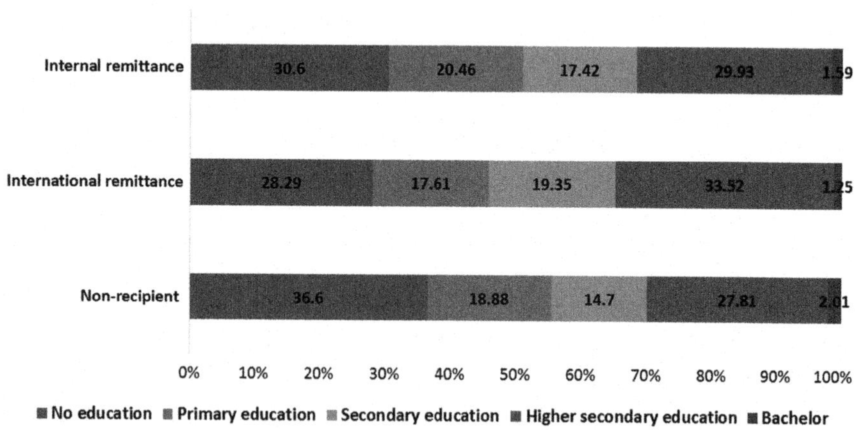

Fig. 12 Level of education by remittance status. *Source* HIES data, 2010

itself can play a role of 'push factor' in case of educational attainment which may further influence the labor market participation decision of those receiving remittance.

4 How Does Remittance Affect the Labor Force Participation (LFP) Behavior and Employment Choice? Insights from Econometric Exercises

To see the impact of remittances on the recipients in their labor market participation decision, we have used the Household Income and Expenditure Survey (HIES), 2010 data where there is a separate section for migration and household remittance information. We have categorized remittance recipients into two specific types based on the sources of remittance they are accruing from: recipient of international remittance and recipient of internal remittance. To see the objected impact of remittances, we first need to define the labor force. For simplicity, we followed the definition of labor force used by the HIES, 2010. According to the definition of HIES 2010, any individual aged 15 or more who have been seeking work during the past 7 days or is willing to work or is in work are considered in the labor force. The definition also includes persons who could not work during the last 7 days due to leave, illness or other issues, and excludes persons who are physically disabled or aged old.

After segregating labor force participants from persons not in labor force, we have separated the labor force participants (considering only the employed) into two categories (i) agriculture and (ii) nonagriculture. The categories are created for individual belonging to both the remittance recipient and non-recipient households. Further, we have segregated the labor force participants into two categories according to their employment status: (i) self-employed and (ii) wage-employed for both the agricultural and nonagricultural sectors.

As our objective is to see the impacts of remittances over (i) labor force participation decision (i.e., whether the recipient is in labor force or not), (ii) likeliness of sector employment (i.e., whether a person belonging to remittance recipient household prefers to engage in agriculture or nonagriculture sector), and (iii) over the employment status (i.e., whether the person receiving remittance is wage-employed or self-employed), our dependent variable is invariably dichotomous in nature. A possible and the easiest way to explore the narrated relationship is running an OLS regression which, in fact, will provide us with linear probability model (LPM) estimates. Despite its simple dexterity, a major drawback of LPM is that it does not guarantee the estimated probability to be constrained between 0 and 1. And, that is why we need to pursue a nonlinear maximum likelihood estimation. In this respect, the choice of logit or probit model depends upon the underlying assumption of the distribution of the error term. If the error term follows a logistic distribution, it is parsimonious to use a logit model. On the other hand, if the error term is assumed to follow a normal distribution, a probit model is suggested.

As stated above, we run following four probit regressions (assuming that the error term is identically and independently distributed with a normal distribution) where our dependent variables take the values as following in the respective equations:

Regression 1: The switch between not in LFP and LFP: 1 if the person is in labor force, 0 otherwise.

Regression 2: The switch between agricultural and nonagricultural sectors: 1 if the person is employed in nonagriculture, 0 if the person is employed in agriculture.

Regression 3: The switch between wage-employed and self-employed in agricultural sector: 1 if the person is self-employed in agriculture, 0 if the person is employed in wage-employed in agriculture.

Regression 4: The switch between wage-employed and self-employed in nonagricultural sector: 1 if the person is self-employed in nonagriculture, 0 if the person is wage-employed in nonagriculture.

To see the impacts of remittances over the objected dependent variables, we have considered dummy of international remittance recipient (1, if the individual belongs to a household that receives international remittances) and dummy of internal remittance recipient (1, if the individual belongs to a household that receives internal remittances) separately for each of the regressions. However, in all of these regressions, our common set of considered explanatory variables are, age, age square, size of the household, rural (dummy, 1 if rural), marital status (dummy, 1 if married), female (dummy, 1 if female), sex of the household head (dummy, 1 if the household head is a female), household income, years of schooling, and dependency ratio. Here, we have calculated the dependency ratio as the ratio of the number of children (0–14 years old) and older persons (65 years or over) to the working age population (15–64 years old) within a household.

4.1 Probit Model Estimation to Determine LFP and Not in LFP (Regression 1)

To observe the impacts of remittances over labor force participation decision we run two separate regressions. In the first regression (regression 1a), we estimated the impact of international remittances over labor force participation decision of the individuals who belong to international remittance-receiving households. The average marginal effects of the regression are presented in Table 1. The results suggest a strong but negative influence of international remittances over the LFP of individuals from recipient households. On an average, the probability of participating in labor force is 8.6 percentage points lower for the individuals from the international remittance-receiving households compared to the individuals from non-recipient households. On the other hand, in the second regression (regression 1b), we see the impacts of internal remittances over labor force participation decision, and we find

Table 1 Average marginal effects from probit regressions

Variables	Marginal effects of regression 1a	Marginal effects of regression 1b
International remittance	−0.086[a](0.007)	–
Internal remittance	–	−0.030[a](0.009)
Age	0.028[a](0.001)	0.029[a](0.001)
Age square	−0.00035[a](0.00001)	−0.00036[a](0.00001)
Household size	−0.003[a](0.001)	−0.004[a](0.001)
Rural dummy	−0.010[a](0.004)	−0.012[a](0.004)
Marital status	−0.015[a](0.005)	−0.020[a](0.005)
Dependency ratio	0.00001(0.00003)	−0.00001(0.00003)
Gender dummy	−0.493[a](0.001)	−0.494[a](0.001)
Household head gender dummy	0.087[a](0.006)	0.068[a](0.006)
Years of schooling	−0.006[a](0.000)	−0.007[a](0.000)
Household income	0.0000001[a](0.000000)	0.0000001[a](0.0000000)
Number of observations	32,810	32,810

Note a, b and c indicate statistical significance at the 1, 5 and 10 percent levels respectively. The figures in parentheses are standard errors

that internal remittance reduces the probability of a person from internal remittance-receiving household to be in labor force by 3 percentage points compared to the person from non-recipient household.

In both of the regressions, the impacts and magnitudes of age and age squared are quite similar and they suggest that the probability of participating in labor force increases at a decreasing rate with the increase in age. The impacts of rural dummy, marital status, and household size are found to have significant negative associations with labor force participation decision. The gender dummy shows that females have almost 50 percentage points lower probability of participation in the labor force. Gender of the household head, years of schooling, and household income are also found to be significant.

4.2 *Probit Model Estimation to Determine Agricultural Versus Nonagricultural Employment (Regression 2)*

In the second set of regressions, our objective is to observe the impact of remittances over the choice of occupational source: i.e., we want to see the role of remittances over the dynamics of choosing occupation in agriculture or nonagriculture.

Like the previous case, we run two regressions to see such dynamics where in the first regression (regression 2a), we see the impacts of international remittances and

Table 2 Average marginal effects from probit regressions

Variables	Marginal effects of regression 2a	Marginal effects of regression 2b
International remittance	−0.125[a](0.009)	–
Internal remittance	–	−0.047[a](0.012)
Age	0.030[a](0.001)	0.031[a](0.001)
Age square	0.0003814[a](0.0000140)	0.0003971[a](0.0000141)
Household size	−0.005[a](0.001)	−0.007[a](0.001)
Rural dummy	−0.144[a](0.004)	−0.145[a](0.004)
Marital status	0.006(0.006)	0.002(0.006)
Dependency ratio	0.0000275(0.0000396)	0.0000213(0.0000395)
Gender dummy	−0.403[a](0.003)	−0.406[a](0.003)
Household head gender dummy	0.110[a](0.008)	0.087[a](0.007)
Years of schooling	0.004[a](0.000)	0.004[a](0.000)
Household income	0.0000001[a](0.0000000)	0.0000001[a](0.0000000)
Number of observations	32,810	32,810

Note a, b and c indicate statistical significance at the 1, 5 and 10 percent levels respectively. The figures in parentheses are standard errors

in the second regression (regression 2b), we see the impacts of internal remittances. The results of average marginal effects for both of the regressions are presented in Table 2. The results suggest that individuals belonging to international remittance-receiving households compared to their counterparts have 12.5 percentage points higher probability to be engaged in the agricultural sector than nonagricultural sector. Although to a lesser extent, we see a similar impact in the case of internal remittance: individuals belonging to internal remittance-receiving households compared to their counterparts have almost 5 percentage points higher probability to be in the agricultural sector than nonagricultural sector. A possible explanation behind this shift could be that remittance-receiving households have higher tendency of purchasing lands with their remitted earnings than their counterparts. Like the previous case, age, age square, household size, gender dummy, household head's gender dummy, years of schooling, and household income are found to be significant in both regressions.

4.3 Probit Model to Determine the Agricultural Employment Status (Regression 3)

In the third set of regressions, our intention is to observe the impact of remittances over the employment status in the agricultural sector: i.e., how do remittances affect the employment choice between wage employment and self-employment in the agricultural sector. The average marginal effects of this set of regressions are shown in Table 3. The results of first regression (regression 3a) suggest that if a household receives international remittances, the probability of getting into self-employment for any individual from that household increases by 21 percentage points compared to the individuals from non-recipient households. In the case of internal remittances (regression 3b), the probability of an individual belonging to internal remittance-receiving household has 16 percentage points higher probability to be engaged in self-employment than wage employment compared to the individuals belonging to non-recipient households. The signs and significances of other major variables are found to be as expected for both regressions.

4.4 Probit Model to Determine the Nonagricultural Employment Status (Regression 4)

In the last set of regressions, our objective is to see the impact of remittances over the employment status in the nonagricultural sector: i.e., how do remittances affect the employment choice between wage employment and self-employment in the nonagricultural sector.

The average marginal effects from the probit regressions are depicted in Table 4. Unlike the previous sets of regressions, we find different impacts of international and domestic remittances over the employment status in the case of nonagricultural

Table 3 Average marginal effects from probit regressions for agricultural employment status

Variables	Marginal effects of regression 3a	Marginal effects of regression 3b
International remittance	0.206[a](0.029)	–
Internal remittance	–	0.160[a](0.035)
Age	0.013[a](0.003)	0.012[a](0.003)
Age square	−0.00007[c](0.00004)	−0.00006(0.00004)
Household size	0.040[a](0.004)	0.043[a](0.004)
Rural dummy	0.082[a](0.019)	0.082[a](0.019)
Marital status	−0.019(0.023)	−0.017(0.023)
Dependency ratio	−0.00052[a](0.00011)	−0.00053[a](0.00011)
Gender dummy	−0.027(0.026)	−0.036(0.026)
Household head gender dummy	−0.019(0.029)	0.006(0.029)
Years of schooling	0.035[a](0.002)	0.036[a](0.002)
Household income	0.0000001[c](0.0000001)	0.0000001(0.0000001)
Number of observations	5,257	5,257

Note a, b and c indicate statistical significance at the 1, 5 and 10 percent levels, respectively. The figures in parentheses are standard errors

Table 4 Average marginal effects from probit regressions for nonagricultural employment status

Variables	Marginal effects of regression 4a	Marginal effects of regression 4b
International remittance	0.131[a](0.021)	–
Internal remittance	–	−0.040(0.029)
Age	0.021[a](0.002)	0.021[a](0.002)
Age square	−0.00020[a](0.00003)	−0.00020[a](0.00003)
Household size	0.017[a](0.002)	0.018[a](0.002)
Rural dummy	0.032[a](0.009)	0.035[a](0.009)
Marital status	0.009(0.015)	0.008(0.015)
Dependency ratio	−0.00007(0.00009)	−0.00010(0.00009)
Gender dummy	−0.175[a](0.015)	−0.179[a](0.015)
Household head gender dummy	−0.092[a](0.019)	−0.081[a](0.019)
Years of schooling	−0.005[a](0.001)	−0.004[a](0.001)
Household income	0.0000001[b](0.0000000)	0.0000001[b](0.0000000)
Number of observations	10,386	10,386

Note a, b and c indicate statistical significance at the 1, 5 and 10 percent levels respectively. The figures in parentheses are standard errors

sector. The probability of an individual belonging to international remittance recipient household to be in self-employment is 13 percentage points higher than an individual from non-recipient household (regression 4a). On the contrary, average marginal effect of internal remittance (regression 4b) is found to be insignificant. This result stylizes nothing but the fact that international remittances play a different role than the internal remittances in the case of self-employment in nonagricultural sector. In fact, self-employment in nonagricultural sector requires more seed capital than self-employment in agricultural sector. Hence, although internal remittances can play a role in the case of agricultural sector to shift an individual from wage employment to self-employment, its efficacy in the case of nonagricultural sector is found to be the opposite.

5 Conclusion

International remittance is an increasingly growing external financial source for Bangladesh. The issue of migration and remittance in Bangladesh is mainly motivated by the search for generating substantial welfare gains and increasing employment opportunities that can play an important role in poverty reduction. Our study has revealed two distinctive findings. First, despite its poverty-reducing effect, remittances can lead to some depressing effect on labor force participation, as individuals from remittance recipient households tend to have less incentive to participate in the labor market. Secondly, remittance has a significant impact over switching individuals from nonagriculture sector to agriculture sector. This may result from the remittance-receiving household's preference for purchasing land with the remitted earnings. Finally, international remittance leads to a transition from wage employment to self-employment significantly, and this may be due to the availability of more investment capital which is essential for setting up own business in nonagricultural and agricultural activities (i.e., poultry farm, fishing, etc.).

Migration is seen as an important element in the process of development. The first finding of our exercise does not suggest migration to be discouraged. In contrast, migration needs to be promoted in a way that cam persuade households with migrants to get involved in better economic activities. Policies can therefore be addressed aiming at the creation of additional economic opportunities that motivate households with migrant to develop entrepreneurship and to reallocate flow of remittance more towards the productive channel.

References

Acosta, P. (2006). *Labor supply, school attendance, and remittances from international migration: The case of El Salvador.* World Bank Policy Research Working Paper 3903, World Bank.

Amuedo-Dorantes, C., & Pozo, S. (2006). Migration, remittances, and male and female employment patterns. *The American Economic Review, 96*(2), 222–226.

Böhme, M. (2013). *Does migration raise agricultural investment?—An empirical analysis for rural Mexico.* Kiel Working Paper No. 1840.

De Hass, H. (2006). Migration, remittances and regional development in southern Morocco. *Geoforum, 37*(4), 565–580.

Epo, B. N., & Baye, F. M. (2013). Implications of farm–non-farm population shifts for household poverty changes in Cameroon. *African Journal of Agricultural and Resource Economics (AfJARE), chap. I, 8*(2).

Funkhouser, E. (1992). Migration from Nicaragua: Some recent evidence. *World Development, 20,* 1209–1218.

Görlich, D., Mahmoud, T. O., & Trebesch, C. (2007). *Explaining labour market inactivity in migrant-sending families: Housework, hammock, or higher education.* Kiel Working Paper Series No. 1391, Kiel.

Jadotte, E. (2009). *International migration, remittances and labour supply: The case of the Republic of Haiti.* Research Paper No. 2009/28, UNU-WIDER (United Nations University, World institute for Development Economics Result).

Justino, P., & Shemyakina, O. N. (2012). *Remittances and labour supply in post-conflict Tajikistan* (Working paper Vol. 2012, No. 388). London: Institute of Development Studies.

Khondker, B., & Raihan, S. (2009). poverty impacts of remittances and garments: A computable general equilibrium analysis. In A. Narayan, & H. Zaman, *Breaking down poverty in Bangladesh* (Chap. 4). Dhaka: The University Press Limited.

Narazani, E. (2009). *Labour supply, remittances and the new flat tax in Albania.* Southeast Europe: Global Development Network.

Ndiaye, A. S., Niang, O. K., Ndione, Y. C., & Dedehouanou, S. E. (2015). *Migration, remittances, labor market and human capital in Senegal.* Working Paper, Partnership for Economic Policy (PEP).

Raihan, S., & Sugiyarto, G. (2012). Effects of global crisis on remittances and poverty: The case study on Bangladesh. In *Remittances and poverty in Asia* (Chap. 4, ADB monograph on Global Crisis). Manila: Asian Development Bank.

Raihan, S., & Uddin, H. (2011). Bangladesh: migration, remittances, and development. In S. Kelegama (Ed.), *Migration*. Remittances and Development in South Asia, New Delhi: SAGE Publications Pvt. Ltd.

Raihan, S., Khondker, B., Sugiyarto, G., & Jha, S. (2009). *Remittances and household welfare: A case study of Bangladesh*. ADB Economics Working Paper Series No. 189, Manila: Asian Development Bank.

Raihan, S., Siddiqui, T., & Mahmood, R. (2014). *Estimating the impact of international remittance on households' expenditure in Bangladesh*. Presented at the seminar organized by RMMRU. Dhaka.

Rodriguez, E., & Tiongson, E. (2001). Temporary migration overseas and household labor supply: Evidence from urban Philippines. *International Migration Review, 35*(3), 709–725.

Schumann, N. (2013). *Differential labor supply response to remittances with respect to human capital*. Center for International and Comparative Studies (CIS), University of Zurich.

World Bank. (2016). *Migration and remittance factbook*. World Bank.

Backward and Forward Linkages in the Bangladesh Economy: Application of the Social Accounting Matrix Framework

Bazlul H. Khondker

1 Introduction

A Social Accounting Matrix (SAM) is a generalization of the production relations and extends this information beyond the structure of production to include: (a) the distribution of value added to institutions generated by production activities; (b) formation of household and institutional income; (c) the pattern of consumption, savings, and investment; (d) government revenue collection and associated expenditures and transactions; and (e) the role of the foreign sector in the formation of additional incomes for households and institutions. In particular, the accounting matrix of a SAM identifies the economic relations through six accounts: (1) total domestic supply of commodities; (2) activity accounts for producing sectors; (3) main factors of productions (e.g., labor types and capital); (4) current account transactions between main institutional agents such as households and unincorporated enterprises, corporate enterprises, government and the rest of the world, and the use of income by the representative households; (5) the rest of the world; and (6) one consolidated capital account (domestic and rest of the world) to capture the flows of savings and investment by institutions and the rest of the world, respectively.

Social accounting matrices can serve two basic purposes: (i) as a comprehensive and consistent data system for descriptive analysis of the structure of the economy;

This chapter contains some excerpts from the author's previous publication as a working paper (see: https://mpra.ub.uni-muenchen.de/41231/1/MPRA_paper_41231.pdf).

B. H. Khondker (✉)
Department of Economics, University of Dhaka, Dhaka, Bangladesh
e-mail: bazlul.khondker@gmail.com

B. H. Khondker
South Asian Network on Economic Modeling (SANEM), Dhaka, Bangladesh

S. Raihan (ed.), *Structural Change and Dynamics of Labor Markets in Bangladesh*, South Asia Economic and Policy Studies,
https://doi.org/10.1007/978-981-13-2071-2_12

and (ii) as a basis for macroeconomic modeling. As a data framework, a SAM is a snapshot of a country at a point in time (Pyatt and Thorbecke 1976). To provide as a comprehensive picture of the structure of the economy, a particular novelty of the SAM approach is that, it brings together macroeconomic data (such as national accounts) and microeconomic data (such as household surveys) within a consistent framework. The second purpose of a SAM is the provision of a macroeconomic data framework for policy modeling. The framework of a SAM can often help in establishing the sequence of interactions between agents and accounts which are being modeled. A SAM provides an excellent framework for exploring both macroeconomic and multi-sectoral issues and is a useful starting point for more complex models (Robinson 1989).

Against this backdrop, this study produces an updated SAM for Bangladesh for 2012 using the newly constructed Input-Output Table 2012, which supplemented with institutional accounts, macroeconomic aggregates, and the Household Income and Expenditure Survey. Using the updated SAM, this study develops the SAM multiplier model and explores the growth impact of injection into selected activities in the economy through that multiplier model.

2 Bangladesh Social Accounting Matrix (SAM) 2012

The 2012 SAM identifies the economic relations through *four types of accounts*: (i) production activity and commodity accounts for the 86 sectors; (ii) 4 factors of productions with 2 different types of labor and 2 types of capital; (iii) current account transactions among the 4 main institutional agents; household members and unincorporated capital, corporation, government and the rest of the world; and (iv) two consolidated capital accounts distinguished by public and private origins to capture the flows of savings and investment. The disaggregation of activities, commodities, factors, and institutions in the SAM is given in Table 1.

The year 2012 was chosen as the base year to update/construct the Bangladesh SAM as most of data of the key components of activity-commodity and institutional accounts are available for the year 2012. Moreover, the newly constructed input–output table is also available for 2012 reflecting the consistent activity-commodity accounts for 2012. The consistent activity-commodity accounts then formed the basis from which the factors and institutional accounts were disaggregated to derive the Bangladesh SAM 2012.

The construction of 2012 SAM is based on several data sets drawn from diverse sources. They are listed below.

1. The Input–Output Table 2012 for Bangladesh; Prepared as a background document for the technical frame for the 75th Year Plan.
2. Social Accounting Matrix for Bangladesh for 2006/07; General Economics Division, Bangladesh Planning Commission.

Table 1 Disaggregation and description of Bangladesh SAM accounts

Set	Description of elements
Activities (86)	
Agriculture (20)	Paddy cultivation, wheat cultivation, other grain cultivation, jute cultivation, sugarcane cultivation, potato cultivation, vegetable cultivation, pulses cultivation, oilseed cultivation, fruit cultivation, cotton cultivation, tobacco cultivation, tea cultivation, spice cultivation, other crop cultivation, livestock rearing, poultry rearing, shrimp farming, fishing, forestry
Mining and quarrying (01)	Mining and quarrying
Manufacturing (39)	Rice milling, grain milling, fish process, oil industry, sweetener industry, tea product, salt refining, food process, tanning and finishing, leather industry, baling, jute fabrication, yarn industry, cloth milling, handloom cloth, dyeing and bleaching, woven, knitting, toiletries, cigarette industry, bidi industry, wood and cork product, furniture industry, paper industry, printing and publishing, pharmaceuticals, fertilizer industry, basic chemical, petroleum refinery, earthware industry, plastic products, glass industry, clay industry, cement, basic metal, metal, machinery and equipment, transport equipment, miscellaneous industry
Construction (04)	Building, kutcha house, agriculture construction and other construction
Electricity, gas and water supply (03)	Electricity, water generation, gas extraction and distribution
Trade and transport (07)	Wholesale trade, retail trade, air transport, water transport, land transport, railway transport, other transport,
Services (12)	Housing and real estate service, health service, education service, public administration and defense, bank and other financial services, insurance, professional service, entertainment, hotel and restaurant, communication, other services, ICT
Commodities (86)	
Agriculture (20)	Paddy cultivation, wheat cultivation, other grain cultivation, jute cultivation, sugarcane cultivation, potato cultivation, vegetable cultivation, pulses cultivation, oilseed cultivation, fruit cultivation, cotton cultivation, tobacco cultivation, tea cultivation, spice cultivation, other crop cultivation, livestock rearing, poultry rearing, shrimp farming, fishing, forestry
Mining and Quarrying (01)	Mining and quarrying
Manufacturing (39)	Rice milling, grain milling, fish process, oil industry, sweetener industry, tea product, salt refining, food process, tanning and finishing, leather industry, baling, jute fabrication, yarn industry, cloth milling, handloom cloth, dyeing and bleaching, woven, knitting, toiletries, cigarette industry, bidi industry, wood and cork product, furniture industry, paper industry, printing and publishing, pharmaceuticals, fertilizer industry, basic chemical, petroleum refinery, earthware industry, plastic products, glass industry, clay industry, cement, basic metal, metal, machinery and equipment, transport equipment, miscellaneous industry

(continued)

Table 1 (continued)

Set	Description of elements
Construction (04)	Building, kutcha house, agriculture construction and other construction
Electricity, gas and water supply (03)	Electricity, water generation, gas extraction and distribution
Trade and transport (07)	Wholesale trade, retail trade, air transport, water transport, land transport, railway transport, other transport,
Services (12)	Housing and real estate service, health service, education service, public administration and defense, bank and other financial services, insurance, professional service, entertainment, hotel and restaurant, communication, other services, ICT
Factors of production (4)	
Labor (2)	Labor unskilled, and labor skilled
Capital (2)	Capital and land
Current institutions (11)	
Households (8)	Rural: landless, agricultural marginal, agricultural small, agricultural large, nonfarm poor and nonfarm nonpoor Urban: households with low educated heads, and households with high educated heads
Others (3)	Government, corporation and rest of the world
Capital institution (1)	
Capital	

Source Author's compilation

3. BBS (2010), Household Income and Expenditure Survey, 2010.
4. Ministry of Finance, Economic Survey of Bangladesh (GoB 2014).

The updating/construction of the SAM proceeded in two steps. In the first step, a "proto-SAM" was constructed using the data collected from diverse sources. Since the data came from different sources as well as for different years, in line with the expectation, the estimated "proto-SAM" was unbalanced. In the second step, the SAM was balanced by adjusting the activity and commodity (i.e., private consumption, intermediate demand vectors) accounts as explained below.

The updating of a SAM is not only an exercise in putting together a complete data set, but also an estimation process on the basis of insufficient and partly inconsistent data. In this current exercise, the first step to generate a consistent and balanced SAM is to build a macroeconomic SAM (i.e., the Macro SAM). The main objective of the Macro SAM is to summarize and to show the circular flow in the economy, in general, and interdependence between commodity, activity, consumption, and flow-of-fund accounts without sectoral or institutional details. Thus, in the second step, a preliminary disaggregated SAM (which is also referred to as the Micro SAM) is constructed using available disaggregated information drawn

Table 2 Bangladesh Macro SAM 2012 (Billion Taka)

SAM Accounts	SNA Accounts	Code		ACT	COM	Factors					
				1	2	3					
						Labor	Capital	Land	Indirect tax	M duty	P subsidy
Activity A/C	Activities	1		0	18,080						
Production A/C	Commodities	2		9,212							
Distribution of primary income	Income generation by Institutions	3	Compensation to employees	4,457							
			Operating surplus	3,672							
			Land return	516							
			Indirect tax	346							
			Import duty		314						
			Production subsidy	−58							
			Export subsidy	−65							
Use of Income	Primary income of Institutions	4	Household			4,457	2,807	516			
			Government						346	314	−58
			Corporation				864				
Consolidated capital AC	Capital Account	5	Capital								
			Inventory								
Rest of world	Rest of the world-imports (current)	6			2949						
Total expenditure A/C				18,080	21,343	4,457	3,672	516	346	314	−58
SAM Accounts	SNA Accounts	Code			Domestic Institutions			Capital		RoW	Total income
					4			5		6	
				E subsidy	Household	Government	Corporation	Capital	Inventory		
Activity A/C	Activities	1									18,080
Production A/C	Commodities	2			6,980	513		2,437	73	2,127	21,343

(continued)

Table 2 (continued)

SAM Accounts	SNA Accounts	Code		ACT	COM	Factors					
				1	2	3					
						Labor	Capital	Land	Indirect tax	M duty	P subsidy
Distribution of primary income	Income generation by Institutions	3	Compensation to employees								4,457
			Operating surplus								3,672
			Land return								516
			Indirect tax								346
			Import duty								314
			Production subsidy								−58
			Export subsidy								−65
Use of Income	Primary income of Institutions	4	Household			470				1,016	9,266
			Government	−65	141		337				1,015
			Corporation			3					867
Consolidated capital AC	Capital Account	5	Capital		2,144	30	530			−194	2,510
			Inventory					73			73
Rest of world	Rest of the world-imports (current)	6									2,949
Total expenditure A/C				−65	9,266	1,015	867	2,510	73	2,949	

Note Based on the SNA-SAM Relationship
Source Author's compilation

from various data producing agencies. Subject to data availability, the disaggregated SAM segregates most of the Macro SAM accounts to desired sectoral and institutional breakdowns. While ensuring balance between the receipts and outlays for all accounts, the disaggregated or micro SAM must reproduce the control totals of the macro SAM. The correspondence between accounts of the aggregated micro SAM and macro SAM thus ensure its desired consistency with the national account data.

The complete Macro SAM for 2012 containing the national accounts and other data including transfers, taxes, and foreign transactions are shown in Table 2. The Bangladesh macro SAM is "anchored" primarily to the "Input-Output Table 2012", "National Accounts" data and other macroaggregates. The distribution of labor value added to households and capital value-added channeled through the enterprise account is derived from information contained in the SAM 2000. Savings of households and enterprises have been adjusted to fulfill the macroeconomic balance of the SAM. Government savings are computed as the difference between total government receipts and total government spending.

3 SAM Accounting Multipliers: Modeling and Analysis

3.1 Determination of the Endogenous and Exogenous Accounts

A social accounting matrix has the principal objective of providing the statistical basis for creating a plausible model in order to analyze how the economy works and predict the effects of policy interventions in order to change it. The move from the SAM structure to a model structure requires that accounts of this matrix be separated into *endogenous and exogenous accounts*. The need for this arises from the fact that there must be an entry into the system, i.e., some variables must be manipulated exogenously via injections in order to evaluate the consequences on the endogenous accounts. In general, the following criteria may be applied to separate SAM accounts into endogenous and exogenous (Alarcon 2000).

Endogenous accounts:

- accounts *a priory* specified as objectives or targets when the SAM was built must be made endogenous.

Exogenous accounts:

- accounts intended to be used as policy instruments must be made exogenous;
- accounts beyond the control of domestic institutions should be made exogenous, e.g., the rest of the world current and capital accounts. This is consistent with the "small economy" assumptions;
- accounts determined outside the system must be made exogenous;

- accounts, which do not exert effects over other accounts within the time horizon under consideration should be made exogenous, e.g., in the short-term, the capital accounts of all accounts. This criterion is consistent with the existence of idle capacity in the economy.

Following the above criteria, a selection has been made for the endogenous and exogenous accounts for Bangladesh SAM case.

(a) The following four accounts have been selected as *endogenous accounts*: Production Activities account (i.e., activity account and commodity account), Factors of Production account, and Households account.
(b) Government account is made *exogenous* because it serves as policy instrument (e.g., government transfers, direct tax, government expenditures, etc.)
(c) Since the rest of the world account and the consolidated capital account are beyond the control of the domestic economy and Bangladesh is a small country, they have been considered as *exogenous accounts*. Corporations have been designated as an *exogenous account.*

3.2 Underlying Assumptions

The assumptions of the SAM model are as follows (Alarcon 2000):

(a) the "average propensities to spend", i.e., the ratios between the particular expenditures and the total expenditure belonging to the same account, are fixed and linear;
(b) the "average propensities to spend" are valued at constant prices, further they are considered stable over the short-to-medium term;
(c) the expenditure shares within each defined expenditure account (the equivalent of the constant market shares in I-O) remain (approximately) constant over time;
(d) price relatives are constant over the time horizon of the model, usually the short-term. This implies that the components which make up any account bunch have substitution elasticities which are zero across accounts and infinite within accounts, i.e., they are homogenous within and heterogeneous across accounts;
(e) expenditure-income elasticities are constant for the fixed-price model, while they are constant and equal to unity for the accounting multiplier model;
(f) there is perfect complementarity between capital and other factor inputs (capital, labor, and land);
(g) the economy has idle capacity utilization, and
(h) a number of accounts are exogenous.

3.3 SAM Accounting Multiplier

For any given injection into the exogenous accounts of the SAM, influence is transmitted through the interdependent SAM system among the endogenous accounts (c.f. *Flow Chart 1*). The interwoven nature of the system implies that the incomes of factors, institutions, and production are all derived from exogenous injections into the economy via a multiplier process. The multiplier process is developed here on the assumption that when an endogenous income account receives an exogenous expenditure injection, it spends it in the same proportions as shown in the matrix of average propensities to spend (APS). The elements of the APS matrix is calculated by dividing each cell by its corresponding column sum totals.

The multiplier analysis using the SAM framework helps us in understanding further the linkages between the different sectors and the institutional agents at work within the economy. Accounting multipliers have been calculated according to the standard formula for accounting (impact) multipliers are as follows:

$$y = A * y + x = (I - A)^{-1} * x = Ma * x$$

where

y—vector of endogenous variables
x—vector of exogenous variables
A—matrix of average propensities of expenditures for endogenous accounts
$Ma = (I - A)^{-1}$ = matrix of aggregate accounting multipliers (or the generalized Leontief inverse).

Since the present multiplier framework has four endogenous accounts, for each account in the SAM, we can calculate four types of multiplier measures:

(1) The activity or gross output multiplier, which indicates the total effect on sectoral gross output of a unit-income increase in a given account *i* in the SAM, is obtained by adding the activity elements in the matrix along the column for account *i*.
(2) The value added or GDP multiplier, giving the total increase in GDP resulting from the same unit-income injection, is derived by summing up the factor-payment elements along account *i*'s column.
(3) The basic need multiplier, showing the total increase in the consumption of basic needs resulting from the unit-income injection, is obtained by summing up the basic need elements along the column of account *i*.
(4) Household income multiplier shows the total effect on household income and is obtained by adding the elements for the household group along account *i*'s column.

3.4 Backward and Forward Linkages (Total and Partial)

Each of the columns of the matrix of accounting multipliers, as indicated before, show the effects of each corresponding exogenous injection on the incomes of endogenous accounts. Analogously to the I-O model, the sum total of a column or a row can be calculated and they will be equivalent to the backward and forward income or expenditure linkages. In SAM models within account, sums of columns or rows are calculated for each of the four endogenous accounts as well as the total column and row sums of all the endogenous accounts taken together. The former can be called "partial backward or forward linkages" or within account backward or forward linkages and the latter "total backward or forward linkages". As shown in the earlier section, partial backward linkages can also be named after their corresponding account multipliers such as backward and forward linkages for activity, factors, households and basic needs.[1] Therefore, in conclusion, we can say that the basic idea of backward linkages is to trace the output increases which occur in *supplying* sectors or accounts when there is a change in the sector or account using their outputs as inputs, and just as with forward linkages, we trace the output increases which occur or might occur in *using* industries or accounts when there is a change in the sector or account supplying inputs (Bulmer-Thomas 1982).

Within the SAM context given an exogenous injection into the system (e.g., government expenditure on education activity), the first effect will be to increase income of the corresponding account (i.e., activity), in turn the increase will trigger off effects on the incomes of all other endogenous accounts (i.e., factors, households, etc., the sum of all these effects constitutes its total backward linkage.

4 Growth Impact of Injection into Selected Activities

4.1 Selection of Activities

The injection may be viewed as an exogenous increase in the demand, e.g., exports; government expenditures, and inventory. For analytical purpose, some particular activities were selected to assess the multipliers and backward linkages to prioritize among the activities in order to attain the highest possible growth impact of equivalent alternative intervention. In this analysis, we have selected four activities such as *Rice Milling, Education, Ready-Made Garments, and Construction.* The

[1]The interpretation of partial (within account) backward and forward linkages within a SAM framework is also similar to that of I-O models. Although the sum of all the elements, in any column (row) of the accounting multipliers matrix, could be read as the backward (forward) linkages of the expenditure-injection multipliers, the interpretation in SAM is not so straight forward because the linkages are composites of the effects of several kinds of accounts.

Table 3 Impact analysis of injection into some selected activities in 2012

Multipliers	Rice milling	Education	Ready-made garments	Construction
Gross output multiplier	**4.203**	**3.300**	**3.213**	**3.531**
Commodity multiplier	3.609	2.666	3.724	2.950
GDP multiplier	1.873	1.873	1.523	1.590
Household income multiplier	1.729	1.733	1.370	1.421
Total backward linkage	**11.415**	**9.571**	**9.830**	**9.492**

Source SAM multiplier analysis

selection was based on criteria like high backward linkages, export-orientation, human capital improvements, and infrastructure development.

The overall impact on all accounts added together (known as total backward linkage); due to a unit injection into Rice Milling, Education, Ready-Made Garments and Construction are 11.415, 9.571, 9.83, and 9.492, respectively, (Table 3). In other words, a unit injection into Rice Milling yields 11.415 units of income in the economy and the same implication holds for other three activities. The decomposition of the total backward linkages into the four "within endogenous" accounts is discussed below.

The impact on all production accounts for the four selected sectors as measured by the Gross Output Multiplier are 4.203 units, 3.300 units, 3.213 units, and 3.531 units, respectively. It is observed that gross output multipliers are the highest backward linkages among all the four multipliers. This is due to the fact that production activities have to meet the increase in final demand as well as intermediate demand. This dual impulse for the production activity accounts translates into the highest values of the gross output multipliers.

The composition of Gross Output backward Linkage for each of the four selected sectors and by the 86 sectors is presented in Table 4. Among all activities, the Rice Milling sector is relatively strongly integrated with sectors such as Paddy (0.986), Trade (0.43), and Transport (0.23). The sectors, which are relatively better integrated with the Education sector, are Other services (0.30), Rice Milling (0.25), Trade (0.24), Transport (0.16), and Housing (0.15). The Ready-Made Garment sector has the lowest BL among the four selected sectors because of its high import intensity in production. Like other two sectors, Ready-Made Garment sector is also relatively better integrated with Trade (0.28), Rice Milling (0.20), Cloth-Milling Yarn (0.12), and Transport sectors (0.17). Similar integration pattern is also observed for Construction.

Table 4 also shows that the sectors which are strongly associated with *Construction* sector are *Trade* (0.29), other services (0.28), *Rice-Milling* (0.21), and *Transport* (0.16). This reveals the fact that rice, which is provided by the

Table 4 Impact analysis of injection into the four selected sectors on all the activities in 2012

Activities	Rice milling	Education	Ready-made garments	Construction
Paddy cultivation	0.98519	0.20072	0.16585	0.17256
Wheat cultivation	0.00586	0.00584	0.00469	0.00485
Other grain cultivation	0.00764	0.00754	0.00615	0.00629
Jute cultivation	0.00159	0.00160	0.00216	0.00129
Sugarcane cultivation	0.00388	0.00380	0.00310	0.00319
Potato cultivation	0.02316	0.02251	0.01842	0.01912
Vegetable cultivation	0.01647	0.01601	0.01310	0.01360
Pulses cultivation	0.00420	0.00416	0.00336	0.00347
Oilseed cultivation	0.00499	0.00492	0.00397	0.00409
Fruit cultivation	0.01804	0.01791	0.01438	0.01485
Cotton cultivation	0.00003	0.00004	0.00026	0.00003
Tobacco cultivation	0.00114	0.00111	0.00091	0.00094
Tea cultivation	0.00161	0.00157	0.00131	0.00133
Spice cultivation	0.01771	0.01730	0.01435	0.01464
Other crop cultivation	0.00576	0.00659	0.00427	0.00443
Livestock rearing	0.04642	0.03967	0.03204	0.03308
Poultry rearing	0.05941	0.05863	0.04781	0.04891
Shrimp farming	0.02463	0.02465	0.02020	0.02053
Fishing	0.07500	0.07373	0.05983	0.06199
Forestry	0.02662	0.02406	0.02022	0.08780
Rice milling	1.26170	0.24951	0.20636	0.21477
Grain milling	0.03178	0.03155	0.02546	0.02635
Fish process	0.00322	0.00321	0.00257	0.00266
Oil Industry	0.02083	0.02070	0.01664	0.01721
Sweetener industry	0.00800	0.00790	0.00633	0.00654
Tea product	0.00098	0.00096	0.00080	0.00081
Salt refining	0.00141	0.00183	0.00113	0.00116
Food process	0.02594	0.02667	0.02084	0.02157
Tanning and finishing	0.00630	0.00627	0.00504	0.00528
Leather industry	0.01490	0.01484	0.01192	0.01248
Baling	0.00004	0.00006	0.00039	0.00004
Jute fabrication	0.00003	0.00003	0.00003	0.00004
Yarn industry	0.00218	0.00267	0.01734	0.00182
Cloth milling	0.00555	0.00989	0.09839	0.00474
Handloom cloth	0.04036	0.04047	0.03235	0.03343
Dyeing and bleaching	0.00494	0.00495	0.00396	0.00409
RMG	0.00420	0.00410	1.00390	0.00339
Knitting	0.00220	0.00216	0.00202	0.00181
Toiletries M	0.00235	0.00336	0.00204	0.00256

(continued)

Table 4 (continued)

Activities	Rice milling	Education	Ready-made garments	Construction
Cigarette industry	0.03741	0.03629	0.02969	0.03084
Bidi industry	0.00287	0.00262	0.00222	0.00233
Wood and cork product	0.01191	0.00700	0.00588	0.01033
Furniture industry	0.00854	0.00835	0.00672	0.00701
Paper industry	0.00433	0.00378	0.00422	0.00382
Printing and publishing	0.00874	0.00685	0.00489	0.00595
Pharmaceuticals	0.02740	0.07351	0.02233	0.02310
Fertilizer industry	0.03438	0.00942	0.00774	0.00810
Basic chemical	0.00136	0.00182	0.00114	0.00348
Petroleum R	0.02371	0.02286	0.02036	0.01907
Earth ware industry	0.00196	0.00197	0.00157	0.00168
Plastic products	0.00502	0.00511	0.00406	0.00737
Glass industry	0.00148	0.00139	0.00115	0.00227
Clay industry	0.00013	0.00014	0.00019	0.01126
Cement M	0.00036	0.00040	0.00047	0.06705
Basic metal M	0.00816	0.00789	0.01124	0.23991
Metal M	0.00596	0.00514	0.01241	0.02598
Machinery and equipment	0.00754	0.00464	0.00402	0.00525
Transport equipment	0.00298	0.00249	0.00301	0.00232
Miscellaneous industry	0.00767	0.00774	0.00691	0.00719
Building	0.00293	0.00336	0.00303	1.00415
Kutcha house	0.00216	0.00245	0.00198	0.00308
Agriculture construction	0.00000	0.00000	0.00000	0.00000
Other construction	0.00369	0.00254	0.00463	0.00261
Electricity generation	0.01628	0.02091	0.03570	0.01636
Water generation	0.00138	0.00188	0.00151	0.00142
Gas extraction and distribution	0.00586	0.00715	0.01630	0.00643
Mining and quarrying	0.00479	0.00514	0.00613	0.04289
Wholesale trade	0.16337	0.09420	0.10768	0.10838
Retail trade	0.26532	0.15120	0.17415	0.17540
Air transport	0.00175	0.00175	0.00136	0.00143
Water transport	0.01321	0.00911	0.02234	0.00935
Land transport	0.23468	0.15910	0.27403	0.16447
Railway transport	0.00201	0.00135	0.00381	0.00140
Other transport	0.00613	0.00564	0.00690	0.00531
Housing and real estate service	0.12849	0.15040	0.13939	0.12017
Health service	0.05460	0.05325	0.04711	0.04631
Education service	0.03877	1.04005	0.03125	0.03210

(continued)

Table 4 (continued)

Activities	Rice milling	Education	Ready-made garments	Construction
Public administration and defense	0.01295	0.01008	0.02002	0.02223
Bank and other financial services	0.02745	0.03164	0.04292	0.04179
Insurance	0.00604	0.00787	0.01044	0.01485
Professional service	0.00103	0.00087	0.00177	0.00139
Hotel and restaurant	0.03994	0.03891	0.03422	0.03299
Entertainment	0.00567	0.00568	0.00449	0.00463
Communication	0.01793	0.02097	0.02232	0.03050
Other services	0.17830	0.30046	0.17078	0.27874
Information technology and e-commerce	0.00062	0.00068	0.00085	0.00082
Total gross output multiplier	**4.203**	**3.300**	**3.213**	**3.531**

Source SAM multiplier analysis

Rice-Milling sector, is a major component of the basic food consumption. On the other hand, almost all the sectors use the products of the *Trade* and *Transports* sectors. Therefore, these three sectors are better integrated into the system. Other services, which encompass variety of services, also emerged as a better integrated sectors to other sectors of the economy.

The generations of factor income, as measured by the GDP multiplier, for each of selected sectors are 1.873 units, 1.873 units, 1.531 units and 1.590 units, respectively (Table 5). This increase in factor income is due to the fact that in order to increase production more of all factors need to be engaged and hence further payments must be made for them.

Decomposition of total factor income between labor and capital factors reveals a mixed pattern (Table 5). More factor income is accrued to labor factor than capital factor in the case of Rice Milling, Education, and Ready-Made Garments sectors. This arises out of higher cumulative effect on labor income as compared to capital income. This means those sectors, which pay more labor income, are triggered by injecting into these activities. On the other hand, only in the case of Construction sector, more factor income is accrued to labor compared to capital. This arises out

Table 5 Impact analysis of injection into some selected sectors on value addition

Factors	Rice milling	Education	Ready-made garments	Construction
Labor	**0.966**	**1.186**	**0.801**	0.793
Capital	0.907	0.686	0.730	**0.796**
Total GDP multiplier	**1.873**	**1.873**	**1.531**	**1.590**

Source SAM multiplier analysis

Table 6 Impact of injection into some selected sectors on households' income

Households	Rice milling	Education	Ready-made garments	Construction
Rural				
Landless	0.09864	0.10032	0.08575	0.08992
Marginal farmer	0.10605	0.09780	0.08292	0.08678
Small farmer	0.22936	0.18655	0.15556	0.16211
Large farmer	0.18294	0.11762	0.09656	0.10013
Day labor	0.13005	0.12219	0.09956	0.10326
Self employed	0.28161	0.26410	0.25115	0.26912
Employee	0.15123	0.15821	0.12974	0.13488
Urban				
Day labor	0.11225	0.10333	0.08676	0.09056
Self employed	0.24351	0.30530	0.21778	0.21896
Employee	0.19363	0.27720	0.17116	0.16504
Total household income multiplier	**1.729**	**1.733**	**1.377**	**1.421**

Source SAM multiplier analysis

of higher cumulative effect on capital income as compared to labor income. This means those sectors, which pay more capital income, are triggered by injecting into these activities. Decomposition of factor income suggests that if the objectives were to promote growth along with more income for *labor*, then intervention in sectors like *Rice-Milling*, *Education* and *Ready Made Garments* be preferred over the sector such as *Construction.*

The next impact is on household income through the interdependence of the system (Table 6). The factorial income is then transferred to household. Household income generation as measured by the multiplier on all household income will be 1.729 units, 1.733 units, 1.377 units, and 1.421 units, respectively, for *Rice-Milling, Education*, *Ready Made Garments,* and *Construction* (Table 6). The estimates of HH income multiplier, when compared with value-added (or factor) multipliers, suggest that the full amount of factorial income is not being transferred to household. For instance, in the case of *Rice-Milling* factor income, multiplier is 2.085 while the household income multiplier is 1.729. The discrepancy between these two income multipliers is because of "leakage" of capital factor income to two exogenous accounts, e.g., *Government* and *Corporation.*

Distribution of total household income between households envisage that as a group self-employed household receives highest income followed by employee and small farmers due to larger sizes of these household groups compared to the remaining other household groups. The lowest income is being accrued to the Landless household group envisaging their weak social and economic integration within the system. However, it is imperative to note that for policy purpose, per capita income estimates are considered rather than the household income because of disproportionate association between income of household groups and their population size.

5 Conclusion

The analysis presented in this paper suggests that an exogenous increase in the demand (e.g., exports, government expenditures, and inventory) in some prioritized activities such as Rice Milling, Education, Ready-Made Garments, and Construction, can lead to large impacts on gross output, GDP, and household income through their backward linkages in the economy. Results from the SAM multiplier model shows that while Rice Milling, Education, and Construction have high backward linkages with different agricultural, manufacturing, and services sectors, the Ready-Made Garment sector has the lowest backward linkages among the four selected sectors because of its high import intensity in production.

Such an exogenous increase in the demand results in the increase in factor income due to the fact that in order to increase production, more of all factors need to be engaged, and hence, further payments must be made for them. However, the decomposition of total factor income between labor and capital factors shows that more factor income is accrued to labor factor than capital factor in the case of labor-intensive sectors such as Rice Milling, Education, and Ready-Made Garments sectors. The opposite result is observed in the case of Construction sector, which is a capital-intensive sector. This suggests that intervention in sectors like Rice Milling, Education, and Ready-Made Garments should be preferred over the sector such as Construction, if the objectives were to promote growth along with more income for labor.

Such an exogenous increase in the demand also leads to a rise in household incomes. However, the distribution of income between households is unequal and it appears that, as a group, self-employed household receives highest income followed by employee and small farmers due to larger sizes of these household groups compared to the remaining other household groups. The lowest income is being accrued to the landless household group envisaging their weak social and economic integration within the system.

References

Alarcon, J. (2000). *Social accounting matrix-based modelling: Extension to wellbeing and environment and computable general equilibrium models (applications using the 1975 and 1980 Ecuador SAMs)* (pp. 17–18). The Hague, The Netherlands: Institute of Social Studies.

BBS. (2010). *Household income and expenditure survey*. Dhaka: Bangladesh Bureau of Statistics (BBS).
Bulmer-Thomas, V. (1982). *Input-output analysis in developing countries*. New York: Wiley Ltd.
GoB (2014). *Economic survey*. Ministry of Finance, Government of Bangladesh.
Pyatt, G., & Thorbecke, E. (1976). *Planning techniques for a better future*. Geneva: International Labour Organization.
Robinson, S. (1989). Multisectoral models. In Chenery, & Srinivasan, *Handbook of development economics* (Chap. 18, Vol. II). North Holland.

Economy-Wide and Employment Effects of Different Scenarios in Bangladesh: Application of a CGE Model

Selim Raihan

1 Introduction

Over the past three decades, computable general equilibrium (CGE) models have become an important tool for empirical economic analysis. CGE models offer a comprehensive way of modeling the overall impact of policy changes on an economy or a region by considering all production activities, factors, and institutions. Such models also include factors such as markets and macroeconomic components: investment and savings, balance of payments, and government budget. CGE models are applauded for being able to incorporate multiple economic linkages that often come handy in explaining trends and structural responses to changes in development policy.

CGE analysis allows for the assessment of the impacts of exogenous shocks within a constrained optimization framework (Raihan 2012). At the core of the CGE model is a set of equations describing the behavior of various economic agents (such as firms and households) when faced with changes in relative prices. In an increasingly market-oriented economy, the variations in prices may be the most important sources of reallocation of resources among competing activities which then may alter the factorial income and hence personal income distribution. Changes in personal income distribution of household groups and consumer price indices may have different implications on the welfare and poverty situations of the

This chapter contains some excerpts from the author's previous publication as a working paper (see: https://mpra.ub.uni-muenchen.de/37882/3/Selim-infrastructure_and_poverty).

S. Raihan (✉)
Department of Economics, University of Dhaka, Dhaka, Bangladesh
e-mail: selim.raihan@gmail.com

S. Raihan
South Asian Network on Economic Modeling (SANEM), Dhaka, Bangladesh

S. Raihan (ed.), *Structural Change and Dynamics of Labor Markets in Bangladesh*, South Asia Economic and Policy Studies,
https://doi.org/10.1007/978-981-13-2071-2_13

distinct household groups. Against this backdrop, this paper employs the CGE model for the Bangladesh economy to explore the impacts of a set of policy and natural disaster shock scenarios. These include a rise in crop productivity, a rise in the demand for labor-intensive exports, a rise in the allocation for social protection to households, and a natural disaster shock. A Social Accounting Matrix (SAM) prepared for the year 2012 serves as the consistent and comprehensive database for the abovementioned exercises.

2 Methodology

2.1 The CGE Model

The Bangladesh CGE model is built using the PEP standard static model (Decaluwé et al. 2011).[1] In the Bangladesh CGE model, representative firm in each industry maximizes profits subject to its production technology. The sectoral output follows a Leontief production function. Each industry's value added consists of composite labor and composite capital, following a constant elasticity of substitution (CES) specification. Different categories of labor are combined following a constant elasticity of substitution (CES) technology with imperfect substitutability between different types of labor. Composite capital is a CES combination of the different categories of capital. It is assumed that intermediate inputs are perfectly complementary, and are combined following a Leontief production function.

Household incomes come from labor income, capital income, and transfers received from other agents. Subtracting direct taxes yields household's disposable income. Household savings are a linear function of disposable income, which allows for the marginal propensity to save being different from the average propensity.

Corporation income consists of its share of capital income and of transfers received from other agents. Deducting business income taxes from total income yields the disposable income of each type of business. Likewise, business savings are the residual that remains after subtracting transfers to other agents from disposable income.

The government draws its income from household and business income taxes, taxes on products and on imports, and other taxes on production. Income taxes are described as a linear function of total income, whether it be for households or for businesses. The current government budget surplus or deficit (positive or negative savings) is the difference between its revenue and its expenditures. The latter consist of transfers to agents and current expenditures on goods and services.

The rest of the world receives payments for the value of imports, part of the income of capital, and transfers from domestic agents. Foreign spending in the

[1] See www.pep-net.org.

domestic economy consists of the value of exports and transfers to domestic agents. The difference between foreign receipts and spending is the amount of rest-of-the-world savings, which are equal in absolute value to the current account balance, but of opposite sign.

The demand for goods and services, whether domestically produced or imported, consists of household consumption demand, investment demand, demand by government, and demand as transport or trade margins. It is assumed that households have Stone-Geary utility functions (from which derives the linear expenditure system). Investment demand includes both gross fixed capital formation (GFCF) and changes in inventories.

Producers' supply behavior is represented by nested CET functions: on the upper level, aggregate output is allocated to individual products; on the lower level, the supply of each product is distributed between the domestic market and exports. The model departs from the "pure" form of the small-country hypothesis. A local producer can increase his share of the world market only by offering a price that is advantageous relative to the (exogenous) world price. The ease with which his share can be increased depends on the degree of substitutability of the proposed product to competing products; in other words, it depends on the price elasticity of export demand. Commodities demanded on the domestic market are composite goods, combinations of locally produced goods and imports. The imperfect substitutability between the two is represented by a constant elasticity of substitution (CES) aggregator function. Naturally, for goods with no competition from imports, the demand for the composite commodity is the demand for the domestically produced good.

The system requires that there is equilibrium between the supply and demand of each commodity on the domestic market. Also, there are equilibriums in the factor markets. Total investment expenditure must be equal to the sum of agents' savings. The sum of supplies of every commodity by local producers must be equal to domestic demand for that commodity produced locally. And finally, supply to the export market of each good must be matched by demand.

2.2 *A Brief Description of the Social Account Matrix (SAM) of Bangladesh for 2012*

This study uses the 2012 SAM for Bangladesh, which has the following accounts: (1) total domestic supply of 10 commodities; (2) production accounts for 10 activities; (3) four factors of productions—two labor types and two capital categories; (4) current account transactions between four current institutional agents—households and unincorporated capital, corporate enterprises, government, and the rest of the world; household account includes seven representative groups (five rural and two urban); and (5) one consolidated capital account. The structure of the Bangladesh SAM is described in Table 1.

Table 1 Description of Bangladesh SAM accounts for 2012

Set	Description of elements
Activity (10)	Grains and crops, livestock and meat products, mining and extraction, processed food, textiles and clothing, light manufacturing, heavy manufacturing, utilities and construction, transport and communication, other services
Commodity (10)	Grains and crops, livestock and meat products, mining and extraction, processed food, textiles and clothing, light manufacturing, heavy manufacturing, utilities and construction, transport and communication, other services
Factors of production (4)	Unskilled labor, skilled labor, capital, and land
Households (7)	*Rural*: Landless, agricultural marginal, agricultural small, agricultural large, nonfarm *Urban*: Households with low-educated heads, households with high-educated heads
Other Institutions (4)	Government; corporation; rest of the world, capital

Source Raihan (2014)

2.3 *Structure of the Economy as in 2012 SAM*

Table 2 presents the structure of the Bangladesh economy as represented in the SAM 2012. In terms of value addition, among the agricultural sectors, the leading sector is the grains and crops with 11.33% share; among the manufacturing sectors, the leading sector is textile and clothing (7.55%); and among the services sectors, the leading sector is transport and communication (27.65%). The textile and clothing sector is highly export-oriented. The export basket is highly concentrated as 88.12% exports come from textile and clothing. The heavy manufacturing sector is highly import dependent. In the case of tariff rate, agricultural sectors have lower tariff rates than the manufacturing sectors.

3 Simulation in the Bangladesh CGE Model and Results

Using the Bangladesh CGE model, four different scenarios are run. They are (i) a rise in the crop productivity by 20%, (ii) a rise in the demand for labor-intensive exports by 25%, (iii) doubling the current allocation of social protection to households, and (iv) a natural disaster shock where the economy's capital stock falls by 5%.

Table 2 Structure of the Bangladesh economy in 2012 as reflected in the SAM 2012

Sectors	1	2	3	4	5	6
	Vi/TV	Ei/Oi	Ei/TE	Mi/Oi	Mi/TM	TAR
Grains and crops	11.33	0.42	0.56	9.09	8.05	4.52
Livestock and meat products	1.25	0.07	0.01	2.25	0.25	8.22
Mining and extraction	6.60	0.16	0.08	2.20	0.75	7.61
Processed food	1.34	1.53	1.59	15.96	10.87	13.38
Textiles and clothing	7.55	51.68	88.12	17.57	19.70	25.33
Light manufacturing	1.74	2.41	1.44	20.83	8.22	19.59
Heavy manufacturing	0.99	1.17	1.26	60.96	43.16	11.77
Utilities and construction	16.86	–	–	–	–	–
Transport and communication	27.65	2.87	6.30	2.42	3.49	–
Other services	24.69	0.28	0.63	3.65	5.52	–
Total	100.00	–	100.00	–	100.00	–

Note Vi = sectoral value added, TV = total value added, Ei = sectoral export, Oi = sectoral output, TE = total export, Mi = sectoral import, TM = total import, TAR = tariff rate, all figures are expressed in percentages
Source Raihan (2014)

3.1 A Rise in the Crop Productivity by 20%

This scenario considers a rise in the total factor productivity in the crop sector by 20%. Under this scenario, a set of closure assumptions are imposed on the CGE model where total stocks of land, tax rates, total real inventories, government savings, and current account balance are exogenous, whereas total investment expenditure and total real government expenditures are held endogenous. Capital is mobile across sectors. Labor supply is flexible with fixed wage rates. The nominal exchange rate is the model's numéraire.

The macroeconomic effects of the crop productivity shock are presented in Fig. 1. It appears that such a positive productivity shock in the crop sector would lead to 2.66% rise in the real GDP. The impacts on gross production and domestic sales would be in similar magnitudes. There will a depreciation in the real exchange rate, and falls in both intermediate input costs and primary factor costs, which would lead to a rise in the exports by 2.24%. Furthermore, the GDP deflator would fall by 2.3%.

Table 3 presents the impacts on the volume of outputs, exports, and imports by broad sectors. The largest impact is observed in the agricultural sector with 8.5% rise in output and 25% rise in exports. However, imports in the agricultural sector would fall by 16.6% as domestic production would expand. There would be positive impacts on outputs and exports in both industrial and services sectors, with a larger effect in the former one.

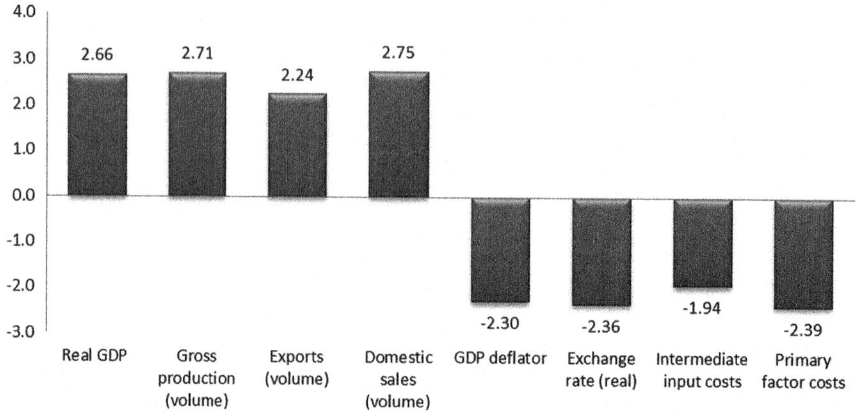

Fig. 1 Effects on key macroeconomic variables for the crop productivity shock (% change from base). *Source* Simulation in the Bangladesh CGE model

Table 3 Effects on outputs, exports, and imports (by broad sector) for crop productivity shock (% change from base)

Sectors	Output	Exports	Imports
Agriculture	8.5	25.2	−16.6
Industry	2.0	2.1	0.5
Services	1.3	1.3	1.9
All sectors	**2.7**	**2.2**	**−0.9**

Source Simulation in the Bangladesh CGE model

Disaggregated sectoral level impacts are presented in Table 4. The largest positive impact is observed in the "Grain and Crops" sector, as output and export in this sector would increase by 11.8 and 28.9%, respectively. There would be positive impacts in all other sectors, except the "Utilities and Construction," due to sectoral inter-linkages and reallocation of factors. Among the other agricultural subsectors, the largest positive impact would be observed in "Livestock and Meat Products"; among the industrial subsectors, both "Processed Food" and "Textiles and Clothing" subsectors' outputs would increase by 2.3%; among the services sub-sectors, the largest positive impact would be observed in the case of "Transport and Communication," which is primarily due to the larger linkage effect.

Figure 2 presents the employment effect of the crop productivity shock. Due to the rise in the productivity in the crop sector, labor (both skilled and unskilled) would be released from the agricultural sector and would be reallocated to the industrial and services sectors. At the aggregate level, there would be positive impact on employment as employment of both skilled and unskilled labors would increase by 1.75 and 0.7%, respectively.

Impacts on real incomes of representative household groups are presented in Fig. 3. All household categories would experience rise in real income. In the rural

Table 4 Effects on outputs, exports, and imports (by sectors) for crop productivity shock (% change from base)

Sectors	Output	Exports	Imports
Grains and crops	11.8	28.9	−18.3
Livestock and meat products	4.3	10.8	−8.3
Mining and extraction	1.2	2.0	−1.4
Processed food	2.3	2.1	0.6
Textiles and clothing	2.3	2.2	0.4
Light manufacturing	1.5	1.1	1.0
Heavy manufacturing	0.9	0.7	0.5
Utilities and construction	−0.5	–	–
Transport and communication	2.5	1.4	2.5
Other services	1.6	0.9	1.6
Total	**2.7**	**2.2**	**−0.9**

Source Simulation in the Bangladesh CGE model

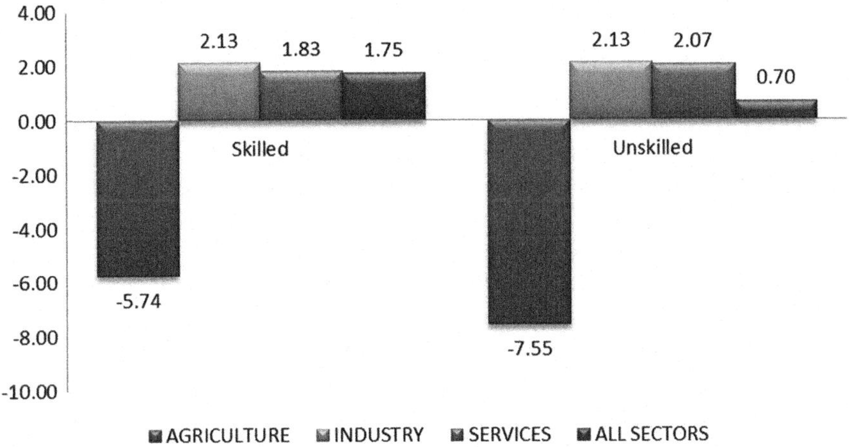

Fig. 2 Effects on employment for crop productivity shock (% change from base). *Source* Simulation in the Bangladesh CGE model

area, the largest rise in real income would be observed for the "rural landless households", and in the urban area the "urban households with low-educated heads" would experience the largest rise. This suggests that such a positive productivity shock in crop agriculture would bring larger gains for the poorer households in Bangladesh.

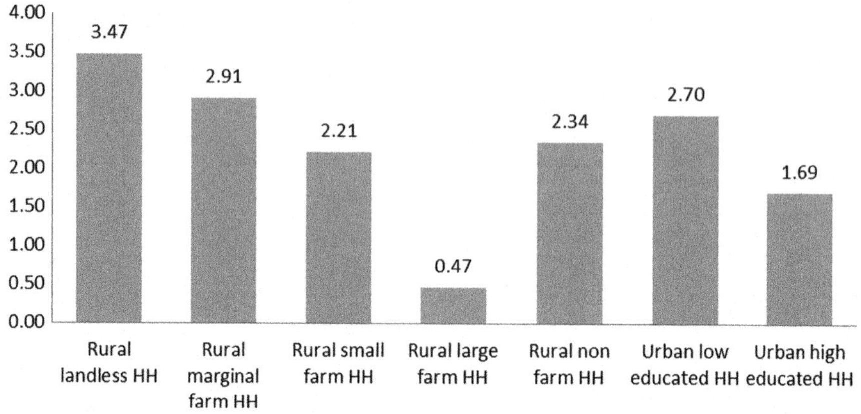

Fig. 3 Effects on households' real income for crop productivity shock (% change from base). *Source* Simulation in the Bangladesh CGE model

3.2 A Rise in the Demand for Labor-Intensive Exports by 25%

This scenario considers a rise in the demand for labor-intensive exports by 25%. Under this scenario, a set of closure assumptions are imposed on the CGE model where total stocks of land, tax rates, technical changes, total real inventories, government savings, and current account balance are exogenous, whereas total investment expenditure and total real government expenditures are held endogenous. Capital is mobile across sectors. Labor supply is flexible with fixed wage rates. The nominal exchange rate is the model's numéraire.

The macroeconomic effects of the export shock are presented in Fig. 4. Such a positive export demand shock would lead to a rise in real GDP by 8%, whereas gross production and domestic sales would rise by 8.3 and 7.8%, respectively. Total exports would increase by 13%. There would be an appreciation of the real exchange rate, and rise in GDP deflator, intermediate input costs, and primary factor costs.

Table 5 shows that the largest positive impacts on both the volume of outputs and exports would be observed in the industrial sector followed by services. As "Textiles and Clothing" is the largest labor-intensive export sector in the country, such effects are quite logical.

Table 6 provides the disaggregated sectoral level impacts. As expected, the largest positive impact would be observed in the "Textiles and Clothing" sector followed by "Light Manufacturing." Among the agricultural subsectors, the largest positive impact is observed in "Livestock and Meat Products." Among the services subsectors, the large positive impacts are observed in the cases of "Other Services" and "Transport and Communication," due to their large linkage effects with the export sectors.

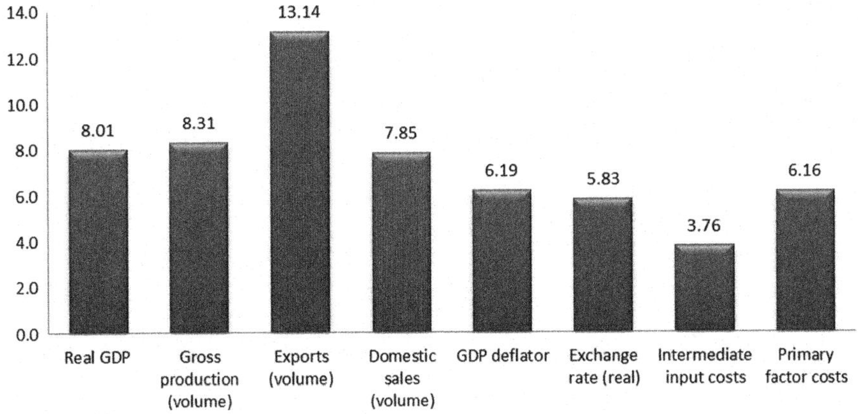

Fig. 4 Effects on key macroeconomic variables for the export shock (% change from base). *Source* Simulation in the Bangladesh CGE model

Table 5 Effects on outputs, exports, and imports (by broad sector) for export shock (% change from base)

Sectors	Output	Exports	Imports
Agriculture	4.3	1.5	20.5
Industry	9.7	14.1	13.7
Services	8.7	2.1	16.4
All sectors	**8.3**	**13.1**	**14.5**

Source Simulation in the Bangladesh CGE model

Table 6 Effects on outputs, exports, and imports (by sector) for export shock (% change from base)

Sectors	Output	Exports	Imports
Grains and crops	3.9	2.6	20.0
Livestock and meat products	5.1	4.2	19.8
Mining and extraction	5.0	−6.5	25.2
Processed food	9.4	12.6	16.7
Textiles and clothing	11.7	14.4	14.2
Light manufacturing	7.2	10.6	15.7
Heavy manufacturing	1.3	−4.4	12.2
Utilities and construction	6.3	–	–
Transport and communication	9.1	2.1	15.0
Other services	10.2	1.9	17.3
Total	**8.3**	**13.1**	**14.5**

Source Simulation in the Bangladesh CGE model

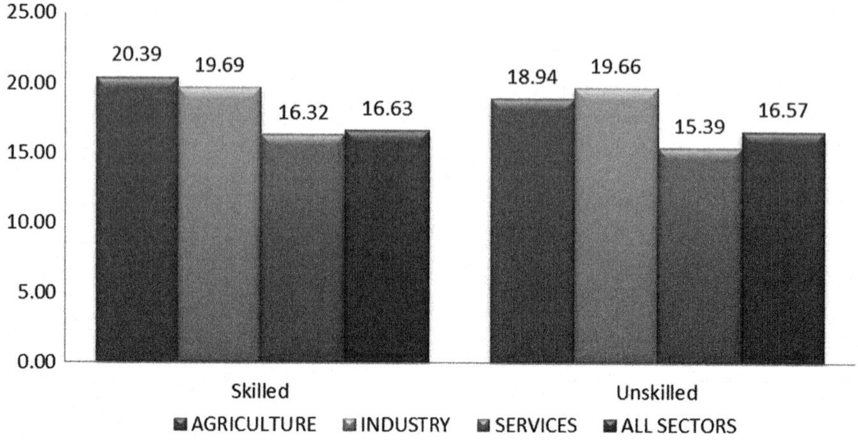

Fig. 5 Effects on employment for export shock (% change from base). *Source* Simulation in the Bangladesh CGE model

The employment effects of the export shock are presented in Fig. 5. Due to the rise in the demand for labor in the labor-intensive export sectors, there would be a large rise in employments of both skilled and unskilled labors in all three broad sectors. In the case of skilled labor, agriculture would appear to experience the largest rise in employment, whereas, in the case of unskilled labor, industry would have the largest rise. As "Textiles and Clothing" is the largest employed for unskilled labor in the labor-intensive export sector, such a pattern of impacts would be compelling.

Figure 6 suggests that real incomes of all representative household groups would rise with much larger effects being observed for the poorer household groups

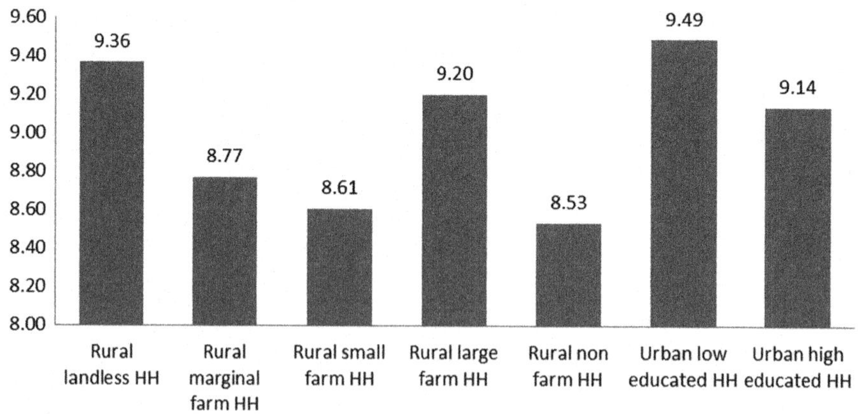

Fig. 6 Effects on households' real income for export shock (% change from base). *Source* Simulation in the Bangladesh CGE model

compared to their counterparts. In the rural area, the largest rise in real income would be observed for the "rural landless households," and in the urban area the "urban households with low-educated heads" would experience the largest rise. This suggests that such a positive export shock in the labor-intensive sectors would bring larger gains for the poorer households in Bangladesh.

3.3 Doubling the Allocation of Social Protection to Households

This scenario considers doubling the current allocation of social protection to households. Under this scenario, a set of closure assumptions are imposed on the CGE model where total stocks of land, tax rates, technical changes, total real inventories, total real government expenditures, and current account balance are exogenous, whereas total investment expenditure and government savings are held endogenous. Capital is mobile across sectors. Labor supply is flexible with fixed wage rates. The nominal exchange rate is the model's numéraire.

The macroeconomic effects of the social protection shock are presented in Fig. 7. Such a rise in the allocation for social protection would not have large macroeconomic effects, as real GDP, gross production, exports, and domestic sales would rise by very small margins. Furthermore, there would be some very small depressing effects on GDP deflator, real exchange rate, intermediate input costs, and primary factor costs.

Also, at the broad sectoral level, the effects on output and exports would be positive but small. Table 7 shows that the largest positive impacts on both the

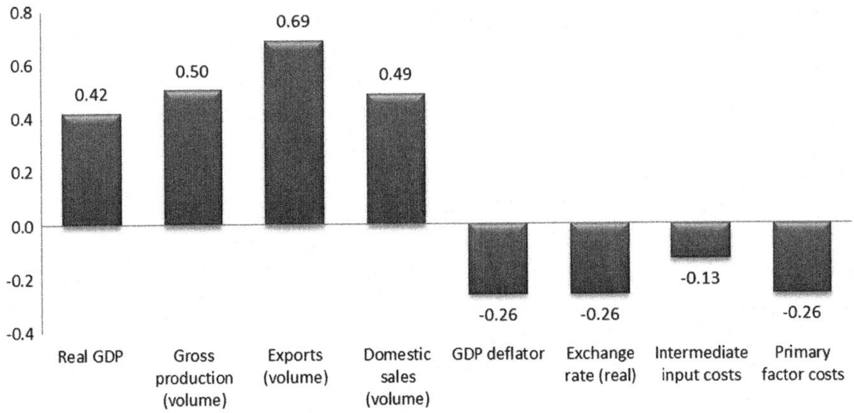

Fig. 7 Effects on key macroeconomic variables for the social protection shock (% change from base). *Source* Simulation in the Bangladesh CGE model

Table 7 Effects on outputs, exports, and imports (by broad sector) for social protection shock (% change from base)

Sectors	Output	Exports	Imports
Agriculture	1.0	0.6	1.4
Industry	1.1	0.7	−0.1
Services	0.0	1.0	1.1
All sectors	**0.5**	**0.7**	**0.2**

Source Simulation in the Bangladesh CGE model

Table 8 Effects on outputs, exports, and imports (by sector) for social protection shock (% change from base)

Sectors	Output	Exports	Imports
Grains and crops	1.4	0.7	1.5
Livestock and meat products	1.4	0.6	1.7
Mining and extraction	−0.3	0.0	−0.6
Processed food	2.4	1.4	2.1
Textiles and clothing	1.1	0.7	1.4
Light manufacturing	1.0	0.7	0.6
Heavy manufacturing	−0.9	−0.2	−1.5
Utilities and construction	−3.9	–	–
Transport and communication	1.4	1.0	1.2
Other services	1.5	1.0	1.1
Total	**0.5**	**0.7**	**0.2**

Source Simulation in the Bangladesh CGE model

volume of outputs and exports would be observed in the industrial sector. As social protection increases poor people's purchasing power, import demand for agricultural products would rise.

Disaggregated sectoral level impacts are presented in Table 8. Among the agricultural subsectors, both "Grains and Crops" and "Livestock and Meat Products" would experience the largest expansion, and among the industrial subsectors, the largest positive impact on output would be observed in the case of "Processed Food." This is primarily due to the increased demand for cereal and processed food products from the poorer households as their incomes would rise due to larger allocation of social protection.

There would be some positive but small employment effects of the social protection shock (Fig. 8). Employments of both skilled and unskilled labors would rise in all three broad sectors. In the case of skilled labor, service sector would appear to experience the largest rise in employment, whereas, in the case of unskilled labor, agriculture would have the largest rise.

Figure 9 suggests that real incomes of all representative household groups would rise with much larger effects being observed for the poorer household groups, both

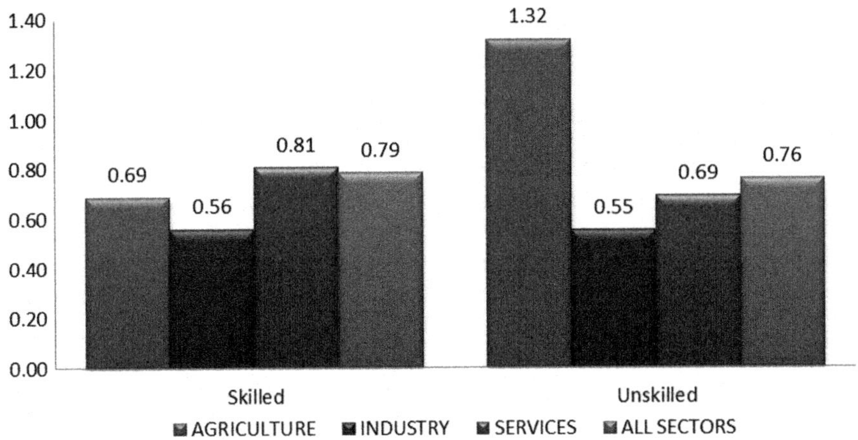

Fig. 8 Effects on employment for social protection shock (% change from base). *Source* Simulation in the Bangladesh CGE model

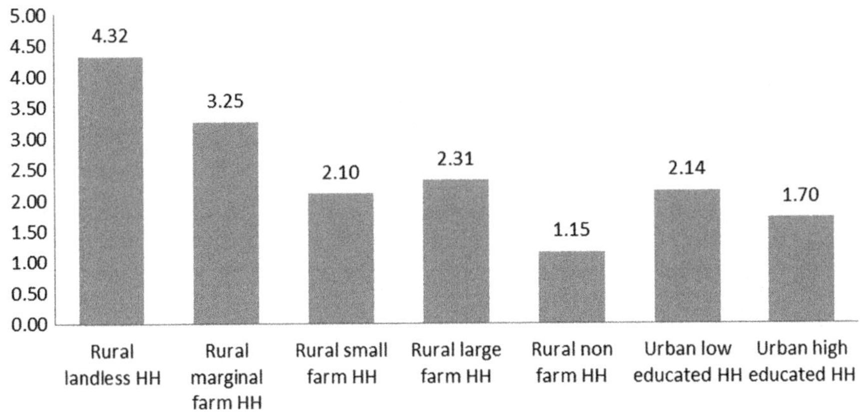

Fig. 9 Effects on households' real income for social protection shock (% change from base). *Source* Simulation in the Bangladesh CGE model

in the rural and urban areas, compared to their counterparts. This is largely due to the fact that social protection programs are targeted primarily toward the poorer households. "Rural landless households," and "urban households with low-educated heads" would be the largest gainers in the rural and urban areas, respectively.

3.4 A Natural Disaster Shock Where the Economy's Capital Stock Falls by 5%

This scenario considers a natural disaster shock (brought about by any earthquake, flood, cyclone, or any other natural calamities) where the economy's capital stock falls by 5%. Under this scenario, a set of closure assumptions are imposed on the CGE model where total stocks of land, tax rates, technical changes, total real inventories, government savings, and current account balance are exogenous, whereas total investment expenditure and total real government expenditures are held endogenous. Capital is mobile across sectors. Labor supply is flexible with fixed wage rates. The nominal exchange rate is the model's numéraire.

The macroeconomic effects of the disaster shock are presented in Fig. 10. It appears that such a scenario would lead to 2.28% fall in the real GDP. The impacts on gross production and domestic sales would also be negative with similar magnitudes. There would be an appreciation in the real exchange rate, and rise in GDP deflator, intermediate input costs, and primary factor costs. These would lead to a fall in exports by 2.63%.

Table 9 presents the impacts on the volume of outputs, exports, and imports by broad sectors. The largest negative impact would be observed in the agricultural sector with 2.7% fall in output and 5.2% fall in exports. This would lead to a rise in agricultural imports by 3.8%. There would be negative impacts on outputs and exports in both industrial and services sectors, with a larger effect in the industrial sector.

We observe from the disaggregated sectoral level impacts, presented in Table 10, that all sectors would experience fall in outputs and exports, with the largest negative impact on output being observed in the "Heavy Manufacturing" followed by "Mining and Extraction." Imports in all agricultural sectors would

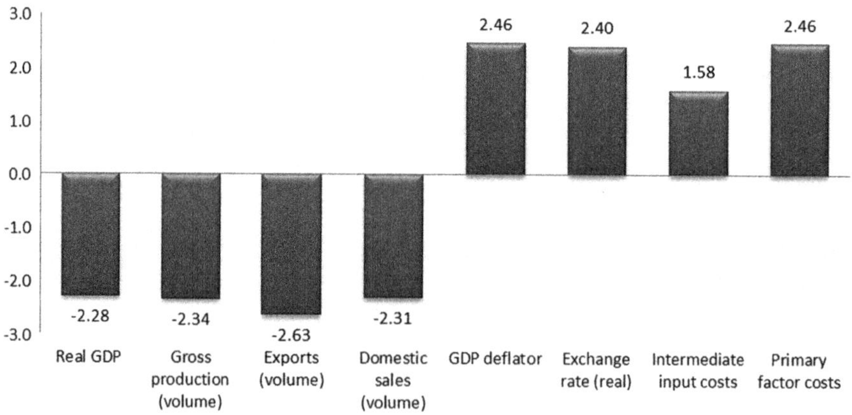

Fig. 10 Effects on key macroeconomic variables for the natural disaster shock (% change from base). *Source* Simulation in the Bangladesh CGE model

Table 9 Effects on outputs, exports, and imports (by broad sector) for the natural disaster shock (% change from base)

Sectors	Output	Exports	Imports
Agriculture	−2.7	−5.2	3.8
Industry	−2.5	−2.6	−0.1
Services	−2.1	−2.3	0.3
All sectors	−2.3	−2.6	0.3

Source Simulation in the Bangladesh CGE model

Table 10 Effects on outputs, exports, and imports (by sector) for the natural disaster shock (% change from base)

Sectors	Output	Exports	Imports
Grains and crops	−2.6	−5.2	3.8
Livestock and meat products	−1.8	−4.5	4.1
Mining and extraction	−3.2	−5.4	4.2
Processed food	−1.8	−2.3	0.8
Textiles and clothing	−2.5	−2.6	0.3
Light manufacturing	−2.7	−3.1	0.4
Heavy manufacturing	−4.4	−4.3	−0.6
Utilities and construction	−2.3	–	–
Transport and communication	−2.2	−2.3	−0.3
Other services	−1.8	−2.4	0.6
Total	**−2.3**	**−2.6**	**0.3**

Source Simulation in the Bangladesh CGE model

increase in much larger magnitudes than those for industrial and services subsectors, primarily due to meeting households' basic food needs.

Figure 11 presents very interesting employment effect of the natural disaster shock. Due to the fall in capital stock, demand for labor (both skilled and unskilled) would increase by small margins. This is primarily due to the effect stemming from some degrees of substitution between labor and capital. Employments in agriculture would rise by some sizeable magnitudes, while those in industry and services would rise very small margins. This suggests that such a natural disaster shock would reverse the structural change in employment in Bangladesh where labor is expected to be released from agriculture for being absorbed in the industrial and services sectors.

All household categories would experience fall in their real incomes (Fig. 12). In the rural area, the largest fall in real income would be observed for the "rural nonfarm households" as this household has the largest share in capital stock in the rural area. For the same reason, in the urban area the "urban households with high-educated heads" would experience the largest fall. However, negative impacts on poorer household groups would also be quite large.

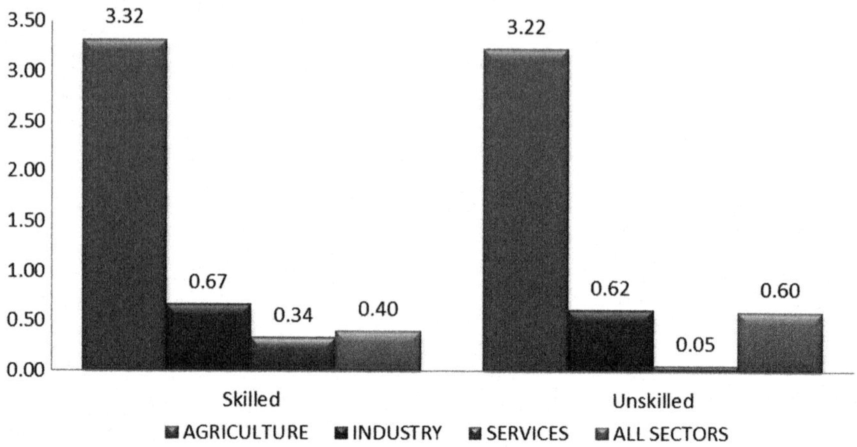

Fig. 11 Effects on employment for the natural disaster shock (% change from base). *Source* Simulation in the Bangladesh CGE model

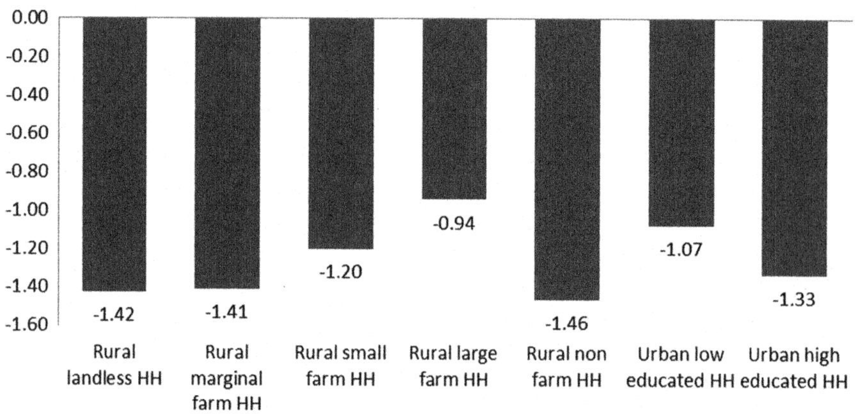

Fig. 12 Effects on households' real income for the natural disaster shock (% change from base). *Source* Simulation in the Bangladesh CGE model

4 Conclusion

This paper presents a CGE model for Bangladesh for the analysis of economy-wide and employment effects of different policy and natural disaster scenarios. These include a rise in crop productivity, a rise in the demand for labor-intensive exports, a rise in the allocation for social protection to households, and a natural disaster shock. This paper provides a description of the CGE model, the social accounting matrix of the Bangladesh economy for the year 2012, and a detailed analysis of the results of four simulations. The simulation results suggest that rise in crop productivity and export demand of labor-intensive sectors can have large positive impacts in the economy in terms of rise in real GDP, exports, employment, and real incomes of the households, with poorer households gaining larger than their counterparts. However, a natural disaster shock can bring depressing effect on real GDP, exports, and real incomes of the households with a risk of reversing the structural change in employment. Finally, even though a rise in the allocation for social protection would have small macroeconomic and sectoral impacts, poorer households, both in the rural and urban areas, would gain significantly due to the increase in their real incomes.

References

Decaluwé, B., Lemelin, A., Maisonnave, H., & Robichaud, V. (2011). The PEP standard computable general equilibrium model single-country, static version. In *Poverty and Economic Policy (PEP) Research Network*. Québec: Université Laval.

Raihan, S. (2012). Infrastructure and growth and poverty in Bangladesh. MPRA Paper No. 37882.

Printed by Printforce, the Netherlands